DAY of LIGHTNING, YEARS of SCORN

DAY of LIGHTNING, YEARS of SCORN

Walter C. Short and the Attack on Pearl Harbor

CHARLES R. ANDERSON

NAVAL INSTITUTE PRESS
Annapolis, Maryland

Naval Institute Press
291 Wood Road
Annapolis, MD 21402

Library of Congress Cataloging-in-Publication Data

Anderson, Charles Robert, 1943–
    Day of lightning, years of scorn : Walter C. Short and the attack on
Pearl Harbor / Charles R. Anderson.
        p. cm.
    Includes bibliographical references and index.
    ISBN 1-59114-011-0 (alk. paper)
    1. Pearl Harbor (Hawaii), Attack on, 1941. 2. Short, Walter Campbell,
1880–1949. 3. Short, Walter Campbell, 1880–1949—Trials, litigation, etc.
4. Generals—United States—Biography. 5. United States. Army—Biography.
I. Title.
D767.92.A717 2004
940.54'26693—dc22

                                2004011495

Printed in the United States of America on acid-free paper ∞
        12 11 10 09 08 07 06 05   9 8 7 6 5 4 3 2
                    First printing

Contents

Foreword

I MET CHARLES R. ANDERSON when he came to work at the U.S. Army Center of Military History (CMH) in the summer of 1987. At that time, he had already written two well-received commercial books based on his experiences as a Marine combat officer in I Corps, South Vietnam. As an established author, Charlie was assigned to the Histories Division of the center, where he spent his career at CMH. Although we worked in different divisions of the center, Charlie and I shared a common interest in Japan and in World War II in the Pacific.

Charlie was taciturn, observant, sometimes sardonic, and always able to gauge the moment. He once said that he resigned his Marine Corps commission because after the real thing in Vietnam, peacetime routine was too boring. That was his succinct and unflinching view of life. If you found things did not suit you, move on. He never complained about the hand he drew, he just played it close to the vest and always in a disarmingly low-key manner. Despite his reserve, Charlie had an intense interest in how things happened and why. Often he would show up at a colleague's office door late in the afternoon and simply ask, "What's up?" His quiet, unassuming personality masked a true professional writer and historian. He was painstaking in his research and writing. He wanted to get it right, down to the last detail. You see this superb craftsmanship in his early unsparing accounts of his Vietnam service, and you see it again in *Day of Lightning, Years of Scorn*.

In the early 1990s, Charlie became deeply involved in researching and writing several of the CMH's World War II commemoration pamphlets. He was a private person, but with this assignment it was natural for us to exchange information, ask questions of one another, and talk about the greatest war in world history. In other words, Charlie's assignment and our shared interest in the Pacific war brought us closer together.

When we talked about the war in the Pacific, Charlie often spoke of his interest in the Pearl Harbor attack, a story told many times. But his approach to examining the Japanese raid was different. He wanted to look at events through the eyes of the Army commander in Hawaii, and Lt. Gen. Walter C. Short caught his imagination. Charlie was curious about Short's professional career, the prewar U.S. Army that produced Short, and why Short was in command of Army forces that Sunday morning in Hawaii. Looking back, I suppose Charlie wanted to fit Short into the context of Pearl Harbor. After all, here was a man who devoted his professional life in the military service of his nation. Short was there through good times and bad, from the hard-scrabble frontier posts to the trenches of World War I, from the era of stagnant promotions and parsimonious Army budgets to the brief period of fulfillment commanding the Army's largest overseas force, the Hawaiian Department. It all came crashing down after a few hours on a Sunday morning in December 1941, as Short's career, like the fleet anchored along Battleship Row, lay in ruins. As much as he was interested in the star-crossed general's career before the Pearl Harbor disaster, Charlie was even more intrigued by Short's response to the bitter recriminations that followed him the rest of his life.

Curiosity led Charlie on his own time to study Short's life and military career. This early research broadened his search for more information about the prewar Army, the various Pearl Harbor investigations, and Short's post–Pearl Harbor activities. Despite his duties at CMH, which by then included writing a major volume in the U.S. Army's Vietnam War series, he used his spare time diligently and efficiently to search archives, interview those who knew or served with Short, assemble unique materials, and, despite serious illness, draft a manuscript that went beyond Short's conduct at Pearl Harbor to encompass the prewar and postwar institutions that Short served faithfully in peace and war.

While Charlie might have sympathized with Short, he did not pity the general or attempt to portray him as a victim. Instead, he evaluated the general based on the available historical records, his own sophisticated understanding of the workings of military institutions, and according to the standards of Short's chosen profession. He did all this with clarity, precision, and, typical of Charlie, with unsparing honesty.

Charlie's evenhanded portrayal of Short acknowledges that the general bore responsibility for certain of the charges made against him. Several allegations, however, were at best debatable, and others shifted blame from senior officers in Washington to the commanders in Hawaii. Charlie's explanation of the reasons and motivations behind the most senior Army and Navy leaders, which differed from those who would investigate the disaster, adds new understanding to the larger issue of the glaring lack of interdepartmental cooperation and coordination among the War, Navy, and State Departments on the eve of the Pearl Harbor attack. The narrative also helps today's reader to understand Short's defensive preparations just before the Japanese attack.

Walter C. Short is remembered in history's harsh verdict as the U.S. Army general who parked his airplanes wingtip to wingtip, making them easy targets for Japanese pilots. A series of post-attack investigations directed and overseen by Washington assigned Short, along with his Navy counterpart, Adm. Husband E. Kimmel, the blame for the disaster at Pearl Harbor on 7 December 1941. In a few hours, Short's lifetime of professional military achievement vanished. Short, of course, did not disappear, but rather patiently bided his time in anticipation of a full and fair hearing.

Thus the attack on Pearl Harbor was the culmination of Short's military career but not his public life. This first full-length biographical treatment of the controversial general demonstrates that Short stoically endured years of investigations, innuendo, and bitter criticism. In contrast, this book offers a balanced assessment of Short's Army career, his role as he understood it in Hawaii in 1941, and, more important, his conduct in the face of blistering, often unfair, criticism in the years after the Japanese attack. As the title suggests, a single day undid an exceptional career but, as the reader discovers, did not undo Short's personal sense of dignity, honesty, and loyalty to the institutions and leaders who shared the responsibility for the disaster at Pearl Harbor.

Charles Anderson died in August 2003 at age sixty after a long struggle with cancer. *Day of Lightning, Years of Scorn* is his legacy to us.

Edward J. Drea
Fairfax, Virginia

Acknowledgments

MANY PEOPLE DESERVE my thanks for their assistance in the preparation of this work. At the National Archives and Records Administration in Washington, D.C., and College Park, Maryland, several archivists were particularly helpful: George C. Chalou, Richard F. Cox, Elaine C. Everly, Timothy K. Nenninger, David Wallace, Howard H. Wehman, and Mitchell A. Yockelson. At the Hoover Institution on War, Revolution and Peace at Palo Alto, California, Elena Danielson and Ernest Thompkins provided valuable assistance.

A larger number of archivists, librarians, and local historians across the country volunteered much time and information. I am especially grateful for the guidance through a variety of collections provided by Marcella White of the Montgomery County, Illinois, Genealogical Society; Josephine R. Motz of the Madison County, Illinois, Historical Society; John Daly of the Illinois State Archives; William Maher of the University of Illinois Archives; Ralph B. Jackson of the Western Military Academy, Alton, Illinois; Dorothy S. Kriete of the Army War College Library, Carlisle Barracks, Pennsylvania; Delores Smith of the Toledo–Lucas County, Ohio, Public Library; Robert W. Viol of the Ohio Historical Society; John J. Grubar of the National Rifle Association; and Paul R. Smiljanich of the 6th U.S. Infantry Association.

I will always be indebted to those veterans and correspondents who greatly expanded my understanding of life in the United States and its army between the two world wars. Their explanations conveyed the experiences, impressions, and judgements which often cannot be found in books and libraries. They include Col. Joffre H. Boston, USA (Ret.), Lt. Col. Samuel Bradlyn, USAF (Ret.), Ruth D. Fleming, Col. Lee W. Haney, USA (Ret.), Lt. Gen. Oren E. Hurlbut, USA (Ret.), J. Robert Judd, Lt. Col. Timothy J. Murphy, USA (Ret.), Joe F. Richardson, Esther McDole Smith, C. L. Traylor, and Lt. Col. Lyman L. Woodman, USAF (Ret.).

Finally, a number of my colleagues at the U.S. Army Center of Military History in Washington, D.C., shared their extensive understanding of the Army in which General Short spent his career and offered research advice and encouragement. They include Graham A. Cosmas, Albert E. Cowdrey, Edward J. Drea, Arnold G. Fisch Jr., John T. Greenwood, Charles E. Kirkpatrick, Clayton D. Laurie, Thomas A. Popa, Edgar F. Raines Jr., and Col. Robert H. Sholly. At the library and archives of the Center of Military History, James B. Knight and Mary L. Haynes helped with bibliographic searches and pointed me toward relevant topical files.

DAY of LIGHTNING, YEARS of SCORN

Son of the Prairie

BENEATH ORNATE CHANDELIERS, POLISHED TABLES FORMED A LARGE T. Oversize maps and charts hung along the walls. Dozens of reporters sat and stood along the sides of the room, many around the tripods of five newsreel cameras filming the proceedings under glaring klieg lights. To the rear of the long room, some four hundred spectators strained for a glimpse of the principals. January in Washington can be bitter cold with the wind off the Potomac. But this room in January 1946 was warm with the press of hundreds of bodies and the anticipation of witnessing a big story, perhaps the biggest in a decade of stunning events.

In decades past, the caucus room of the Senate Office Building had been the scene of countless hearings, many of them aimed at exposing national scandals like Teapot Dome. Now again, a joint committee of Congress had convened to investigate a major event. This time it was the most spectacular defeat ever administered to the armed forces of the United States, the Japanese attack on Pearl Harbor. The ten members of the committee sat along the top of the T–shaped arrangement of tables, each witness at the bottom. The chairman of the committee was the senior senator from Kentucky, silver-haired Alben W. Barkley. At the witness table sat Maj. Gen. Walter C. Short, United

States Army (Ret.). Only a few years earlier, General Short had been the vigorous commanding general of the Hawaiian Department, an officer respected by soldiers and civilians alike, and one destined, it was believed, for a major role if the Japanese started anything in the Pacific. But now Walter Short was a thin, graying man who had been forced into retirement after the attack on Pearl Harbor and then subjected to some of the most vitriolic abuse any American official has ever had to endure. He had recently recovered from a bout with pneumonia and spoke in low tones.

The treatment General Short got from the committee did nothing to improve his health. On the general's fourth day of testimony, one of the junior members, Representative John W. Murphy (D-Pa.), referred repeatedly to Short's statements in previous investigations in an effort to rattle the witness and force a contradiction. Murphy's purpose had less to do with uncovering facts than destroying the credibility of a witness. He wanted the American people to take from his performance the impression that General Short really was so incompetent as to let the Japanese get into Pearl Harbor and disable the Pacific Fleet. After reading each statement, the demanding interrogator fired the same question with the force and monotony of a machine gun: "Did you make that statement? . . . Did you make that statement? . . . Did you make that statement?"[1]

Murphy's verbal assault did not have its intended effect. Short stood firm under the shrill barrage. In controlled tones, he responded to each question, occasionally adding a comment to make clear the context in which he had spoken earlier. But the older man's reasoned approach did nothing to moderate his much younger interrogator. General Short finally fired back, demanding that Murphy stop misquoting him. Another committee member, Representative Frank B. Keefe (R-Wisc.), underlined Short's demand for accuracy, and a ripple of applause came from spectators. But Murphy would not be put off. He continued his machine-gun questioning until the chairman interrupted to recognize another committee member.

Although Representative Murphy was one of the few intemperate interrogators he would face, General Short was well aware that there were many others throughout the country who would like to get at him. For years the American people had awaited this investigation, though many did not wish it to be as acrimonious as Murphy was making it. For years citizens of all stations, from Cabinet officer to cab driver, had been carrying the maddening burden of an unanswered question: How could the Japanese have sailed all the way across the largest ocean in the world and sunk the backbone of the Pacific Fleet without being detected before the attack or caught after? For too many the answer was simple: somebody had been "asleep at the switch," in the idiom of the day. For most, there were two guilty somebodies, General Short and Admiral Kimmel, commander of the Pacific Fleet in 1941.

The fury of the American people at the Japanese was nearly matched by their anger at Short and Kimmel for, it was assumed, allowing a humiliating defeat. In the weeks after the attack, thousands wrote the White House demanding a complete investigation of the debacle, some adding the hope that Short and Kimmel would commit suicide. Representative Dewey Short (R-Mo.) declared to the press, "It's high time we were getting rid of these incompetents. We've got a lot of gold braiders around here who haven't had a new idea in twenty years. They should be court-martialed!" Dozens of editors agreed with their colleague at Wheeling, West Virginia's *News-Register* that the two commanders in Hawaii should be "shorn of their rank and drummed out of the service." One senior member of Congress appeared to lose all control. Representative Andrew May, chairman of the House Military Affairs Committee, told a Pikeville, Kentucky, audience that Short and Kimmel should be shot. And thousands again flooded the White House mail room with protest letters when the two officers were granted full pensions after being involuntarily retired.[2]

For years after that awful day in Hawaii, General Short had silently endured the scorn of officials and citizens alike, waiting for the day when he could tell his story to the American people. The ordeal tested severely the patience of a man known for his self-control. But he never betrayed anger, never shot back at the braying mob of tormenters. Instead, he waited in dignified silence. At long last, Congress granted Short his say before the nation and the recorders of history. But even now, in what might have been his hour of vindication, he was dogged by the hounds of abuse. Finally, after five days of exhausting testimony, the general was excused from the witness chair, and he went back into quiet retirement.

LONG BEFORE GENERAL SHORT was subjected to the critical inquiry of his government and the scorn of his countrymen, the Shorts had felt directly the force of historical events. The American Shorts are of Scottish-Irish stock, descendants of Protestants who in the 1730s began emigrating from Ulster Province to escape exhausted farmland and hostile Catholics. Toward the end of the eighteenth century, the family name was appearing on ships' manifests with increasing frequency. The first forebears to pass along more than dates of birth were the general's paternal grandparents. Lemuel Short, a Quaker, was born in Guilford County, North Carolina, on 24 February 1814. Lemuel had the opportunity to gain more formal education than most and trained as a teacher. He took Mary Haskett for his wife, and they raised eleven children. Their second child was Hiram Spait Short, Walter Short's father.[3]

At the age of thirty-nine, Lemuel risked everything on a better life beyond the Appalachian Mountains. He decided to move his family, which by then included at least eight children, seven hundred miles west to the wilderness of southern Illinois. The Shorts settled in Fayette County, near the village of Ramsey, some sixty–five miles northeast of St. Louis. For the rest of his life, Lemuel moved his family to whichever town offered the best teaching salary. In 1856, he found a job in Shelby County, and the family moved a dozen miles north. Only two years later the itinerant educator found still another school district interested in his services, this one in Missouri, and the family crossed the broad Mississippi. But Lemuel had barely begun his new assignment when death took him at the age of forty-four.

Hiram Spait Short was a well-traveled teenager by the time his family arrived in Illinois. He attended what were then called "common schools," and for much of his early education his teacher was his own father. In 1856, Hiram was sent to the Quaker High School of Westfield, Indiana, for one year, long enough for him to graduate. While his father and most of the family followed teaching jobs, Hiram stayed behind in Ramsey, dividing his time between teaching area children and studying medicine in the office of physician J. C. Jones.

In 1861, twenty-one-year-old Hiram interrupted his medical studies and volunteered for what everyone thought would be a brief campaign to reunite the states. Less than three months after the bombardment of Fort Sumter, Hiram rode a few miles north into Shelby County and signed on with Capt. James Williams's Company C, 35th Illinois Volunteers, Col. G. A. Smith commanding. Company C and the 35th Illinois saw much action, participating in major engagements at Pea Ridge, Arkansas; Perryville, Kentucky; Stone River, Chattanooga, and Knoxville, Tennessee; Corinth, Mississippi; and Chickamauga, Georgia. Hiram's final campaign began with General Sherman's entry into Georgia, and he accepted his discharge at Atlanta on 27 September 1864, as Sherman's huge force prepared for its march to the sea.

Curiously, the war that divided families and traumatized the young nation seems to have touched Hiram Short very lightly. He was neither wounded nor struck ill, and after more than three years' service he resumed his medical studies. His social affiliations soon reflected the elite profession to which he aspired. He accepted invitations from the masonic lodge and the Modern Woodmen camp. In the summer of 1869, with no more training than his apprenticeship in J. C. Jones's office, Hiram began practicing medicine in Fillmore, ten miles west of Ramsey.

On 31 October 1871, in Ramsey, the doctor without a degree married a girl more than eleven years younger than himself, Sarah Minerva Stokes. The new Mr. and Mrs. Short wasted no time starting a family. On 27 July 1872, Sarah gave birth to a son, William Tecumseh Short, four days before she could say she had been married nine months. The proud father soon decided he had better get official recognition of his unofficial medical experience before his family grew any larger. He enrolled in the Eclectic Medical Institute at Cincinnati. His observations in Jones's office were apparently convincing, for the Eclectic faculty conferred the M.D. degree after only two terms. Following graduation in the spring of 1873, the new Dr. Short took his wife and son back to Fillmore, where a second child, Mary Lutie, was born the following year. In 1875, the doctor moved his practice to his wife's hometown of Ramsey. But after three years and two more children, Ramsey had not fulfilled Short's hopes, and he moved family and furniture to Fillmore for the last time. His practice finally flourished, and Short bought a forty-acre farm a few miles southeast of the village.

The couple's fifth and sixth children, both boys, were born in 1880 and 1883, and they were sources of great pride to the doctor, who now had four sons. In an age when sons pursued careers and daughters pursued husbands, Short had four careers to influence. As he examined each of the pink bawling boys, he could not know that three would follow him into medicine while one would take a different path. But he did know that by the time his boys made career choices they would be as well educated as he could make them. The son who would take a different path, the son who would go from a village on the prairie to national prominence was born at home on 30 March 1880. His mother's attending physician was his father, and he was given the name Walter Campbell Short.

Fillmore, Illinois, is one of a handful of towns named after the thirteenth president, Millard Fillmore. The Fillmore in which Walter Short was raised was a busy prairie village with a bright future. Horse-drawn wagons bumped up and down rutted Main Street, raising clouds of dust as they serviced a promising local economy. Farmers drove wagonloads of grain and herds of livestock to the elevator and pens beside the tracks. The Cloverleaf Road, officially the Toledo, St. Louis, and Western, brought enough businessmen, entertainers, and other travelers to justify a hotel. By the last decade of the nineteenth century, the village also boasted its own newspaper, the *Recorder,* a bank, mill, livery stable, saloon and several shops, two physicians, a barber, three churches, and a masonic lodge, as well as a full-time station agent, postmaster, and schoolteacher.

But the bright future of Fillmore never materialized. By the time war broke out in Europe in 1914, growth had leveled off. The population never topped seven hundred. Boarded-up buildings on Main Street became a common sight, especially during the Great Depression, and every year more young people looked elsewhere for career opportunities. Most businessmen and professionals moved their services twelve miles west to the county seat of Hillsboro.

To a curious young boy growing up in Fillmore in the 1880s and 1890s there was nothing small-town about the village. It was full of new and wondrous things to experience. There were frogs and fish to catch in Hurricane Creek, trees to climb, and the other sides of hills to explore. On nearby farms a village boy could find a fascinating variety of animals to watch, chase, and try to ride. From his father, uncles, and cousins Walter could hear thrilling stories of the American wilderness and several wars, and older neighbors could remember when Indians outnumbered settlers in the county.

The seasons brought a succession of adventures and sensual delights. In the spring there were flowers to pick—more than boys could be expected to name—and dozens of newborn animals to watch in barnyards and woods. The best way to cool a hot summer day was to dig into a bowl of homemade ice cream topped with fresh berries. In the fall, the smells of canning filled the house, and every year a few more colorful leaves found their way into the family album. With the trees bare, a boy could help his father choose a turkey for Thanksgiving, then pluck the big bird and make a quill pen. Just weeks later, mother called for young fingers to help string popcorn and tie decorations on the Christmas tree. In the winter, there were snow-covered hills to sled and ponds to skate. When a freezing rain put a crystal crust on the snow, an adventuresome boy could skate down the street and right across the fields. And after a day on the ice, nothing brought back the warmth like a cup of hot cider with a cinnamon stick.

In Fillmore, young Walter got an early, though insulated, view of country living in the nineteenth-century Midwest. Life on the farms of Montgomery County was hard and just beginning to be mechanized. Most of the work was done by horses and by men with calloused hands and iron determination. Their wives worked twelve-hour days in front of wood–burning stoves and soapy washboards or behind a team of horses, and they still found the strength to bear a dozen or more children and raise at least half of them to adulthood. Hunting and fishing were not merely recreational pastimes for those of sporting inclination but activities necessary to supplement a diet of little variety. Young Walter probably sampled the work on the farm owned by but not worked by his father, enough to get blisters or an occasional callous. But his father's profession shielded him from the spirit-sapping drudgery of plowing and harvesting a section of land year after year, the despair of watching crops die or prices drop in response to quirks of climate and market.

More realistic education for a boy being steered toward a profession started in his father's white frame house on North Main Street. Dr. Short combined the hardy work ethic of the prairie pioneers with much respect for the "book learnin'" scoffed at by many of those pioneers. His home was full of books, newspapers, and medical journals. By the time they started school, Walter and his brothers and sisters were much more familiar with the printed word and how it conveyed things of value than were most other country children. Everyday observation in the home yielded many more lessons. By watching his father deal with stricken patients and repeated requests for credit, Walter received valuable demonstrations of compassion and self-control. The doctor could give his children firsthand accounts of the family migration from North Carolina and the Civil War. Since Dr. Short was prominent in village and county, his support was no doubt sought by candidates for local office. In his comments on who was and who was not his man, the doctor made known his prairie Republicanism. Walter's mother was active in the Methodist Episcopal Church and made sure her children had a thorough grounding in Christian values.

At his father's side, Walter got his first lessons in dealing with the community. In the close-knit society of Fillmore, neighbors sat on front porches and talked across hedges and fences, confided in one another, shared jokes, recipes, fishing holes, and business advice, and always paid their debts. But sometimes there were disagreements, raised voices, a refusal to talk for months or years. In his father's home, Walter learned there was only one way for a man of education and character to handle a dispute. An honorable man looked the other party straight in the eye, laid his cards on the table, and listened to what the other man had to say. When the problem was resolved, both sides shook on it and shared a drink or a cigar. An honorable man never refused the chance to settle a problem, never stomped off and started rumors behind the other's back, never held a grudge.

By the time he was in his early teens, Walter Short's course of development was firmly set on the path determined by his parents. The image that comes through the record is of a quiet, studious boy mindful of his parents and always in control of himself. His schoolboy and Halloween pranks were probably among the tamest in town. It is difficult to imagine him even dipping a girl's pigtail in the inkwell of his classroom desk. An excellent student, he was probably teased for always doing what his teachers directed. If he ever sneaked out behind the barn to puff on a cigar or sip corn whiskey, the first time was likely the last.

Only one thing worried his parents. His father noticed the boy was not showing the interests and tendencies that would point him toward a career in medicine, the vague mix of curiosity about cells and compassion for the living whole, of faith in science and awe of nature. Walter showed those things individually, but they did not coalesce in his father's eye in such a way as to cause him to think that he and his wife had another doctor in the house. Walter could parse a sentence as well as most students, but words sparked no unusual interest. When his teachers turned to arithmetic, however, Walter's mind lit up. He felt an immediate affinity for numbers and the way they could reduce confusion to logic. Numbers and formulae were unchanging, dependable.

Walter's high school graduation in June 1897 was the local event of the season, and not only because he was in it. The Short family accounted for three Fillmore High School graduates that year, out of a total of seven. Apparently, neither parents nor school officials were very strict about the pace of students' progress through the system, for although Walter was right on schedule at age seventeen, his brother Ulysses was nineteen and sister Emma twenty. Nor was graduation 1897 an event of merely local note. The high school principal succeeded in attracting the state superintendent of public instruction for an address to the tiny class. During commencement exercises in the Lutheran Church, Ulysses was salutatorian, Emma spoke on "Some of the Beauties of Nature," and Walter was valedictorian and delivered an oration.[4]

The question of what Walter would do after high school was never much of an issue. He had been raised in an educated family, and he would not be satisfied with a diploma from a village high school. Of course he would go to college, but what would he study? Soon the new law school at the University of Illinois caught his attention. On his application form he answered the question "What course of study do you desire to pursue?" with "Preparatory to Law." Walter was accepted with the class of 1901.[5]

Fillmore was small, but in any direction stretched a range of opportunities as wide as the open midwestern horizon. Every morning, noon, and evening the wailing whistles of Cloverleaf Road trains echoed across broad fields, calling those who would hear to new worlds down the shiny rails. His father had taught him how to listen, so young Walter Short heard the call, and at the age of seventeen he started down those shiny rails. On a bright September morning, he shaved, dressed, and ate a big breakfast. He hefted a bulging carpetbag onto the back of his father's buggy and rode with his parents to the station. A smoke plume grew above the ripening corn, and a rush of anticipation overtook parents and son. Last-minute parental reminders were largely drowned out as the train hissed and sighed to a stop. Walter kissed his mother, shook hands with his father, and stepped up into the stuffy coach. As the train chugged and jerked through the cornfields, the bright young man knew he was leaving behind more than his hometown. An arrangement of values, a whole way of life, receded into the smoky past behind the train, and nothing would be the same again. Walter Short would return to Fillmore many times in his life but he would never again live the quiet rhythms of a prairie village.

WHEN WALTER ARRIVED at the University of Illinois, he walked into an educational revolution. Andrew Sloan Draper, a transplanted New Yorker, was in the middle of a ten-year presidency that would transform Illinois from an agricultural and industrial academy into a true university addressing the varied problems and opportunities of a fast-developing world power. From 1894 to 1904, the university added seven departments or schools, including the law school that had aroused Walter's interest. During Draper's tenure, the number of buildings nearly doubled and the enrollment more than tripled.[6]

For a young man from a tiny village, the University of Illinois opened vast new horizons. The numbers measuring the new experience suddenly exploded. In Fillmore, Walter had been 1 of 7 members of his high school class; at Illinois his freshman class numbered 217, 44 of them women. The 1897–98 enrollment of 1,034 was twice the population of Fillmore. And Walter, along with most of his classmates, probably described the towns on either side of the burgeoning campus as big cities. Champaign counted 9,100 people, Urbana 5,700.[7]

The range of activities was similarly dazzling. Beginning early on the university's unofficial calendar of events, and no doubt shocking to many new students, was the annual freshman-sophomore war, the ritualized violence by which each of the lower classes crashed and trashed social events of the other throughout the year. More civilized entertainment could be found at football and baseball games, with the big crowds orchestrated by jumping-jack cheerleaders, all of them men. Fraternities offered strong camaraderie and mysterious rituals. Clubs promoted dozens of interests, from animal husbandry to Greek literature, astronomy to oratory. And at the Saturday hops in the armory, Walter could meet and dance with more girls than he had ever seen in one place.[8]

With the class of 1901 groping for an identity—they began by calling themselves the "Terriers of Umpty-One"—Walter settled into the life of a student. In the 1890s, dormitories were not yet among the standard structures on American campuses. Most students lived in boardinghouses, and Walter found a room at 603 East Healey Street in Urbana, just three blocks from campus. For extracurricular activities, he chose the *Illio,* the university's yearbook, and the Mathematical Club. In his sophomore year, he was popular enough to be elected class historian.[9]

Of all the activities available to Walter, the Illinois Battalion won his strongest interest. As a land-grant college, Illinois was required to offer military instruction to all male students every year of their enrollment. Over the years the military requirement had been relaxed so that by the time Walter arrived on campus, the course was an elective for juniors and seniors. Freshmen and sophomore men studied tactics once a week for six terms. For Walter the policy relaxation was irrelevant. He remained in the battalion throughout his years at Illinois, except during his sophomore year, when the Military Department was closed because of the Spanish-American War.[10]

Fully accredited by the federal government, the Military Department was staffed by commissioned Army officers and supplied with three hundred rifles and two field pieces. Uniforms were patterned after those worn at West Point. During Walter's freshman year the battalion consisted of four infantry companies, an artillery detachment, and a band. In his senior year, Military Department enrollment jumped, probably in response to the flush of patriotism which swept the nation during the war against Spain, and the Illinois corps of cadets was expanded to a regiment of two battalions, three companies each. Leadership positions were filled by faculty appointment. In his junior year, Walter was named a sergeant in Company A, and in his senior year captain of Company B.[11]

Academically, Walter got off to a hesitant start. At the beginning of his first term he had to request a postponement of his entrance exam because of eye trouble. Soon no one could remember this early hitch in his progress. From his first term he wrote a brilliant record. According to academic policy of the day, students remained in a probationary status for two years, a practice necessitated by the wide range in quality of high schools at the time. Those with satisfactory grades were allowed to "matriculate" and continue work toward a degree. For Walter, the policy was unnecessary. His grades, recorded on a 100-point system, remained in the 90s with monotonous frequency. Only twice in four years did he receive a score in the 80s. He won his highest grades in the Military Department; of eleven courses taken, he earned perfect 100s in eight.[12]

Although Walter did well in his military studies, he did not decide on a military career while at Illinois. He seriously considered two other fields. University counselors advised him to study German as preparation for law school. After several terms of German, however, in addition to the usual variety of liberal arts courses, he developed an interest in teaching mathematics. Six weeks before his graduation, he wrote President Draper of his desire for an appointment to the new American school system in the Philippines. But parental objection forced a change in this plan only two weeks later. Thoughts of career choices were set aside as Walter finished his mathematics thesis, "Continuous Functions without Derivatives," and took final exams. In his Military Department final, he finished first with a near-perfect score of 99.76. With the end of exams, the class of 1901 jumped into a round of parties and farewells.[13]

As one of the top students in his class, Walter was due a number of honors, and they started coming on Class Day. Following several orations and musical performances in the chapel, the university band gave an outdoor concert, and ten seniors presented farewell addresses to buildings and grounds. Appropriately, Walter delivered the farewell to the armory. That night everyone attended the Senior Ball. More honors came at the university's thirtieth commencement. Governor Richard Yates presented Walter and seven classmates commissions as brevet captains in the Illinois National Guard. In addition, he was one of three graduates reported to the adjutant general in Washington as a distinguished cadet for listing in the Register of the United States Army. On top of all that was induction into Phi Beta Kappa.[14]

The few surviving photographs hint at the personality behind Walter's impressive record of scholarship and leadership. A serious, handsome face projects a friendly, optimistic attitude toward the future. The hair is parted in the middle and combed straight down the sides. Large eyes full of trust fix the viewer. The lower lip is full, the mouth holds a slight smile. No cynicism, no guile creases the clean-shaven face. The forthright set of the shoulders and head suggests self-control. The young graduate was certainly aware of his intelligence, and like so many others of his time he was willing to use it for the benefit of less fortunate people, as shown by his interest in teaching in the Philippines. There is no reason to doubt his acceptance of the widely held convictions of his generation: that every person should strive to improve the world according to individual abilities, and that hard work combined with faith in God and one's fellow man were the prerequisites of success. It seems appropriate to view Walter Short at this early stage of his career as a brainy Horatio Alger.

After graduating, Walter returned to Fillmore for a well-deserved vacation. He answered the perennial need of the new graduate for income by taking a job teaching mathematics at Western Military Academy in Upper Alton, Illinois, across the Mississippi River from St. Louis. There must have been some raised eyebrows in the Short household at this decision, for Dr. Short remembered all too well the frequent moves and low pay of his father's teaching career. Walter may have made his first job choice acceptable to his parents by explaining it as a useful activity while awaiting an opening in the Army's strictly controlled quota of commissions.

Walter faced his first class at Western Military Academy on 15 September 1901. Founded in 1879, the academy offered a War Department-approved secondary curriculum to about one hundred boys. The life of a teacher at the academy had little in common with the university-centered routine he had just left. Outside the classroom there were faculty teas and church socials, but not much more. The three-mile trip by horse or buggy from Upper Alton on the high ground east of the Mississippi to Alton on the riverfront required most of the day, and once there, the newcomer found the social life geared more to the hard lives of men working on the river than to young college graduates. There was ample opportunity for the new teacher to read the books he had not had time for at Illinois.[15]

Even before his first semester of teaching had ended, Walter received a suggestion about a different career. Late in November, President Draper wrote from Champaign-Urbana, asking if he would be interested in a Regular Army commission. Draper recalled Walter's "personal qualities, your good scholarship, and your interest and proficiency in military work." Without waiting for a reply, Draper submitted to George Cortelyou, secretary to President Theodore Roosevelt, the names of two Illinois graduates for Army commissions. One, of course, was Walter Short, who Draper described as being of "thoroughly sound character." In December Draper wrote again, reporting his recommendation of Walter for an Army commission and concluding with the hope that the young graduate would "properly represent your university."[16]

Things began to move quickly for Walter in the new year of 1902. On the morning of January 22, he and six others presented themselves before a board of Army officers in the Pullman Building in Chicago. During a full day of written tests and interviews, Walter won high marks from the board, and he made arrangements to leave his teaching position. He was sent an infantry commission, backdated to 2 February 1901, and returned to Fillmore to prepare for another momentous change in his life, this one even more dramatic than the transition from his home village to a major university community.[17]

2

A Zealous Young Officer

THE WORLD OF 1902 GAVE EVERY INDI-
CATION THAT A YOUNG MAN BEGINNING a military career would find ample opportunity to practice his chosen profession. The volatile international situation
generated enough tension to produce wars with startling frequency and far-
reaching consequences. Only two years earlier, the Western Powers and Japan
had joined forces to suppress the Boxer Rebellion in China and then imposed a
punitive settlement that virtually guaranteed future conflict. In Europe, the
Balkan states were already the warm tinderbox that would soon flash into the
deadliest war the world had yet seen. In vast empires controlled by a small number of nations, subject peoples resisted their colonial status, and by so doing
ensured that their conquerors would have to continuously dispatch punitive
expeditions and occupation forces. Even the United States, despite its formative
experience with imperialism and frequent denunciations of the system, took territories after its victory over Spain in 1898. To justify the policy reversal, Americans adopted an ideology that combined their traditional Manifest Destiny and
a newer faith in the products of the Industrial Revolution. In the words of Senator Albert J. Beveridge of Indiana, "God has marked the American people as
His chosen nation to finally lead the regeneration of the world. . . . We are
trustees of the world's progress, guardians of its righteous peace."[1]

The United States of 1902 was at peace, and according to American tradition, that meant there was no need for a large army. Between the Civil War and the Spanish-American War, the U.S. Army numbered only about twenty-five thousand men, which to defend some seventy million people was by European standards a ridiculously small land force. But victory over Spain in 1898 brought new territories to administer—Cuba, Puerto Rico, Guam, and the Philippines —and in 1901, Congress approved an expansion of the Regular Army from forty-two to fifty-eight regiments. To help lead the new regiments, Congress authorized the commissioning of 837 new first and second lieutenants of the line. More than ten thousand men applied for the new vacancies, and the War Department stacked the odds against civilian applicants like Walter by giving preference to West Point graduates, qualified enlisted men, and former volunteer officers, but the young Illinoisan won his commission.[2]

The Army of 1902 was small, isolated from the society it served, and highly conscious of its traditions. Four years after the Spanish-American War, it numbered 81,275 men, 4,049 of them officers. The senior officer carried the rank of lieutenant general and the title Commanding General of the Army. He presided over a headquarters of ten bureaus in Washington, D.C. Outside the capital, Army organization was based on the regiment. In the early years of the twentieth century, the Army had thirty infantry, fifteen cavalry, and the equivalent of thirteen artillery regiments serving on forty-five posts in the United States and overseas possessions. Each regiment was divided into a headquarters staff and twelve companies of three officers and about sixty men each. At the head of each regiment was the colonel, a grandfatherly figure who might be left in command of the same unit for more than a decade. Many were Civil War veterans, and most were experienced Indian fighters. Official photographs of turn-of-the-century colonels show white-haired or balding men with carefully trimmed beards and moustaches. Some carried so much weight under their blue kersey tunics that they required assistance in mounting their horses. But the fire was still in the eyes, to keep the headquarters staff from getting too comfortable behind their desks.[3]

For the soldiers of 1902, isolation was as much a fact of life as uniforms and regulations. Although the last campaign against the Indians had ended in 1890, most soldiers more than a decade later still garrisoned distant frontier posts. Travel to and from most of these forts required several days. Units posted near cities were avoided by most townspeople. Few daughters made their parents happy by announcing plans to marry soldiers, and everyone knew the worst credit risks were soldiers. Pay was low, still based on legislation of 1871.

Privates rated thirteen dollars a month, with an extra two dollars if the man scored as a marksman on the rifle range and five dollars if he qualified as an expert. Unskilled factory workers earned almost twice as much. Troops on pass had to read demoralizing signs on the doors of some establishments—No Dogs or Soldiers—and were routinely directed to gin mills and red-light districts. A 1911 federal law imposing a five-hundred-dollar fine on proprietors discriminating against soldiers in uniform did little to change public attitudes. Antiquated and prejudicial laws added political restrictions to the soldier's lot. At the turn of the century no one had yet thought of the absentee ballot, and many states specifically withheld the franchise from "idiots, paupers, Indians, soldiers and sailors."[4]

While white Americans directed their more talented sons away from military service, black Americans viewed the Army as an opportunity. The Army was one of the very few American institutions that welcomed black participation and gave equal pay to all soldiers of the same rank and experience. Once in uniform, however, black recruits had to conform to racial attitudes prevailing in civilian society. The Army of 1902 was segregated. Four regiments, the 9th and 10th Cavalry and the 24th and 25th Infantry, were officially designated "colored." All officers, however, were white, and few of them considered assignment to a colored regiment helpful to their careers. White Americans may have accepted the idea of black soldiers defending the nation, but few tolerated the idea of armed blacks garrisoned near their communities. In deference to the majority attitude, the War Department posted the four regiments to the arid expanses of the southwestern states and territories or, after 1898, overseas.

White or black, the individual soldier's life centered on his company, a community of three officers and about sixty men whose cohesiveness could rival that of a family. In the early years of the twentieth century, U.S. Army companies were much more self-sufficient than those in later periods. Companies typically had their own messes, gardens, barbers, and tailors, their own specialists such as carpenters, painters, and plumbers to maintain the barracks, and their own funds to provide extras like condiments for the mess and athletic equipment. The training schedule allowed ample time for practicing these unofficial specialties. Mornings were taken up with drill, which implied everything from close-order and extended marching to tactical problems, practice marches, and firing and cleaning of weapons. Afternoons were reserved for fatigue details: uniform and equipment repair, post maintenance, and mess preparation, which included gardening.

Promotions and transfer policies gave much stability to the company.

Among officers, typically six or seven years' experience was required for promotion from second lieutenant to first, another seven or eight years to make captain. Enlisted men came on active duty under an initial five-year term, all of which was spent in the same company. Those who reenlisted for a career could look forward to spending twenty years or more in the same regiment if not the same company. Promotions came slowly, but few left the service for that reason. A surprising number of troops valued camaraderie and steady but low pay more than rank; every company had its "career privates." Those who thought they would like a change of scenery found no official encouragement; transfer to another unit depended on a vacancy at the same rank or demotion to private. The stability of the company protected soldiers from civilian indifference and bureaucratic alienation. The individual could always count on the advice of experience, a sympathetic ear, a loan to tide one over until the next payday, even a surreptitious drink from a sergeant's locker when stress built up. War Department bureaucrats and regimental officers could issue all the orders and regulations they wanted but the family of the company offered the consolation that made virtually any garrison or field adversity tolerable.

Venerable traditions reinforced the camaraderie. Daily life on post was regulated by the sharp notes of the bugle at reveille, meals, drill, fatigue details, retreat, tattoo, and taps. At morning and evening formations, sergeants counted heads, passed along news, and announced fatigue and guard duty assignments. There was even a little pomp to add glitter to the weekly routine. The spectacle of evening parade, with dress uniforms, well-groomed horses, snapping flags and pennants, snappy band music, and booming salute gun often attracted a crowd of civilians. Saturday morning inspections and the annual inspector general's visit threw everyone into a frenzy of scrubbing and polishing. The regimental anniversary was marked by a sumptuous mess which began as a formal affair but later improved to a friendly or riotous condition after the colonel left and the troops adjourned to company supply sheds to retrieve unauthorized bottles. There were unofficial traditions as well. Every company had its old-timers who could be counted on to pass along to recruits the tricks of passing inspections, supplementing meager pay, or sneaking out of the barracks after taps.

The most pervasive of all traditions was the rank structure, which governed everything from duties, pay, and living quarters to styles of speech and dress. The operative principle behind the tradition was expressed in a brief sentence maddening to recruits but comforting to career men: Rank has its privileges. Congress clearly underlined the principle in the pay scale it voted its men in uniform. Company first sergeants earned $45.00 a month, more than triple a private's pay. A new second lieutenant earned $116.67 a month, and the regimental colonel $333.00 monthly. On-post housing expressed the principle physically: the higher the rank, the bigger the quarters. Bachelor enlisted men lived in the barracks. Those who married had to rent an apartment or home off post at their own expense; married housing was not yet provided by the government. Communication was also much influenced by rank. Enlisted men did not speak directly to their company commanders without the first sergeant's permission, and when they did they referred to themselves in the third person, as in, "Sir, the private requests permission to marry," one of the most common reasons to seek a meeting with the captain.

The officer-enlisted relationship was not the dictatorship it appeared to outsiders. Lines of communication, including complaints, were as open between officer and enlisted man as between officers, as long as the protocol was observed. While officers could deal directly with each other, enlisted men had to negotiate a circuitous route to get the attention of officers. If Corporal Smith thought Lieutenant Jones was doing a lousy job, he told the nearest sergeant, who told the first sergeant, who told the company commander, who then counseled Lieutenant Jones on his deficiencies. The monopoly of authority among officers by no means implied a monopoly of expertise. As Lieutenant Short well knew, junior officers depended on the experience of long-serving noncommissioned officers. The officer who ignored the advice of his NCOs risked losing the loyalty of his men and the effectiveness of his command.

SECOND LIEUTENANT SHORT's first orders directed him to the 25th Infantry, one of the regiments on occupation duty in the Philippines. His journey to the 25th began at Jefferson Barracks, Missouri, a few miles south of St. Louis. The newest lieutenant walked purposefully up to an imposing stone gate, took the sentry's salute, and asked directions to the headquarters building. On 4 April, the adjutant endorsed his orders. Then Short did what soldiers have always done and always hated doing when they are keyed for action. He waited. For a week he waited while the personnel officer tried to figure out how to unite him with his regiment eight thousand miles away. Finally, he was given a rail ticket to one of the Army's West Coast posts, the Presidio of San Francisco. Arriving on the sixteenth, he expected to stay only until the next ship left for the Philippines. Instead, his orders were changed by a rotation of units overseas. The 25th Infantry would be returning to the United States soon, and rather than crossing the Pacific twice only weeks apart, Short would await his unit in

San Francisco. He would not be participating in the "regeneration of the world" that Senator Beveridge had held up as a worthy American goal, at least not yet.[5]

As a temporarily unattached officer, Short was a welcome sight to the base commander at the Presidio, who, like his counterparts at other posts, always had a few undesirable jobs to fill but no volunteers. Until the 25th tied up at dockside, Short would be supervising casuals, the catch-all category of men on their way to another post, back to civilian life or to the stockade. In casual barracks Short saw the best and the worst of the Army. He was in daily contact with wide-eyed young recruits and gravel-voiced old sergeants as well as the sick, lame, and lazy of casual barracks: malaria-wracked and wounded men just back from the Philippines, cynical deserters, desperate men who saw the Army as a refuge from poverty or the law, thirty-year men who knew every trick in the book, even convicted criminals under guard. The job was not much different from that of a jail warden. Rather than an aberration in his Army experience, Short's time with casuals was realistic preparation for the range of character and capability he would have to deal with.

Finally, on 13 August, the 25th Infantry sailed into San Francisco Bay aboard the U.S. Army transport *General George Crook*. While troops streamed off the ship, Short met his first regimental commander, Col. Alpheus H. Bowman, and his first company commander, Capt. Frank H. Albright of Company E. After a week of sorting out gear and personnel, the 25th made a four-hour march to Oakland and boarded trains for permanent stations, the 1st and 3d Battalions to Fort Niobrara, Nebraska, and the 2d Battalion with Short to Fort Reno, Oklahoma Territory.

Second Lieutenant Short began his Army career with more authority than expertise. Even officers who had marched up and down their university football fields for four years knew little about the inner workings of a line regiment. To remedy the ignorance of new junior officers, post commanders conducted garrison schools. At the Fort Reno garrison school, lieutenants studied company administration, close-order and extended drill, manual of guard duty, small-arms firing regulations, troops in campaign, minor tactics, military law, field engineering, military topography and sketching, and international law. Short also tried to sneak in some cavalry training, equestrian and hippology, since he loved to ride horses, but this had to be primarily a weekend activity. To add realism to their training, student-officers served brief tours as assistants to post staff officers in quartermaster, commissary, ordnance, and other specialties. Tests determined whether they were excused from the training or repeated courses.[6]

Social life on post revolved around married officers and their families, but even unmarried lieutenants had social obligations, and they occasioned as much anxiety as a major inspection. A timeless Army tradition required new arrivals on any post to make a social call on their commanding officer and his lady. On the appointed day, usually a Sunday, the lieutenants would put on carefully pressed uniforms and walk to the colonel's home. After dropping their cards in a silver tray, they would introduce themselves to the colonel and his wife and, the young officers hoped, a pretty daughter, then join inane chit-chat and admire the colonel's souvenirs from the Indian wars or teak furniture and water buffalo horns from the Philippines.

In preparation for the event, Lieutenant Short and his peers ordered name cards in flowery script, then checked with the adjutant to see when the colonel would be receiving. In the brief time Walter and his fellow officers had to present themselves to their commanding officer, they could only wonder at the mysterious process by which naive second lieutenants became knowledgeable colonels. They knew it would take a long time, especially if the peacetime conditions of 1902 held, and they passed around a bit of barracks doggerel to describe the long, slow career path: "Keep your bowels open, your feet dry / And you'll be a colonel before you die!"[7]

But few lieutenants could appreciate the potent role of political favor in advancing careers in a stable, if not stagnant, institution or the blatant self-promotion that many engaged in to win that favor. Ambitious officers took months of leave and used much of it to patrol corridors and cloakrooms in Washington pleading their individual causes. Mid-career officers were known to write letters to the War Department recommending decorations, prime assignments, and promotions for one another, and to append notes of support from as many congressmen and generals as they could talk into describing their sterling qualities.

For a junior officer at Fort Reno there was much more sweat, dirt, and gun oil than anxiety about social obligations or career patterns. Unless Congress cut the military budget so severely that ammunition had to be rationed, every company made a monthly visit to the rifle range. This gave each man the chance to get down in the prone position and inhale the Oklahoma dust while sighting in on a distant target. Most of the garrison routine involved more strenuous activity. Short got his first physical test in uniform when he began taking Company E out on practice marches, and as the newest officer in the company he probably got the duty more than he wanted. The weekly ordeal was designed to keep the troops tough and trim by sending them over twelve miles of rough terrain under the weight of full packs and rifles at 105 paces to the minute. Afterward, Short put the men back in their barracks and inspected feet. The march generated not only sweat and blisters but also a report, which had to be couched in gentlemanly formality. Addressing the regimental commander, Short began with "I have the honor to submit the following report," then went on to describe the route and elapsed time of the march as well as the condition of feet at its end.

Drill, tactical exercises, dusty practice marches, and fatigue details still left free time for most of the men, except those assigned a stint of guard duty for the night. In the days before USO tours and Rest and Recreation leaves, the War Department made minimal provision for the leisure activities of its men in uniform. Each company had its own dayroom equipped with parlor chairs, pool tables, and a few magazines. Units fielded their own athletic teams, usually football, baseball, and boxing. Standard post buildings included a library, canteen, and chapel, but post movie theaters had not yet appeared. At a time when the proportion of foreign-born in some regiments topped 25 percent, some men had to spend their off-duty time studying the language of their new homeland. For the underpaid soldier on pass, the only alternative to those activities was the "soldiers' town" just outside the main gate. In these towns, often no more than one block-long street and an alley, a small number of legitimate concerns, such as a general store, restaurants, tailors, and cobblers, was always outnumbered by businesses less savory if not illegal—bars, gambling and tattoo parlors, and houses of prostitution. Carefully following his sergeant's directions, the soldier on pass looked for the street full of uniforms, then bellied up to a bar and proceeded to get as drunk as his money and curfew allowed.

As with most aspects of Army life, the situation differed for officers. Higher pay made a weekend in Oklahoma City a real possibility for Short and his peers. Otherwise, he spent most of his free time on post. Getting drunk and consorting with ladies of the evening violated every value his parents had taught him. His taste in entertainment tended toward the prosaic. A rubber of bridge or a good book provided diversion enough of an evening. On weekends he either polished his marksmanship on the pistol range or went hunting on the farther reaches of the post.[8]

Lieutenant Short had barely completed his first year in uniform when he heard the most stunning news to come out of the War Department since the call-up of 1898. The Army was reforming itself. The war with Spain had revealed serious shortcomings at the highest levels of Army administration. Enthusiastic volunteers had been inadequately trained then hurriedly shipped to ports of embarkation. Army authorities soon discovered they had not contracted for enough ships to carry units to the battle fronts, so large numbers of troops languished in unsanitary camps and fell victim to diseases. The quartermaster had clothed the troops in wool for a war fought in tropical areas. During most of the war rumors swirled about soldiers having to eat "embalmed beef." Most troubling for future mobilizations, there was no single center of planning and command with sufficient authority to coordinate all bureaus and field commands. Instead of one head, the Army had several, and their cooperation depended on the chemistry of personality.

Soon after Spain surrendered, President McKinley appointed Elihu Root secretary of war. The new official, who had no military experience, began a study of the most respected foreign armies of the time to discover their strengths. Between 1901 and 1903, Root, either by his own authority or that of Congress when necessary, expanded and modernized the Army. A general staff was established to conduct all military planning. Root and the Congress resolved the competing claims to authority by the commanding general of the Army and the bureau chiefs in favor of the former, who became a presidentially appointed chief of staff and the direct subordinate of the secretary of war. The War Department strengthened service schools to prepare officers for successively greater responsibilities and added a war college to teach senior officers a broad strategic perspective. Promotion depended on examination results rather than seniority, and all officers periodically rotated between line and staff assignments. The regular Army took an active role in training state militias to bring them closer to the ideal of an effective reserve force. Increased funding supported the development of new weapons, and a Joint Army-Navy Board initiated continuous interservice planning. Annual unit maneuvers tested the new system. With the adoption of Root's reforms, the U.S. Army became a more professional force and a more effective agent of national policy. For Walter Short and his peers, Secretary Root had laid out new paths to traditional career objectives.[9]

ALL INDICATIONS ARE that Walter Short had no difficulty adjusting to either the Army or his lowly position in its officer corps. Efficiency reports from his early years in uniform describe a conscientious, intelligent young officer gradually gaining more administrative than troop-leading experience. Short's first evaluation covered his first months in the Army to 30 June 1902. He was judged "Excellent" in habits, general conduct, and bearing, "Very good" in professional zeal and ability, and "Good" in capacity for command. But his reporting senior diluted the marks with the concluding notation that he had had to report on a large number of officers coming to the post for brief periods and he could not get to know them well.

Short's second efficiency report, for one year beginning 1 July 1902, reflects his first regimental duty. His reporting senior found him to be "a man of good abilities and will prove capable officer with experience." Reports of the next several years show him growing steadily in the estimation of his superiors. His attention to duty and professional zeal were considered "Excellent," and in his studies at the Fort Reno Officers' school, he "stood No. 1 in his class, second years course." He showed "peculiar fitness or marked ability" in hippology, engineering, and topography. To the question "Would you have any objection to this officer being under your immediate command?" his reporting senior in 1904 wrote, "No, he would be one of my first selections." The same officer judged him suited for wartime duty with a battalion staff section, such as those headed by the quartermaster or commissary officers. Two years later, Short's company commander noted that he "rarely touches liquor," was "perfectly competent to command a company," and was "not by nature diplomatic, but is discreet and has good judgement." The same report concluded with one sentence in the remarks section: "He is very intelligent & keeps all his work right up to date." His 1907 report concluded in glowing praise: "I consider this officer the most promising of any of the second or first lieutenants I have known in the eight years I have been in the Army with one exception. He is extremely quick in handling any question which requires mathematical skill."[10]

Like all new infantry officers, Short was given experience in a variety of additional duties. He spent brief periods, as little as three weeks in some cases, supervising the Fort Reno firing ranges, mess hall, recruiting office, stockade, and ordnance and signal sections. He also filled in for company commanders on leave. He spent longer periods as battalion and post quartermaster and commissary officer, a dual job which doubtless gave him headaches as he struggled with all the details involved in feeding, clothing, equipping, and housing a large number of men, horses, and mules. These duty stints occasionally spared Short some rigorous field work with his regiment. He missed the entire fall maneuvers of 1903 in Kansas, including a 120-mile march from the rail station at Wichita to Fort Riley. But he did take part in the ordeal of a twenty-one-day, 204-mile practice march in October 1906.

One of his additional duties took Short away from his regiment's home post. The War Department periodically updated its maps through a project known as the Progressive Military Map of the United States. Teams of one officer and several enlisted men surveyed areas measuring about thirty-five miles by sixty while living out of a mule-drawn wagon. Supervising engineers from the nearest department headquarters issued skeleton maps to officers in charge of each team and directed them to fill in terrain details on a scale of one inch to two miles. Ground distances were measured either by attaching an odometer to the wagon wheel or, if a railroad ran through the area, walking along the track bed and counting rail lengths. Short served two tours on the project. He spent all but a few days of July 1906 near Jarilla Junction, New Mexico Territory. Six months later, he walked an area around Sierra Blanca, Texas, for seven weeks. The engineer officer supervising the project commended him for covering "a large territory in a remarkably short time" and judged his work "complete and eminently satisfactory."[11]

No matter how many extra duties he was given, Short still found time for his favorite pastime, target shooting. He early established himself as an outstanding marksman, especially in the pistol, a skill he developed while growing up in Fillmore. In small towns and on farms of the nineteenth century, almost everyone owned guns, and any young man, doctor's son or not, could at least hit a fence post at fifty paces, even if he were not experienced at hunting elusive game like squirrel, rabbit, or pheasant. Short's marksmanship was further refined in the Illinois Battalion. He first gained recognition in 1905, when he outshot everyone on the Fort Reno pistol range and then represented his regiment's parent headquarters, the Southwestern Division, at the annual Army matches at Fort Sill, Oklahoma Territory. In this, his first major competition, he won a bronze medal. The next year he did even better, gaining selection to teams on three levels of competition—Southwestern Division, Army, and U.S. National. The matches were held first at Fort Sill, then at Fort Sheridan, Illinois. Again, Short won a medal. Between his first match in 1905 and his last in 1913, he won ten medals in pistol competition.[12]

In January 1906, the garrison routine at Fort Reno came to an abrupt halt. The 25th Infantry was ordered to garrison three posts in Texas. Although unit changes of station had long been part of Army life, the receipt of signed orders always provoked a round of bellyaching. Not only did all equipment have to be cleaned, inspected, and packed, but the troops had to endure an around-the-clock ride in a cramped train. On married soldiers the change of station imposed a financial burden as well, for in 1906 the government paid no moving expenses.

Because the 25th Infantry was a black regiment, the transfer drew more attention from civilians than did the periodic moves of white regiments. As War

Department officials watched nervously from a distance, the regimental head-quarters and 2d Battalion completed the 834-mile move to Fort Bliss near El Paso without incident. But when the Army announced a few months later that the other two battalions of the regiment would participate in summer maneuvers with the Texas Militia, clear opposition developed. A number of influential Texans, including the governor, made known their displeasure at the assignment of a black regiment to their state. Col. R. W. Hoyt, commanding officer of the 25th Infantry, wrote the War Department requesting his regiment be excused from the Texas maneuvers. The secretary of war granted Hoyt's request, and the two battalions went directly to their assigned posts, 1st Battalion to Fort Brown, near Brownsville at the southern tip of Texas, and 3d Battalion to Fort McIntosh near Laredo.[13]

On 28 July, 1st Battalion arrived at Fort Brown to a hostile reception from townspeople. The troops went about their soldierly routines, going out of their way to avoid friction with civilians, but the feared racial outbreak occurred only two weeks later. On the night of 13 August, about twenty armed men moved through the streets of Brownsville, shooting into buildings at random. A bartender was killed and a policeman wounded. President Roosevelt immediately appointed an investigator, who concluded the shooting had been done by black soldiers whose names he could not determine. The tense situation was defused locally when a few days later the battalion was sent north to Fort Reno where the investigation continued. A second presidential investigator reached the same conclusion as the first but failed to uncover the names of the alleged offenders. Despite the lack of evidence, the president accepted the recommendation of his investigator that all troops who had been at Fort Brown the night of the shooting be discharged from the Army. In November 1906, the men of Companies B, C, and D were discharged without honor, and without court-martial, denied all benefits including pension, barred from reenlistment, and excluded from civil service employment. Among the 167 men discharged were 26 with more than ten years' service and 19 who had been decorated or cited for bravery in the Spanish-American War.[14]

By a quirk of scheduling, Short missed the racial outbreak at Brownsville. While the 25th Infantry was losing three companies under questionable circumstances, he was winning his first medal for pistol marksmanship. Given the racial attitudes of the time, a clash like the shooting at Brownsville and discharge of 167 troops made no difference to the careers of officers in the regiment, all of whom were white. The Army regrouped, recruited new black soldiers, and resumed the usual garrison routine. Nearly five decades would pass before racial integration came to the Army, and not until 1972 would the U.S. government make amends to the soldiers discharged for what was known as the Brownsville Affray.

IN THE EARLY MONTHS of 1907, Lieutenant Short marked his fifth year on the bottom of the officer corps rank ladder, not an inordinately long time to be a second lieutenant, but enough to make him wonder if the War Department bureaucracy far away in Washington needed a reminder of his existence. Apparently someone had been watching the paperwork, for in April he received a summons to a promotion board meeting at Fort Leavenworth, Kansas. He did well on written tests and in an interview and was placed on the promotion eligible list to await a vacancy at his new rank. Two months later, Short learned that the year 1907 held still another milestone for him, his first overseas assignment. After five years in the United States, the 25th Infantry was being sent back to the Philippines for its second tour of duty in the islands. The move overseas began in June when the regimental headquarters, band, and 2d Battalion, with Company E and Short, participated in the annual Joint Army and Militia Coast Defense Exercises of the Department of California. Following a few weeks of garrison routine, 2d Battalion was joined at the Presidio by its sister battalions, and on 10 August the entire regiment sailed aboard the transport *General George Crook*. Steaming west at a leisurely pace, the ship made port calls at Honolulu, Nagasaki, and Manila before debarking the 25th Infantry at Parang on the west coast of Mindanao on 13 September. Three days later, 2d Battalion was sent to its station thirty-five miles farther down the coast at the town of Malabang. Here Short settled in for his first close-up experience with a foreign culture.

Short and his comrades walked down the gangplank into a situation that was still new to the U.S. Army, the occupation of foreign territory. After the Spanish surrender in 1898, the McKinley administration decided to keep the Philippines. The Filipinos had a different idea—national independence—and thousands took up arms against their liberators. During three years of sporadic guerrilla warfare, the Americans learned how to fight in the jungles and gradually subdued the outgunned freedom fighters. By the time President Roosevelt issued his peace and amnesty proclamation on 4 July 1902, all but a few Filipinos accepted American control. The Army then turned to military government and economic assistance. Soldiers trained a national constabulary—the Philippine Scouts—and local police forces. They supervised elections, collected and disbursed tax and license revenues, regulated commerce, and enforced new sanitary standards. Army engineers reclaimed malarial swamps and built roads, bridges, port facilities, schools, and clinics. Army medical teams conducted vaccination campaigns on every island. In all, nearly five hundred military government teams were at work throughout the Philippines.[15]

A young man from a small town on the Illinois prairie could not be expected to embrace immediately the dry administrative routines of military government. Mindanao offered too much of the exotic. Steaming tangled jungles, so beautiful from a distance but so exhausting to patrol, were home to dazzling floral explosions, huge teak and mahogany trees, skittering scorpions, undulating centipedes, and huge, somnolent pythons. Less dangerous creatures were at first wonders to write home about but soon became enormously irritating, especially the flying cockroaches and little green lizards that crawled across ceilings and too often dropped onto desks and dinner plates. From villages of nipa huts came a luxury undreamed of by American soldiers: loyal servants easily affordable on Army pay. But lurking in the background of this tropical wonderland was the possibility of cholera or malaria and of combat against fierce Muslim tribesmen, the Moros.

The mere sight of Moro warriors was enough to instill fear. Strapped around or hidden in turbans, loose jackets, and sarongs or trousers of garish colors were more daggers and sabers than they could use at once. They liked to deal in slaves, kill Christians, and make war on anyone outside their tribes. Short took the advice of those more experienced at living on Mindanao, sleeping with not only his pistol close by but a baseball bat as well, since bullets alone sometimes would not stop determined Moro raiders.[16]

While still acclimatizing to the debilitating heat and humidity of Mindanao, Short faced a desk piled high with paperwork. During his first month in the islands, he served as 2d Battalion adjutant. To that was added the familiar job of post commissary the next month. In November, he got some firsthand experience with military government when he was selected municipal president of Malabang. The position embodied the full breadth of what the Americans were trying to accomplish in the Philippines. Basic to the American concept of democracy was strong local government supported by an active citizenry. The Spanish had governed the islands through a centralized system which the Americans determined to root out by going into every village and building institutions of self government. The municipal president, in the person of an appointed Army officer, was the all-important contact between American policy makers and Filipino villagers. Each municipal president had to demonstrate a wide knowledge of democratic procedures and public administration, a sense of justice, and an incorruptible civic spirit. Short's duties included collecting customs and internal revenues, presiding over civil and criminal court cases, supervising the town council and police, and enforcing sanitation standards.[17]

The War Department ended Short's term as municipal president with the good news that a first lieutenant's billet had opened up in the 16th Infantry. An overseas tour of two or three years had been reduced to a two-month interruption of stateside duty. With transfer orders in hand, Short gave himself over to the slow workings of the Army transportation system. It took him twelve days to get to Manila, where he waited two weeks for a transport back to San Francisco. In Manila, Short got his only taste of the servant-softened life in the colonial capital. He could pass long sultry afternoons sipping exotic drinks on the Manila Hotel veranda, take dinners at the Army and Navy Club, and attend dances amid the scent of hibiscus.

Eleven days before Christmas, Short walked up the gangplank of the Army transport *Buford* and promptly got stuck with paperwork for the voyage when he was appointed adjutant for troops embarked. Thirty-five days later, the *Buford* tied up in San Francisco. A generous peacetime Army policy allowed Short seven weeks' leave and three days' travel time to his next post, Fort Crook, Nebraska, ten miles south of Omaha. On 12 March 1908, four months after he left the 25th Infantry and Malabang, he stepped up to the main gate at Fort Crook.[18]

SHORT'S FIRST PROBLEM in Nebraska was learning how to dress, not for style but for survival. On tropical Mindanao a single shirt would be sweat-soaked by noon, but on the Great Plains in winter four or five layers might be necessary to prevent frostbite in temperatures as low as forty-five degrees below zero. While making the transition, the new first lieutenant and his new unit, Company E, Capt. Martin L. Crimmins commanding, carried out the timeless routines of soldiering. Regimental returns of the period reduce an entire month's activities to the same three words with monotonous frequency: "Usual garrison duty." Almost all soldiers realized sooner of later that the usual garrison duty, if allowed to run its repetitive course, could erode morale. Short countered the routine with reading and bridge in quarters and riding and hunting on weekends. But he spent most of his free time, including much of his leave, on the post firing range. His skill came to fruition in the summer of 1909 when he won the National Pistol Championship at Camp Perry, Ohio.[19] This triumph made him for a time one of the best-known junior officers in the Army, and at the same time the subject of intraservice bragging by men of the 16th Infantry.

The following year, Short got his second overseas assignment, but it would not take him as far as the Philippines. The 16th Infantry was ordered to Alaska, with several of its companies assigned to garrison scattered posts. Along with the move came increased responsibility. Short was given Company A, an acknowledgment of his leadership ability, since company commanders were normally one rank above him. En route to Alaska aboard the Army transport *Buford*, the regimental commander, Col. Cornelius Gardener, described Short in an efficiency report as a "zealous Young Officer with no bad habits."[20]

After a month at sea, regimental headquarters debarked at Fort Davis, near Nome. But Short could not unpack yet, for Company A was sent 425 miles overland and up the Yukon River. For the next two years the company would garrison Fort Gibbon, at the mouth of the Tanana River and only one hundred miles south of the Arctic Circle. The mission was to guard and maintain part of a 395-mile stretch of the recently constructed military telegraph line connecting Alaska with the War Department in Washington. Duty in the interior of Alaska, with its extreme isolation, subzero temperatures, and disorienting midnight sun, imposed such severe noncombat strain on soldiers that units sent there experienced dramatic increases in rates of alcoholism, insanity, and suicide. Short decided to counter the challenging environment with an intense literary exercise. He bought multivolume sets of Alexandre Dumas, Guy de Maupassant, James Fenimore Cooper, and Edgar Allan Poe—a total of forty-one volumes. Besides reading, soldiers could take in the spectacular scenery of the mountainous Alaskan interior, hunt caribou, and fish with the Eskimos to stave off boredom. Otherwise, soldiering in the frigid northern territory came down to discipline or drink. Even the regimental historian passed off the experience with a yawn: "The tour of duty in Alaska was uneventful." Short's reading may have expanded his horizons, but it also imposed changes on his routine and appearance. On his return to the Presidio of San Francisco in July 1912, he was fitted for eyeglasses.[21]

Coming from the most frigid outpost of American influence, Short went to the California coast for a prime staff assignment. From November 1912 he was to be the secretary of the School of Musketry at the Presidio of Monterey. A direct result of the reforms of Elihu Root, the School of Musketry trained small units in techniques of fire control for various weapons, and developed methods of employment for new weapons. At Monterey, Short became fascinated with a new weapon the Army was not yet sure how to use, the machine gun. Rapid-fire weapons had been integrated into European armies for nearly a decade when the U.S. Army adopted the French Benet-Mercie in 1910.[22] When Short joined the School of Musketry staff, a committee of officers was experimenting with techniques of employment and crew structure for an infantry unit equipped with machine guns.[23] As secretary of the school, Short spent more time behind a desk than in the field with the test committee. When not tending to his paperwork, he repeated garrison school courses in military hygiene and infantry drill regulations. In the summer of 1913, he entered the Army pistol competition and topped everyone, winning the First Gold Medal.[24]

While at the School of Musketry, Walter met the young woman who would change his life. In February 1913, the school moved from Monterey to Fort Sill, Oklahoma. Weekend social events at Fort Sill included a Friday night bowling party, Saturday night hop at the Officers' Club, Sunday morning hunt breakfast, and afternoon polo matches. These events attracted civilians, including young women, from as far away as Oklahoma City, eighty-five miles to the north. For most single officers such affairs turned out to be welcome changes of routine and nothing more. Social attitudes and demographics discouraged bachelors from expecting too much. In an age when unmarried young ladies went nowhere without a chaperon, dating involved a rather elaborate protocol. If the bachelor and his date were farther apart than a buggy ride, a married couple had to be talked into accepting a house guest for a weekend. The need for married hosts and the social disdain for soldiers which kept many "proper" young women away from military installations ensured a chronic shortage of marriage-age women at post functions.[25]

At a Friday night bowling party in the fall of 1913, Walter decided to buck the odds. He spotted an attractive young girl with dark hair and asked a friend for an introduction. He did not back off when informed that the young lady in question was already engaged. "Well, she isn't married, is she?"[26] Thereupon the lieutenant was introduced to Miss Florence Isabel Dean of Oklahoma City. One of the first things she told her new suitor was not to call her Florence. She was Isabel to all her friends.

Photographs and other records of the time give an idea of what each saw at their first meeting. Isabel stood just over five feet and barely topped one hundred pounds. She had a vivacious personality, and her sparkling eyes easily melted Walter's disciplined demeanor. According to a report of physical examination dated 9 October 1914, Walter stood five feet ten inches and weighed 155 pounds. Rather narrow at the shoulders, his chest "at inspiration" measured thirty-six and three-quarters inches, "at expiration" thirty-two and one-quarter inches.[27] Around Isabel, Walter was mostly inspired, and he moved to monopolize her time.

Things said were much more telling than physical dimensions. She learned that he was the son of a small-town doctor and had been in the Army over twelve years. He learned that she was the daughter of a jeweler and she was only twenty-one. But Walter was not to be put off by what people might say about their ages. Already thirty-four years old and painfully aware that attractive young women did not walk through the gate of Fort Sill every day, he moved fast. He asked Isabel to return on subsequent weekends and made arrangements for her to stay with friends of his, Capt. Lesley and Clare McNair. Isabel accepted, and broke her engagement.

At post parties, Walter soon learned Isabel's unusually fine singing. She had studied voice at Belmont College for Young Women in Nashville and developed into a contralto of professional quality.[28] But the entertainment world was not in her plans. Walter did not have to hear or see much to reach a lifetime decision. One summer evening he took Isabel for a walk, and under a starry Oklahoma sky he proposed. One wonders if his well-developed professional aplomb wavered a bit under the emotional strain. However it came out, Isabel agreed, and a date for the wedding was set.

On 4 November 1914, Isabel and Walter were married in St. Paul's Cathedral, Oklahoma City, by the Right Reverend Francis Key Brooks, Episcopal bishop of Oklahoma. The ceremony began at eight in the evening of a Wednesday before 150 guests. Lloyd Jones of the 5th Artillery stood as Walter's best man, and Lucy Porter Terry of Glasgow, Kentucky, served as maid of honor. The groom and groomsmen, all Army lieutenants from Fort Sill, wore dress uniforms, and bride and groom left the church under an arch of crossed swords. Two of Walter's physician-brothers, William and Lemuel Byrd Short and their wives, made the long journey from the St. Louis area. The most dazzling gift to the newlyweds came from the bride's parents: a 250-piece silver service. During the couple's month-long honeymoon in Cuba, Walter met the island pistol champion and bested him in a friendly match.[29]

Back from their Caribbean idyll, Walter and Isabel bounced and lurched in a Daugherty wagon drawn by four mules from the rail station at Lawton to their new quarters on post. Army-supplied furnishings were minimal, and Isabel soon learned the meaning of the old saying among the ladies on post that all an Army wife needs to make a home is a few packing crates and a bolt of chintz. Small fireplaces often produced more smoke than heat. For cooking, Isabel had a monster to tame, a coal-burner that was either red hot or stone cold. But a hint of conveniences to come was already present. Electric lighting had been installed on post the year before the Shorts married.

As soon as the curtains were up and the furniture arranged, the Shorts began the obligatory round of social calls and return visits. Isabel's lively personality and musical talent took much of the strain out of the old Army customs. In the days before fully equipped post clubs, movies, and visiting civilian performers, officers and wives generated their own entertainment from available talent. Isabel formed a quartet soon in demand at dinner parties. The group included violinist Capt. Edmund L. Gruber, who in 1908 had written the well-known "Caisson Song" that later became the official Army song, pianist Clare McNair, and violinist Mrs. Fox Connor.[30]

Looming over the School of Musketry assignment was the possibility of involvement in warfare on a scale far larger than anything the United States Army had seen in its 140-year existence. A new war had broken out in Europe, and it quickly became large enough to make millions of Americans wonder if it would affect life across the Atlantic. The war began in a traditional enough way, with confident predictions by national leaders and bold movements on the battlefields. But by the time Walter and his bride walked under their arch of sabers and into a rose-colored future, the conflict had stabilized in a new and forbidding type of warfare. Two enormous armies dug into trench networks and bombarded each other for days on end across broad expanses of barbed wire and land mines called No Man's Land. The subterranean war provoked a new vocabulary to describe the mole-like existence of its soldiers: trench coat, trench knife, trench foot. During the Shorts' first year of marriage the hideous character of the new war came clear for all to see. On land, advances of only a few hundred feet or yards might cost several thousand dead and wounded in a single afternoon. Exotic new weaponry—poison gas, tanks, submarines, zeppelins, more efficient machine guns—failed to bring the breakthrough that would end the slaughter. Along with the new weapons came a new and sinister morality that threatened to drag all nations into the war. The German policy of unrestricted submarine warfare denied the choice of neutrality.

No doubt the European war dominated conversation in officers' clubs and barracks throughout the Army. Some thought the Europeans would settle it among themselves in a matter of months, while older cynics knew the United States and its Army would have to get into it sooner or later. But before the debate could play out, the U.S. Army had to take care of trouble closer to home.

To Arms

EVEN AFTER ITS LOCATION HAD BEEN FIXED BY THE WAR OF 1845–48, THE Mexican-American border was a porous and insecure boundary. Mexicans occasionally raided to the north, Americans retaliated to the south, and Apache bands hunted and looted in both directions. The coming of the Mexican Revolution in 1910 intensified border violence. Concerned about not only security along the border but also American investments in Mexico, President William Howard Taft put together a "Maneuver Division" of thirteen thousand men at San Antonio for possible duty on the border.

Taking office in 1913, President Woodrow Wilson was determined to avoid war with Mexico, but some of his early decisions raised tensions. Openly siding with one of several factional leaders vying for Mexican leadership, Wilson enraged all others. One of the others, the politically inept but charismatic and violent Francisco "Pancho" Villa, rebelled and gained control over most of northern Mexico. Denied recognition by the Wilson administration, Villa instigated a series of violent incidents on both sides of the border. In January 1916, his men murdered seventeen American employees of the Cusi Mining Company in Chihuahua state. Cross-border raids culminated in an attack by five hundred of Villa's men on Columbus, New Mexico, the night of 9 March 1916. This time the raiders killed fifteen Americans and destroyed much property before cavalry-men drove them off. The next day, Wilson ordered Brig. Gen. John J. Pershing to lead a force into Mexico to capture Villa and his band.

The American force, officially named the Punitive Expedition, U.S. Army but popularly known as the Pershing Expedition, was organized as a provisional division of two cavalry and one infantry brigades. Each cavalry brigade con-sisted of two cavalry regiments and one battery of field artillery. The infantry brigade had two infantry regiments, the 6th and 16th, and a long support train of engineer, medical, transportation, and communication units. The force also included the first aviation unit in the Army, the 1st Aero Squadron, which con-sisted of eight biplanes. The provisional division numbered over ten thousand men when formed, and two more cavalry and two infantry regiments were later added.

Pershing planned to enter Mexico in two columns and close in a pincers movement at Colonia Dublan, eighty miles south of the border. If the columns moved quickly enough, they would trap Villa before he could reach the moun-tains of western Mexico. The eastern, or Columbus, column, with the infantry brigade and seven troops of the 13th Cavalry, would march south from Colum-bus on the Palomas-Ascension road. The western, or Culberson, column, with the rest of the cavalry units, would ride south from the Culberson Ranch, seventy-five miles southwest of Columbus, on the Ojitos road. At noon on 15 March, General Pershing sat high in his saddle, looked back on a long col-umn of cavalry, infantry, and supply wagons and swung his arm high in the signal to move out. The first armed American movement into hostile foreign territory since 1898 had begun.[1] After only an hour on the move, the eastern column reached the border and stopped to make a bow to tradition. The 13th Cavalry stepped aside and let the 6th Infantry lead the column across the border, a reenactment of 1845, when the 6th had been the first American regiment to set foot on Mexican soil. On the Mexican side of the border, the 13th Cavalry resumed its point position and the chase continued.[2]

The eastern column spent its first night in Mexico at Palomas, nine miles south-southwest of Columbus. Before the sun came up again, the troops were wondering if they had been chosen the subjects of a monstrous War Depart-ment joke. Someone in Washington had classified Mexico a tropical country, assuming that high daytime temperatures carried through the night. Supply sergeants saved room in their wagons by leaving behind overcoats and extra blankets. The troops carried only one blanket apiece, and shivered through the night. The next morning they found the water in their canteens frozen.[3]

After a day in camp, the eastern column marched a demanding twenty-six miles on 17 March, the first twenty-one miles without water breaks. For the next five days the eastern column kept up an exhausting pace, averaging nineteen miles per day. Field conditions were among the worst to be found in North or Central America. Cavalry columns raised thick clouds of alkaline dust which the infantry behind had to breathe. In miserable contrast to freezing nights were blazing hot days, with temperatures frequently above one hundred degrees. Winter winds in northern Mexico, still strong through March, caused cracked and bleeding lips and raw swollen faces and hands. When passable roads could not be found, the troops had to fight their way through arroyos, chaparral, ravines, mesquite, and cactus. Water was not as easily found as expected, and Pershing had to put into effect strict water discipline. The field ration of hard-tack, bacon, coffee, and sugar—seasoned liberally with dust—did nothing to improve morale.[4]

On 22 March, the eastern and western columns linked up at Colonia Dublan. But the meeting occasioned no celebration, for Villa had escaped the trap. Pershing's pincers had caught little more than rumors of Villa's whereabouts.

Although the news of Villa's Columbus raid and the formation of the Punitive Expedition were known throughout the Army, the move into Mexico seems to have caught Lieutenant Short by surprise. Isabel was visiting her parents in Oklahoma City the weekend after Villa's raid. On Sunday, Walter called, reporting that he had orders to rejoin the 16th Infantry for the expedition. Without waiting for Isabel to return to Fort Sill, he took the next train to El Paso. There he found his regiment frantically packing and loading equipment at the rail yards. On the train to Columbus and during a day of final preparations, he found himself reassigned to the same unit he had joined eight years before, Company E. But this time he was the company commander.[5]

While the cavalry chased Villa and dominated the headlines, Short's company and the rest of the infantry brigade performed the much less glorious roles of patrolling suspect areas and guarding supply points. The 16th Infantry stayed with division headquarters at Colonia Dublan for a month from 22 March. Here the weather worsened, with the swirling dust and sand flurries augmented by snow storms. But the patrolling continued, day and night. The next series of marches took the regiment 120 miles deeper into Mexico to San Geronimo

Ranch, the unit's patrol base for most of May. A twenty-two-mile march brought the 16th to Namaquipa, where it remained until 19 June. A two-day march of 31 miles earned the troops a ten-week stay at El Valle. Short and his fellow company commanders occasionally captured small groups of bandits and, if they could not be connected to Villa, turned them over to the Mexicans. Wherever their loyalties lay in the turmoil of revolutionary Mexico, local authorities agreed on the proper treatment for bandits: on-the-spot execution.[6]

The rigors of the Punitive Expedition proved an ordeal for Lieutenant Short. In June he developed a case of diarrhea and lost eleven pounds. The next month his condition worsened, and he was hospitalized on 24 July for a stay that eventually reached six weeks. His misery was partially compensated by advancement to captain effective 1 July. A well-deserved promotion, coming after fourteen years in the Army and seven years since his last, had reached him at a time when he was in less than heroic form. Nor did the increase in authority signal the end of Short's medical problems. Back on duty the second week of October, he was again hospitalized in late November, this time for a week.[7]

At the same time he was part of a shooting war against Villa in Mexico, Short was carrying on a paper war against his superiors at Fort Sill and in Washington. At the School of Musketry the year before, he had taken some innovative action to solve a problem that had interfered with training. Much of Fort Sill was taken up by firing ranges, some of them crossed by roads the Army could not close to civilians. Whenever a rancher rode or drove onto a range, firing had to be stopped while a soldier rode out and escorted the unknowing offender through the danger zone. But a man on horseback was too slow, so Short decided to put his sentries on wheels. He sent a purchase order for two motorcycles to the base quartermaster. The order came back disapproved, with the explanation that the Army budget for the next fiscal year had already been approved and could not be increased to allow range personnel to chase down civilians more efficiently. Short promptly resubmitted the requisition. This time it went all the way up the bureaucracy to the War Department auditor. That official, too, rejected it.

Unwilling to wait for the next budget cycle, Short in August ordered two Harley-Davidson motorcycles from a civilian dealer. He paid $531 for the machines out of his own pocket, then sent a request for reimbursement to the Quartermaster's Department. Then the fireworks began. Short's superiors reminded him of the quartermaster's time-honored policies regarding the acquisition of new equipment, and their superiors reminded them of the need to keep a sharp eye on impatient subordinates. For six months irritable memos flew back and forth between Fort Sill and Washington collecting endorsements and recommendations for action. The motorcycle flap finally ended in complete victory for Short when in February 1917, U.S. senator Robert L. Owen secured passage of an amendment to reimburse Short for the cost of the machines, and the commandant of the School of Musketry recommended that no disciplinary action be taken for the hasty purchase.[8]

WHILE CAPTAIN SHORT was battling illness and the Army budgeting process, conditions for the troops in Mexico gradually improved. When the cavalry pursuit of Villa ended in June, General Pershing stabilized his front some 150 miles south of the border. Duty then came to center on the base camps, the two largest at Columbus, New Mexico, and Colonia Dublan, 85 miles south of the border. Both grew into broad expanses of conical troop tents, adobe huts, supply sheds, stables, and truck parks. Many smaller and temporary camps grew wherever one or more regiments stopped for a few days. The camps soon attracted many Chinese, who were surprisingly eager to cook and launder for the Americans in exchange for the protection of the compounds. A few questions revealed that the volunteers were not motivated by agreement with American policy but by fear of Villa, known to kill any Chinese he found. In all camps the universal characteristics of the rear echelon soon set in: endless working parties and boredom, the latter countered by baseball, boxing, deer hunting, authorized prostitution, and plenty of unauthorized gambling. Another diversion grew out of the constant struggle against the snakes, scorpions, centipedes, tarantulas, and swarms of flies that made their way through tent flaps and into empty boots. When Pershing's aide, the young Lt. George S. Patton Jr., shot two rattlesnakes, a new sport was born among expeditionary troops.[9]

By the end of the summer it was clear that Villa and his band had eluded the Punitive Expedition despite a massive manpower advantage enjoyed by the Americans. On 1 September, more than 158,000 Army troops and National Guardsmen were on duty either in Mexico or on the American side of the border. The American press jabbed at Wilson's policy and Pershing's tactics by picturing Pancho Villa running circles around the larger and slower American force, a journalistic slant that overlooked the success of the expedition and the lessons learned by the Army in Mexico. American operations so thoroughly dispersed Villa's band that the cross-border violence which brought the expedition into being ended. As for Villa, he was removed not only from the border regions but his country's political stage as well; others decided the course of revolutionary Mexico.[10]

The Pershing Expedition held more benefits for the Army than for Walter Short. The Army that was keeping an anxious eye on the war in Europe gained valuable experience coordinating a large force of both regulars and volunteers. Even more important, the Mexican experience accelerated technological improvements in the Army. Major problems appeared in communications, aircraft, supply, and intelligence, and the Army initiated research to correct them. Ironically, the most important single innovation was the gift of the Mexican Revolution. When political turmoil shut down the railroads of northern Mexico, the Army had to augment its horse- and mule-drawn wagon trains with trucks. The War Department purchased 663 trucks of various types for use in Mexico and touched off extended debate about their value to a modern military force.[11]

For the commander of Company E, the Punitive Expedition lived up to none of its promise. What began as Short's first combat experience turned into an extended bout with illness. But even a healthy infantry officer would have been hard pressed to find professional growth in Mexico. The necessary method of the expedition, an extended cavalry dash, relegated the infantry to the low-profile, no-glory roles of supply line security and local patrolling. Neither activity posed the challenges that would sharpen skills or bring forth new leaders.

In January 1917, President Wilson ordered Pershing's force back to the United States, and on 1 February, Short led Company E on the march north. Five days later they reentered American territory at Columbus to bring the eleven-month expedition to an end.

FOR MORE THAN two years after the start of war in Europe, President Wilson pursued a policy of neutrality, and he was strongly supported by the American public with its generations-old view that Europe's wars were none of America's business. Not even a shock like the sinking of the *Lusitania* in May 1915, with the loss of 114 American lives, shook Wilson from neutrality, and in 1916 he was reelected on the "He kept us out of war" theme. No less sensitive than the president to the national mood, a majority in Congress nevertheless believed a measure of preparation in order at a time of rising tension along the Mexican border and increasing risk that German submarines would sink American ships in the Atlantic. In passing the National Defense Act of 1916, Congress broke with the American tradition of a small army in peacetime. The Army could now expand to 175,000, nearly doubling of the average manpower during the previous five years. In case of war the president could call to arms a total of 286,000 men.[12]

The rush of events in the early weeks of 1917 confirmed the wisdom that underlay the National Defense Act of 1916. On 31 January, Germany announced the resumption of unrestricted submarine warfare. The next day the president broke diplomatic relations with Germany, and warned that any aggressive acts would be followed by a strong American response to protect freedom of the seas. On 28 February, the secretary of state made public the Zimmerman note, which contained the suggestion that Mexico be induced to join Germany in making war on the United States in exchange for the return to Mexican control of Arizona, New Mexico, and Texas. In March, four American ships were sunk by German torpedoes. With neutrality no longer a viable policy, Wilson in April asked for, and Congress voted, a declaration of war.

The next month the president approved a War Department plan to send one division, about 25,000 men, to France and asked lawmakers to provide for more. Congress responded with a Selective Service Act authorizing the president to call a million men, half immediately and the rest whenever he considered necessary. As a result, Army strength for fiscal 1917 nearly quadrupled over that of the previous year, from 108,399 to 421,467, while War Department expenditures more than doubled, from $183 million in 1916 to $378 million the next year. To lead the new American Expeditionary Force (AEF), Secretary of War Newton Baker chose the commander of the recently returned expedition to Mexico, John J. Pershing.[13]

While the commander in chief and the Congress made their momentous decisions in Washington, Pershing brought together the 16th, 18th, 26th, and 28th Infantry Regiments and the 6th Field Artillery to form the 1st Infantry Division. On 28 May, the general and a staff of 190 sailed from New York to set up AEF headquarters on the continent. In England and France, Pershing was dined and toasted by battalions of VIPs. Behind the glitter he recognized the desperation in London and Paris. The British had lost so many men in 1916 that they could no longer replace casualties, and the French were paralyzed by mutiny with the Germans only fifty miles from Paris. But before the Americans could influence the bloody stalemate on the western front they would have to undergo months of hard training.[14]

BACK ON AMERICAN SOIL after service in Mexico, Short resumed garrison duty with the 16th Infantry, now at Camp Cotton near El Paso. Camp Cotton was part of Fort Bliss, which name not only honored an Army personality but provoked cynical comment from barracks pundits. Short laughed with other new arrivals at the greeting of post veterans: "Welcome to El Paso, where ignorance is bliss, and we've got a whole fort full of it!"[15]

Isabel joined Walter within a week in a small off-post apartment. She found a new appliance to help her cook—a gas stove—but the west Texas climate imposed a new hardship. El Paso in 1917 had few paved streets. With a daily wind storm and the scarcity of rain, the Shorts' apartment quickly filled with dust and static electricity, and Isabel had to shovel dust and mop floors several times a day.[16]

The Shorts' dusty ordeal did not last long. Within a few weeks Walter had orders to General Pershing's Southern Department staff at Fort Sam Houston near San Antonio. Six weeks later, Congress declared war on Germany, and Short was again transferred, this time to Fort Oglethorpe, Georgia, to train officer candidates. Isabel took a hotel room in Chattanooga. On weekday afternoons, she and several other wives boarded an interurban electric car and rode the few miles to the post just over the Georgia line to join their husbands for dinner. On weekends, Walter and others made the return trip to reunite with wives in the city. Short enjoyed his two-month tour with the young officer candidates, for they were eager to learn and put their training to use in France. At the end of the training cycle they presented their captain with an engraved watch. Only a chance encounter with a mosquito marred the Fort Oglethorpe episode. While in the field Short picked up a case of malaria, which over the years proved no worse than a recurring nuisance.[17]

On a bright Sunday morning in June, breakfast at the Short house was interrupted by a telephone call. Walter listened to an officious voice report that the 1st Division had been ordered to France, and he was to rejoin his regiment immediately. He called Fort Bliss to find out how much longer his regiment would be there and was told it had already left by rail. Guessing the troop train would pass through St. Louis, the couple hurriedly packed and caught a train out of Chattanooga. In St. Louis, they found railroad officials unwilling to give information about troop train movements. Isabel then called on a relative with railroad contacts and learned the 16th Infantry train would be in at midnight but would remain out in the yards rather than come into the station.[18]

At midnight, the Shorts went through the terminal and followed the shiny rails out into the darkness. With Isabel in tow, Walter took off on a confused search for his company. For hours they walked over endless rows of rails, dodging switch engines and freight trains, calling up to every passenger car they found, "What unit are you?" Finally, someone answered, "16th Infantry." The captain kissed his wife goodbye and climbed up into the train just before it pulled out. But his search was not over. Now he had to walk the length of the train, through several companies and attached units, looking for familiar faces. Not until the train reached Harrisburg, Pennsylvania, did he find his Company E, ending one of the most bizarre movements to war in the AEF. Isabel went back to her parents' home in Oklahoma City. In four and a half months, she had followed her husband through four household moves.[19]

At the end of a destroyer-escorted voyage through U-boat-infested waters, the 1st Division stepped ashore at St. Nazaire, France, on 25 June. As soon as his company settled into its first bivouac, Short sent his wife a two-word telegram: "Arrived safely." An Oklahoma City reporter interviewed Isabel and announced her husband's arrival with a burst of local pride: "Oklahoma City Man Is Among 'Go-Getters' in France with Pershing / Captain Walter C. Short, Who Was Stationed at Fort Sill, Wires Wife Here of Safe Landing Yesterday."[20]

Before the Americans moved up to the front lines, their hosts asked a favor. Desperate to lift national morale, the French government invited the AEF to mark the Fourth of July by joining in a public display of Franco-American strength. Pershing accepted, and a battalion of the 16th Infantry—2d Battalion, including Short's Company E—was chosen to march with a French battalion from the Court of Honor at Les Invalides, where Napoleon is buried, to Lafayette's tomb in Picpus Cemetery. A huge crowd of Parisians threw flowers and cheered wildly for "the men in cowboy hats." The doughboys still wore broad-brimmed campaign hats while awaiting issuance of helmets.[21]

Less than three weeks after the parade, Captain Short was detailed from his regiment as a temporary instructor in the 1st Division automatic weapons school. In this assignment he began dealing with a major problem of the AEF. After winning grudging approval for an independent American force, General Pershing did not want to have to send his trainees to French and British specialty schools. He wanted to build his own American military school system, a huge task not only because of the large number of trainees involved but also the variety and continuing development of equipment and weapons.

In Pershing's original training concept, the first graduates of the various schools would return to their units as instructors in specialties like machine guns, trench mortars, field fortification, personnel administration, intelligence, communications, and sanitation. But the rapid growth of the AEF soon rendered this concept obsolete. Instead of being sent back to their units, many graduates, Short among them, were held as instructors on rapidly expanding staffs. While studying automatic-weapons doctrine, Short's brilliance in mathematics and experience in teaching allowed him to stand out among his peers. He had found a role in the AEF, and by the end of the year he was no longer on the rolls of the 16th Infantry.

As a MACHINE-GUN INSTRUCTOR, Short had to work with the confusion that was American automatic weapons policy in 1917, a policy representing in microcosm American unreadiness for the three-year-old war. For several years before Congress declared war, the standard machine gun in the U.S. Army was the Benet-Mercie, a French automatic rifle developed in 1909. In 1913, the Ordnance Department declared the Benet-Mercie obsolete and began conducting tests to select a successor. Half a year of range firing, accompanied by extended wrangling between inventors, the Ordnance Department and Congress, resulted in selection of the British Vickers machine gun in 1914. But when war broke out in August, the British needed every Vickers they could manufacture for their own forces on the Continent, and the U.S. Army had to retain the Benet-Mercie. American troops, then, were forced to continue using an obsolete foreign weapon because the War Department had chosen to adopt another foreign weapon it could not acquire in sufficient numbers. Faint consolation to this farcical situation came with the announcement that the Browning Company was in the process of developing an American machine gun that, if successful in tests, promised to end embarrassing dependence on foreign manufacturers. But with neutrality the national policy, no institution that could have influenced automatic weapons production or any other aspect of military preparedness felt any urgency about the issue, and technical development proceeded at a leisurely pace.[22]

In France, and only weeks away from his first battlefield test against the Germans, General Pershing could not wait for engineers and politicians back in the United States to come up with something. He had to make an immediate improvement in AEF firepower. Appealing to the French, he arranged a large purchase of two types of weapons, the light Chauchat automatic rifle and the heavy Hotchkiss machine gun. This stopgap weapons buy created technical problems for Short and his fellow instructors as well as the troops. For one, training manuals had to be translated and reprinted. A second problem involved that old irritant to Americans, the metric system. Probably because they expected delivery of a heavy Browning machine gun within a year, AEF officers decided to continue using the Hotchkiss Model 1914 in its original 8-mm caliber.

But with no development of light machine guns under way in the United States, ordnance officers decided to adapt the Chauchat to their own standards. After buying sixteen thousand 8-mm Chauchats, the Americans requested rechambering and rebarreling of the gun and bought another nineteen thousand in .30-caliber configuration. While seeming to serve the concept of organizational consistency, this decision forced the AEF supply system to handle two sizes of ammunition for the same weapon. A third problem was never solved. The Chauchat, nicknamed the "cha-cha" by the troops, was notorious for malfunctions.[23]

Organizational questions compounded technical problems. No one knew how many machine guns to put in a division, or even how large a division should be. At the outbreak of the war, the machine gun was already thirty years old but had made only a tentative impact on the U.S. Army. The typical American regiment had only four machine guns in 1917. Years before they went to war in 1914, European armies had incorporated much larger numbers of machine guns. Congress finally moved to bring the U.S. Army up to date by voting $12 million for automatic weapons development in 1916. But the fluctuating size of the American division put off decisions about the numbers of machine guns to allocate and instructors to assign. At its arrival in France, the 1st Division numbered over twenty-five thousand men, almost twice the size of British and French divisions. On Allied advice, the unit was reduced to seventeen thousand, but it gradually returned to its original size as support units grew and machine-gun battalions were added. With division size finally fixed at one artillery brigade and two infantry brigades of two regiments each, AEF headquarters allocated 260 machine guns and 768 automatic rifles to each division. These numbers implied a huge training effort even for one division, since at least three men were required to operate the Hotchkiss and two for the Chauchat. Thus each division required at least 2,316 trained machine gunners. With forty-three American divisions eventually in France, the total AEF requirement for machine gunners, allowing for casualties, was well over 100,000.[24]

As the American Expeditionary Force grew with the increasing flow of troops across the Atlantic, Short quickly gained responsibility and rank. On 26 August, he was promoted to major in the National Army, the name given the amalgamation of prewar regular troops, National Guardsmen, and new citizen soldiers raised by the Selective Service Act. He remained an instructor in the 1st Division school system until 8 October, when he was named director of the Automatic Weapons School of the larger 1st Corps school system. Five weeks later he became an instructor at the Army School, an AEF headquarters-level facility with a curriculum including much more than automatic weapons. On 12 January 1918, Short was named director, Infantry Weapons School of the 2d Corps school system. Three months later he won an assignment coveted by many involved in preparing the growing AEF for combat operations. On 21 April, he was named a member of the G-5 Section (Training) of General Headquarters, AEF, located at Chaumont, 135 miles southeast of Paris. In addition to his general staff duties, he would now supervise all machine-gun training.[25]

The commander of the training section, Col. Harold B. Fiske, had plenty of work for Major Short, and there was good reason for the heavy responsibility. The French command had finally turned over to General Pershing part of the western front on 5 February, nearly eight months after the doughboys arrived. The Ansauville sector was regarded as quiet but the Americans were primed to prove themselves in battle. On 28 May, the 1st Division kicked off the first American offensive of the war, a successful assault against Cantigny ridge. Although Short had no direct connection with the Cantigny attack, he was deeply involved in all subsequent American offensives. After Cantigny the AEF mounted its first multidivision operation, the Aisne-Marne campaign against the Marne salient, a German strongpoint dangerously close to Paris. To do the job, Pershing assigned seven divisions, which, with support units, totaled 270,000 men. Short's job was to help make sure those men were as well trained as possible when the attack began.[26]

During preparations for an offensive, staffs at all echelons worked at a frantic pace. Short's duties included preparing and revising training manuals, translating useful French texts, writing course curricula and instruction schedules, issuing training bulletins, and organizing new courses as needed. He also had to leave Chaumont frequently to inspect schools and supervise instruction, listen to recommendations from unit commanders, and maintain liaison with French and British training staffs. He was distracted the first week in June, when he received word that his wife had contracted smallpox, frequently disfiguring or fatal at the time. When the Aisne-Marne offensive began on 18 July, he spent much time in assembly areas just behind attacking units directing machine-gun training at every opportunity. After eighteen days of hard fighting in fortified woods, across farms, and through hedgerows and streams, American troops occupied the Marne salient, and the Germans retreated northward. Major Short was a happy man in August, for reasons both professional and personal. American staff work was progressing faster than the French had predicted, Isabel had recovered from her bout with smallpox, and he won another promotion, to temporary lieutenant colonel, effective 8 August.[27]

But there was no time to celebrate. The AEF staff immediately turned to preparations for the next offensive, scheduled for mid-September. The Allies wanted another salient eliminated, this one at St. Mihiel, 140 miles east of Paris. To do the job, AEF planners put together a force of nine divisions, plus six in reserve, totaling some 550,000 men, the largest American force committed to battle since the Civil War. This time victory came after only five days of fighting. Once again Short and the rest of the AEF staff turned to the next operation, scheduled to follow St. Mihiel by only ten days. The Meuse-Argonne offensive would be the largest operation ever conducted by the Unites States Army. For the massive push against the German line north of Verdun, the AEF assembled twenty-seven divisions totaling 1.2 million men.[28]

As the Americans gained experience in planning and conducting huge operations, they began to innovate and put a recognizable stamp on their methods. General Pershing had already directed American infantry tactics away from the static trench warfare the French and British had fallen into nearly three years earlier. In his view, infantrymen skilled in the use of the bayonet, and led by commanders who understood the tactics of a war of movement, would defeat the Germans. But innovation in automatic weapons policy was a different matter. In their 1917–18 state of development, machine guns were burdened with technological limitations. Overheated barrels were all too common, as were malfunctions in feeding and ejection, especially in the Chauchat automatic rifle. Another limitation was weight. The water-cooled Hotchkiss weighed fifty-two pounds unloaded. The Browning machine gun, also water-cooled, was a great improvement at thirty-two pounds but did not arrive in appreciable numbers until the last few months of the war. Only the Chauchat, at twenty pounds, could be moved easily enough to keep up with infantry assaults.[29]

Weight and lack of motive power confined machine guns to the primarily defensive role of reinforcing forward positions. Advancing infantry left machine guns in their wake to ward off counterattacks on territory gained. With German defenses beginning to crack in the summer of 1918, the Allies found an offensive role for automatic weapons. They concentrated large numbers of machine guns and used them for direct and indirect long-range fire, much like artillery. One particularly devastating innovation that Short taught was overhead fire. Machine-gun companies would fire from concealed positions over the heads of friendly units on the trench line. If the range were great enough, German troops would not hear the rain of bullets cutting through their ranks. In teaching calculations of the range, elevation, search and traverse, and windage required for overhead fire, Short made full use of his skill in mathematics.[30]

Lieutenant Colonel Short's hectic routine of planning, instructing, and inspecting continued as the Meuse-Argonne offensive ground its bloody way north toward Belgium. In November, rumors of German willingness to talk peace swirled through Chaumont but did not affect the headquarters routine, for many still believed a 1919 offensive would be necessary. The AEF personnel section diligently pursued its record keeping while statesmen probed and parried and came through with another promotion for Short, to temporary colonel from 7 November. When the armistice went into effect four days later, he was not yet used to the feel of silver eagles on his shoulders. For his wartime service, Short was decorated by two armies. The French inducted him into their Legion of Honor, and his own Army awarded him the Distinguished Service Medal, the latter pinned on his chest by General Pershing himself. His citation noted that "he rendered conspicuous service in inspecting and reporting upon front-line conditions" and "efficiently directed the instruction and training of machine-gun units at every available opportunity during rest periods."[31]

The sudden end of the war caught Short in the middle of some original tactical thinking. His study of machine-gun unit battle reports convinced him that the potential of automatic weapons was not being realized by American divisions. Contemporary doctrine on machine guns called for their use as defensive weapons, to consolidate a decisive hold on ground just taken by the infantry and inflict maximum casualties on enemy counterattacks. Before machine guns were set up to hold a position, their crews simply walked behind attacking infantry formations with other support elements, carrying but not firing their weapons. Short believed this passive role at the beginning of offensives increased casualties among both leading infantry elements and trailing machine-gun crews even before the latter began to fight. In reviewing 1st Division unit reports of the Battle of Soissons, Short found that on 18 July 1918, one machine-gun company lost fifty-seven men without firing a shot, and another company lost sixty-one men while firing only ninety-six rounds.[32]

Short believed the most effective assault was one in which maximum firepower remained close to the front from start to finish, and the best way to maximize firepower at the front was to keep machine-gun units close to the infantry. The problem, however, was the weight of ammunition. Machine-gun crews, like the infantrymen they supported, began offensives by carrying their own supply of ammunition. But if they had to stop and fire to help the infantry maintain forward momentum, their faster rate of fire soon exhausted their ammunition, and they fell behind while awaiting resupply.

In the latter months of the war, Short worked at involving machine-gun units in an offensive role along with the infantry, and had some success. During inspection visits to training sites, he urged unit staff officers to utilize as many machine-gun companies as they could support near the leading edge of assaults, and challenged them to use any means available, including carts drawn by men or mules, to keep ammunition moving forward. Several divisions acted on Short's advice and recorded measurable progress in coordinating infantry assaults with supporting arms. In the battle of St. Mihiel, fought from 12 to 16 September 1918, the 90th Division made little use of its automatic weapons, but on 1 November, in the Meuse-Argonne offensive, the division's machine-gun units fired more than one million rounds, enough to cover the infantry advance for most of the day. The 2d and 5th Divisions made similar adjustments, both using only eight of fourteen machine-gun companies in the St. Mihiel operation but adding automatic weapons units later. On 1 November, the 2d Division involved not only all fourteen of its own machine-gun companies in its advance but borrowed ten more companies from the 42d Division. The 5th Division used all of its machine-gun companies in its 1 November advance and tried a new fire support technique, clearing the path of advance for lead elements by firing over the assaulting infantry from behind.[33]

But borrowing machine-gun units and relying on human or animal power to transport ammunition did not solve the problem of keeping automatic weapons firing near the front of infantry assaults. The obvious need was for some kind of vehicle capable of carrying at least one thousand pounds of ammunition over rough terrain. The British had already developed what they called a "tankette," a tracked vehicle operated by two men, to fill the role of battlefield weapons and ammunition carrier. The Americans were interested in developing a similar vehicle for the same purpose, but the war ended before the project could be initiated. Short and others interested in machine-gun tactics and equipment put their ideas on hold, hopeful that an automatic weapons carrier would be among peacetime development projects.

Six days after the shooting stopped, Short took up duties as assistant chief of staff, G-5 (Training) of the new Third Army, the headquarters designated the American Army of Occupation in Germany. His new assignment began with the unpleasant task of writing his wife that he would not be coming home for some time. In its new occupation mission, directed from Coblenz, the AEF was much smaller and much less active. With the German people more interested in securing the next meal than resuming war, American soldiers spent almost as much time sightseeing as policing. Colonel Short's role in the occupation had little to do with machine guns. While he supervised all Third Army training, his main duty was to head the newly established American University on the Rhine. The school offered a broad curriculum, including vocational training and college preparatory classes, designed to equip soldiers with job skills to assist their adjustment to civilian life upon returning to the United States.[34]

No sooner had he become familiar with his new educational responsibilities than Short was detailed to a new type of study group called into being by General Pershing. The Superior Board, AEF, was charged with extracting from the just-concluded war lessons that might prove useful to the Army in future conflicts. The first formal lessons-learned effort by the U.S. Army, the Superior Board was yet another modern battlefield function—like automatic weapons, aircraft, tanks, and military intelligence—in which the Americans lagged behind their British and French allies. During April and May 1919, officers from each military branch examined the performance of their specialty on the western front and made recommendations on tactical employment and organization. Short was one of ten officers on the Machine Gun Board, itself one of ten specialty, branch, or functional panels comprising the Superior Board. The Machine Gun Board recommended that the infantry division be equipped with 154 heavy machine guns organized in twelve companies of 12 guns each, with 10 guns held in a mobile ordnance repair unit. Each machine-gun company was to consist of 6 officers and 184 enlisted men. During the war, a number of American officers came to believe that automatic weapons had assumed such tactical prominence in field operations that they should be organized as a separate branch specialty, as the British did, but the board advised against the establishment of a new separate arm.[35]

Seven months after the armistice, Short boarded the *Leviathan* for the voyage home. In the unhurried days before the Statue of Liberty came into view, he had plenty of time to evaluate his unique if not always exhilarating wartime experience. He came out of the war with a reputation as a master trainer of large numbers of men. It was not a headline-generating skill, but as the methods and machines of war became increasingly sophisticated, effective training gained importance. On the way to earning that reputation, he had found personal rewards beyond anything he had thought possible when he accepted his commission seventeen years earlier. In less than two years, he had rocketed up the rank ladder, from junior captain to full colonel, and shouldered heavier responsibilities in the largest field headquarters ever formed by the United States Army. Furthermore, in the rarified atmosphere of General Pershing's headquarters, he had worked with many officers he would meet again in his career. He also acquired his first experience with foreign military personalities and methods at Chaumont when he dealt with liaison officers from several allied nations. In working with French and British officers, Short developed respect for the former and their mobile operations, but like many other Americans, he was not impressed with British generals, whom he found unimaginative and slow to react to the unexpected.[36]

Back to Barracks

THE DOUGHBOYS OF THE AMERICAN
EXPEDITIONARY FORCE CAME HOME TO an America intent on resuming the
quiet rhythms of Main Street at peace. Despite their brief participation and relatively light casualties in the Great War—in nineteen months, 53,000 Americans
lost their lives in battle and another 63,000 died of other causes, while in four
years, 945,000 British, 1.4 million French, and 1.8 million German troops were
killed—the vast majority of Americans believed they had sacrificed enough in
the crusade for world peace and were eager to turn away from international
commitments. Most Americans approved the U.S. Senate's refusal to ratify participation in the League of Nations, and the new Republican president, Warren
G. Harding, was perfectly in tune with the voters of 1920 when he called for a
return to "normalcy."

Part of normalcy was a small U.S. Army. The American military tradition
included rapid demobilization at the end of hostilities, and after the Armistice
of November 1918, the Army wasted no time in returning soldiers to civilian
life. On the day the fighting ended on the western front, the Army counted 3.76
million men at all posts. Six months later, 864,000 soldiers were on duty, and at
the end of another year of demobilization, the Army totaled only 204,000.[1] The
American public and its diplomats were comfortable entrusting their hopes for

peace not to large standing forces but to naval limitations treaties signed in 1922 and 1930 and the 1928 Pact of Paris, an attempt to outlaw war.

As strong as was the popular desire to return to peacetime pursuits uninterrupted by foreign crises, it conflicted with new realities. The United States had already taken on new responsibilities beyond its borders and had seen the rise of a serious rival in the Pacific. Victory over Spain in 1898 brought the United States extensive territories in the Caribbean and Pacific oceans, including Puerto Rico, Guam, and the Philippines. In the same year, Congress approved President McKinley's bill to annex Hawaii. The administration and defense of these areas required significant and sustained budgetary and manpower investments. Most recently, President Wilson's frequently stated internationalist views raised the expectation that the United States was poised to assume a more prominent role in world affairs.

In preparation for expanded missions, Army leaders planned a large peacetime force. In January 1919, the chief of staff, Gen. Peyton C. March, proposed a standing army of half a million men. Aghast, members of Congress looked for an alternative. Months later, General Pershing added his prestige to a proposal for a smaller army, and Congress, more than a year after taking up the issue, passed the National Defense Act of 1920. The act reduced General March's strength request to a maximum authorization of 280,000 men and erected a framework for responding to contingencies beyond the nation's borders. National command and strategic planning aspects of the 1903 Army reforms were strengthened by increasing the General Staff personnel complement from only nineteen officers to four assistants and eighty-eight officers under the chief of staff, and by transferring responsibility for war planning from the War College to the General Staff. Three functions improvised during the war—in finance, chaplaincy, and chemical warfare—became permanent branch specialties. One of the more promising of the new technologies demonstrated in the World War, aircraft, was given enhanced status when the Air Service was separated from the Signal Corps to become an independent combat arm. Another institutional change addressed the woeful lack of coordination between the war effort and private industry. A new office, assistant secretary of war, took responsibility for industrial mobilization and procurement of all military supplies.[2]

But the promise of the 1920 act was never fulfilled. In elections later the same year, the Republicans took over the White House and strengthened their hold on both houses of Congress, then proceeded to enact new economies in national defense. They cut the War Department budget from $1.6 billion in 1920 to $336 million in 1925.[3] In 1923, the Army bottomed out at about 135,000 men, where it would remain for more than a decade.[4] More damaging to the future, the War Department research and development budget was reduced from $5 million in 1921 to $2.85 million four years later, severely limiting Army efforts to develop the doctrine and weapons that could prevent a repeat of the tactical nightmare of the western front, the stalemate of trench warfare, and the horrific casualties taken in attempts to break it.[5] The department also had to deal with an imbalance between missions assigned before the war and resources available after. Army commanders, especially those in the Caribbean and Pacific overseas outposts, drew up optimistic plans to stretch small troop contingents over vast territories and reduced tactical principles and interservice agreements to words on paper, all the while hoping no adversary would move to exploit glaring vulnerabilities.[6]

Within a few years, continued budget-cutting lowered the military efficiency and living standard of all soldiers. When wartime stocks of parts for everything from trucks to typewriters ran out, broken-down equipment went unrepaired. The Army depended for several years on a huge wartime supply of ammunition, built up when the Allies expected Germany to continue fighting well into 1919, but by the mid-1920s stocks were so low that target practice had to be curtailed. Pilots remained grounded for lengthening periods as reductions in the Air Service fuel budget forced cuts in prescribed flight time, and their obsolescent planes required more frequent maintenance. Barracks and housing deteriorated, and on many posts sanitary hazards and firetraps developed.[7] Several deaths by fire spurred Congress to approve a ten-year $110 million housing construction program in 1926, and in the same year ammunition replacement was authorized.[8] Both programs were paid for not by increased appropriations but by government property sales and further personnel cuts. The civilian components of the Army—National Guard, Organized Reserves, Reserve Officer Training Corps, and Civilian Military Training Corps—began to show major deficiencies in readiness because Regular Army personnel cuts had depleted training cadre. A major morale problem developed when postwar inflation ate into the modest Army pay schedule. Congress provided some relief with the Pay Act of 1922, the first since 1908, but inflation soon nullified its effect. While soldiers struggled with worsening conditions on and off duty, successive secretaries of war proudly announced that the United States was spending less on national defense than any other major power and lauded nonmilitary returns to the nation such as civil engineering projects, colonial administration, technical education, and even improved national physique and preservation of the art of horseshoing.[9] Hardly aware of either military or nonmilitary activities of their Army, taxpayers annually spent six times the War Department budget on candy and soda pop.[10]

In 1926, Congress seemed to halt the pattern of military budget cuts, at least for one specialty. The Air Corps Act of that year gave military aviators a new name, semiautonomous status, and a five-year expansion program calling for eighteen hundred planes and 16,650 officers and men. But relentless pressures soon compromised the intent of the act. Instead of recruiting new personnel to fill out the Air Corps, which would have increased the Army payroll and with it the overall military budget, the War Department transferred men from ground components of the service, a policy which reduced efficiency and morale in all branches. At its expiration, the five-year program fell short of its goals, and the United States fell further behind other nations in air power development.[11]

Unemployed in the view of its government and people, the Army reverted to an inbred clubby life-style. Young officers resigned themselves to low pay and the prospect of a decade or more between promotions, and searched for new ways to fill the duty day. They read and debated the tactical concepts of imaginative foreigners like the British mobile warfare advocates J. F. C. Fuller and B. H. Liddel Hart and the Italian air power enthusiast Giulio Douhet. They also wooed colonels' daughters, refined dinner party patter, sneaked bootleg whiskey into quarters, bought tailored uniforms, and engaged in the gentlemanly violence of polo. Senior officers polished their Sam Browne belts and puttees and reminded dinner party hostesses how close they had been to General Pershing in France. Some plumbed new depths of detail in an effort to uphold standards and appear useful. Maj. Gen. Charles P. Summerall disliked the droppings of automobiles more than those of horses as he watched the number of privately owned vehicles increase on Army posts in the 1920s. Commanding in Hawaii, he ordered auto owners to wash oil stains from the pavement in front of officers' quarters at Schofield Barracks.[12]

While their tiny Army struggled to maintain itself amid neglect, Americans felt their way into a postwar existence bearing less and less resemblance to prewar "normalcy." Seemingly irresistible social and economic developments changed the rhythms and scenery of life. The 1920 census revealed that for the first time in American history, more than half the population lived in cities and towns. The automobile replaced the horse and buggy, and new communities and businesses appeared to service the new machine and its passengers: gas stations, roadside restaurants, motor hotels, and suburbs. Women got the vote. Everyone got Prohibition, and millions soon ignored it. A Red scare, labor strikes, race riots, and sharp inflation punctured wartime idealism. But within a few years a booming economy made it easy for most Americans to forget postwar dislocation. With the spread of radio and large-circulation publications, a new mass culture appeared as millions tried to keep in step with the latest fads and fashions. Public attention bounced back and forth between trifles and tragedies. One month it was rising skirts and falling moral standards, the next it was beauty contests and gang wars, and so on through the decade with hip flasks and flappers, sensational murder trials, anarchist plots, Teapot Dome, flagpole sitters, and marathon dancers.

BY THE TIME Walter Short stepped off the *Leviathan* on 5 July 1919, most of the enthusiasm for the homecoming soldiers had faded. But Isabel made up for the lack of public recognition with a surprise dockside welcome at Hoboken. The couple toured New York City for a week, then took a train to Illinois and Oklahoma to visit families. Walter reported to Fort Leavenworth, Kansas, as an instructor at the General Service Schools the first week of August. Like most other officers coming from service in France, he soon took a tumble down the rank ladder, reverting to his prewar rank of captain. At their new posting, the Shorts found good friends from courtship days, Lesley and Clare McNair.[13]

The General Service Schools, renamed the Command and General Staff School in 1923, offered mid-career training in staff and command procedures of large units. The schools system included the School of the Line, the Staff College, the Signal School, and the Field Engineer School, with curricula taught by a faculty of thirty-two. In the immediate postwar years, duty at Fort Leavenworth was anything but a slack peacetime assignment, for doctrine in all specialties needed rewriting to reflect the lessons of the European War. After a day of teaching, Walter and the other instructors wrote new course manuals far into the night. Short continued his wartime work with machine-gun units and produced a text used throughout the Army for years. *The Employment of Machine Guns*, published by the War Department in 1922, updated automatic weapons doctrine and presented exhaustive treatment of angles of tangent elevation, lateral wind allowances, and frontal and oblique barrages. The experience earned him the nickname that would follow him the rest of his career: Machine-gun Short.[14]

After a few weeks, the Shorts and Fort Leavenworth society settled into the familiar Army-post routine of social calls and bridge and dinner parties. Isabel added something new by performing as the lead singer of a musical group she formed with her friend Clare McNair. Although Walter's days and evenings were full of teaching and writing, he decided he had better become a student as well. Advanced professional development depended on more than the garrison school courses he had mastered at the beginning of his career, and he was already at the Army's premier education center. He was accepted for the School of the Line course convening 1 September 1920. Designed to prepare middle-rank officers to function as members of a division staff, the curriculum included nineteen subjects presented as lectures or map problems followed by terrain exercises and tactical rides. Students spent most of their time on tactics and troop leading, less on duties of the division commander and staff, the writing of plans and orders, military history, field engineering, military intelligence, supply, and military government.[15]

One day near the end of 1919, Isabel gave her husband news that made him forget all about his academic routine. She was "in a family way," as they said at the time. The months crawled by as Walter taught, studied, and looked forward to fatherhood at age forty. About the time Isabel went to her parents' home for the birth, her husband passed another professional milestone. Captain Short became Major Short on 1 July 1920. Ten days later, the good news flashed from Oklahoma City: it was a boy, six pounds, two ounces. The infant was named Walter Dean Short, after his father and maternal grandfather.[16]

Within a few weeks the newest family on post reunited. The parents were soon struggling with a new routine that often had them awake long before reveille. Isabel took an occasional respite from infantile demands, leaving the baby with the new father as she went off to bridge parties at the Officers' Club. Upon completion of his School of the Line course, Walter's name came up on the Initial Eligible List for General Staff Duty of 24 December 1920. The following month, he got the opportunity to use his new qualification when orders came through for the 6th Division staff at Camp Grant, Illinois.[17]

At Camp Grant, near Rockford, Short found an assignment more impressive in name than content. Taking up duties as assistant chief of staff for both operations and supply, he learned he would be working on nothing more glamorous than the orderly demise of his new unit. The War Department was demobilizing the 6th Division, as well as many other units. Returning to his quarters each night, Short saw the housing deterioration that resulted from continued budget cutting. His government-issue home consisted of two twenty-foot-square sheds placed end to end. With remarkable linguistic license, the post quartermaster termed the structure a "bungalow" and a flimsy lean-to on one side a "screened porch."[18]

When Isabel arrived with the baby, tension in the Short bungalow rose dramatically. Winter drafts, frozen pipes, and a balky stove strained the new parents' patience. Spring rains revealed a sieve-like roof, and the Shorts had to transform the floor into an obstacle course of pots and pans. When summer weather turned the shack into an oven, Isabel gathered up the baby and went to Cape Cod. The War Department soon came to the rescue, ending the Camp Grant ordeal in its fifth month with orders to general staff duty in Washington.[19]

For the next two decades Short filled billets in the three areas every ambitious officer had to experience: staff, school, and line. A four-year tour in Washington, three with the Far Eastern Section of the Military Intelligence Division, provided welcome relief from the privations of Camp Grant as well as occasional splashes of capital glitter. Then came three years in balmy Puerto Rico as executive officer of the 65th Infantry; another stint as an instructor and, concurrently, assistant chief of staff, G-3 (Operations), at the Command and General Staff School, Fort Leavenworth; and four more years in Washington, this time as finance officer and later executive officer for the chief of the Bureau of Insular Affairs.[20]

While with the Military Intelligence Division in the early 1920s, Short's routine was affected by a change in the mood of his countrymen toward the Army and its triumphant experience in France. Only two years after cheering the troops returning from the western front, many Americans began to suspect that their government had somehow been tricked into the European war in 1917 by British and French diplomats and international bankers. Alive to the potential for image problems always present in Washington, a city unusual for its concentration of military and naval installations, the War Department promoted a "low-visibility" policy. Major Short and his fellow Army officers on duty in the capital worked in civilian clothes so as not to encourage the impression of a government under the influence of militarism.[21]

In 1924, Short got the break that gave him a good chance at a better-than-ordinary military career. He was accepted for the War College class of 1925. Unlike the lower echelons of Army education, the War College did not admit all officers who had reached a certain rank. Short's selection confirmed the evaluations of superiors going back to his earliest years in the Army that he was among the minority in his peer group with the potential for high command. A lieutenant colonel since 6 October 1923, Short and seventy-five other selectees reported to Washington Barracks in the capital, where they were greeted by War College commandant Maj. Gen. Hanson Ely. The class of 1925 began its course of study with an unprecedented gesture when it nominated General of the Armies John J. Pershing as an honorary member. The general, a national hero since leading the AEF in the World War and recently retired as Army chief of staff, had begun studies with the first War College class in 1904, but duty in the Philippines had precluded his completion of the course.[22]

Founded as one of Elihu Root's reforms of 1903, the War College boasted a sizable number of alumni by the time the United States entered the war in Europe in 1917. But the performance of War College graduates on the western front revealed a number of deficiencies, the most glaring among them a lack of appreciation for the influence of nonmilitary activities on war. Accordingly, the postwar curriculum included studies of international relations as well as military, economic, political, and psychological analyses of the United States and other powers. The ten-month course consisted of an informative phase devoted to analysis of War Department General Staff functions and a war-plans phase, during which students prepared plans based on strategic estimates of various nations and regions. Both phases were divided into subcourses, the first four of which followed the standard general staff organization of personnel, intelligence, operations and training, and logistics, those numbered one through four, respectively. Additional subcourses in 1924–25 included "Command," during which students tested their plans in a war game, and "The Assistant Secretary of War," which focused on issues relating to industrial mobilization.[23]

In each subcourse, officer-students formed committees to examine various aspects of problems, and made presentations to the student body and faculty. In their preparations, students enjoyed access to a vast body of source materials, including the records of all major participants in the World War as well as the Crimean and Sino-Japanese Wars. In the G-1 subcourse, Short chaired the five-man Committee 1, titled Estimate of Military Manpower of the United States. In the G-3 subcourse he worked with Committee 3, Indoctrination as the Basis for Military Training. In the Command subcourse, he sat on Committees 5, Movements by Rail, Truck and Marching, and 19, Unlimited and Limited Objectives. Students also prepared staff memoranda as assigned. Short's included the following titles: "Interchange of Infantry and Field Artillery Officers," "Necessity for Greater Uniformity in Methods of Training and for Stressing Morale," "Overseas Shipping During War," and "How Is the Influence of National Policy Felt in Connection with the Preparation of Specific War Plans?" In addition to their committee work, students heard frequent lectures by both military and civilian specialists in a variety of fields. Titles included "Strategic Minerals," "The Canning Industry," "War Industries Board," "War Department

General Mobilization Plan," "A Solution to the Cavalry Problem," "The Relation of Psychology to Leadership," and "The Joint Army-Navy Problem in the Pacific." Several tours rounded out the curriculum. The class made a reconnaissance trip to Camp Dix, New Jersey, and viewed an Air Service demonstration at Bolling Field, Virginia.[24]

Despite the extensive overhaul of the War College curriculum following the world war, promising technologies emergent during the conflict received only cursory attention from faculty and students. The airplane and the tank demonstrated great potential to affect the course of events on the battlefield but the Americans, unlike both their allies and enemies in Europe, did little to exploit either weapon. The failure to develop air power is especially curious, since the airplane, unlike the tank, had an obvious civilian application, soon manifested in the new civil aviation industry. A small number of enthusiasts in the Army urged rapid development of the airplane. Their loudest voice, Brig. Gen. William "Billy" Mitchell, demonstrated how easily air power could sink a warship in 1921 and organized an around-the-world flight of four Army amphibian planes in 1924. But such events changed no minds in the upper reaches of the Army, and Mitchell's forceful advocacy of air power development earned him a court-martial for insubordination in 1925. Aircraft remained restricted to the missions of observing enemy troop movements and adjusting friendly artillery fire, the same tasks they had performed on the western front. Of some thirty committee presentations Short and his fellow students heard, only one concerned air power. Committee 27 presented a study titled "Fundamental Principles for the Employment of the Air Service." And of more than one hundred lectures delivered to the class of 1925, only two related to air power.[25]

SOLDIERS WHO REMAINED in uniform after the World War found their loyalty to the Army brought with it the penalty of slow promotions. The huge officer corps built up to lead the four-million-man wartime army was much too large for the postwar force, and the War Department had to involuntarily discharge many officers. Those allowed to stay formed a "hump" in the once orderly career pattern, a large number of officers of nearly the same age and experience who in some cases had to wait well over a decade for promotions that formerly took half as long. For those behind the hump, professional advancement came at an insultingly slow pace. Lucian K. Truscott Jr., fifteen years younger than Short, just missed service in France, and after the war he languished as a captain for a decade and a half. Fortunately for the nation, Truscott and others in the same situation, such as Dwight Eisenhower, stayed in uniform until perceptive superiors recognized their abilities and in another Army expansion rose to high rank, full general in Truscott's case. But many others became discouraged at the lack of recognition and resigned from the Army, even after the Great Depression seriously curtailed opportunities in civilian life.[26]

In the middle of the promotion hump rather than behind it, Walter Short continued to rise. The pace of his midlevel promotions, three years from captain to major and another three to lieutenant colonel, placed him in the vanguard of his generation. With each promotion came a prime assignment. As a lieutenant colonel he was selected for the War College, served as regimental executive officer in Puerto Rico, and held important staff posts at Fort Leavenworth and in Washington. Promotion to colonel on 1 October 1933 made him eligible for his first regimental command, and the War Department came up with a premier unit for him. The 6th Infantry, one of the Army's oldest regiments, had fought in every war after the revolution, including Indian campaigns before and after the Civil War. The 6th was then garrisoned at Jefferson Barracks, Missouri, which brought Short back to the post where he had started his Army career thirty-two years earlier.[27]

Socially, Jefferson Barracks proved both pleasant and pressing. As the highest ranking Army officer in the area, Short found himself in demand on many social and patriotic occasions. His regimental reviews on post, with him erect in the saddle atop an immaculately groomed mount, attracted spectators and reporters from several nearby towns. Family visits now became easier with a number of relatives living on both sides of the Mississippi River between St. Louis and Fillmore. In the summer of 1935, the War Department added a pleasant temporary duty to an already desirable assignment when it appointed Short executive officer of the National Rifle and Pistol Matches at Camp Perry, Ohio, the same competition in which he had triumphed with the pistol twenty-six years earlier. The growth of their son Dean was a source of special pride to the Shorts. Not satisfied with the boy's performance in school in Puerto Rico a decade before, Isabel had tutored him intensively at home for several years. Dean more than justified his parents' hopes and labors when he graduated from Cleveland High School in St. Louis a year ahead of his peers.[28]

An experienced colonel after two years in command of the 6th Infantry, Short went on to another prime assignment, this one at Fort Benning, Georgia. In July 1936, he took up duties as assistant commandant of the Infantry School. The primary school of the Army's primary branch, the Infantry School trained company grade officers in the techniques of leading small units, and enlisted men in a variety of skills, even horseshoeing. Welcomed in a post newspaper puff piece as "a sandy-haired son of Illinois," Short took charge of the academic department, which made him responsible for the curriculum and instructional staff serving more than five hundred soldier-students.[29]

Only three years after putting on the eagles of a colonel, Short's name appeared on a list with six others confirmed by Congress for promotion to brigadier general. The small-town boy from Illinois had exceeded the most realistic career goal available to him when he had accepted his commission thirty-four years earlier. In a career pattern defined by attrition more severe than that found in most other professions, he had thrived. At the time of his selection, Short stood 269th in a population of 634 colonels, and he was one of only 17 tapped for the next rank in 1936.[30]

More than a few officials and many citizens as well were likely interested in the particular mix of character, attitudes, and abilities that had allowed Short to stand out among his peers. He did not present an imposing figure. At five feet ten, about one hundred fifty-five pounds and narrow at the shoulders, he let others demonstrate the physical aspects of command presence. Short had a deceptive resilience that those impressed by size overlooked. He surprised family and associates by walking away from a riding accident at Fort Leavenworth in which his mount tripped, threw him, and then rolled completely over him. His light blue eyes conveyed a warm midwestern affability. He could also project the searching look of the demanding inspector, alert to all details. The narrow face and slightly protruding lower lip he inherited from his mother gave a stern set to his mouth, cautioning others not to trifle. His voice was evenly modulated, low in volume, not underlined by expansive gestures. His smile and laugh came easily, but no one considered a slap on the back appropriate.[31]

Short compensated for his rather ordinary appearance with a penetrating intellect, which helped him generate intensity among a full room but did not translate into the charisma to move masses. Quick to take action and thorough in executing his own duty assignments, he did not tolerate a leisurely approach to problem solving in others. Subordinates considered him strict and somewhat austere but always fair. Punctuality was almost a fetish with him. Usually terse, he expressed approval with "That's good," "All right," or simply "Okay." Disapproval could be expressed at greater length and intensity depending on the magnitude of the mistake. Short usually responded to earnest mediocrity with paternalistic patience, and made a mental note to shuffle duty assignments. But sloppy performance from those he considered capable provoked irritability, a flushed face, and sharp commentary. Criticism might be underlined with a steely glare from the light blue eyes but not a roaring voice, sarcasm, or profanity.[32]

On social occasions Walter's professional staff conference demeanor warmed to a more genial manner. He initiated conversation easily, smiled and laughed quietly. Not one to tell jokes or ribald stories, he enjoyed recalling among peers humorous incidents from Army assignments. Conversations with him usually included competition shooting, hunting, and horses. Supremely self-disciplined, Short limited himself to one drink before dinner, and he stopped smoking about the time he married. After decades of "at homes" and Officers' Club parties, he had developed a social facility that went beyond the exchange of inane pleasantries. By the time he became a general he was known for his ability to get along well with civilians and Navy officers, two forms of life considered natural adversaries by many in the Army. Women remembered him as charming in an intellectual way, an attentive listener, and never patronizing, even toward those who may have deserved such treatment.[33]

Between 1898 and 1940, a total of 465 men held general officer rank in the United States Army for at least one year. In some respects, Walter Short reflected faithfully the experiences and attitudes of those officers, but in others he stood apart. His origin and earliest identities put him in the mainstream of early-twentieth-century military leadership. He was born in a small midwestern town, his father practiced one of the professions, and his family worshiped with a Protestant denomination. Either a plurality or majority of his fellow generals shared those experiences. In terms of professional preparation Short stood apart from other generals in one obvious respect: he was not among the 68 percent who graduated from the military academy at West Point.[34]

Early-twentieth-century generals were basically pessimistic about human nature but optimistic about America's role in the international order. They viewed war as an ineradicable pattern of human behavior, and peace movements and attempts to outlaw war, such as the Pact of Paris, as not only idealistic but also threats to national security because they weakened the nation. At the same time, the generals embraced the religion of progress and believed the key to its continuation lay in a combination of laissez-faire economic theory and the rugged individualism personified by Theodore Roosevelt. They thought of the ideal citizen as a healthy, disciplined individual who respected authority and cheerfully fulfilled the obligation of military service to the nation. They also saw the ideal citizen-soldier as white; the generals accepted the prevailing majority civilian racial theories of white superiority, genetic and intellectual. Recurring labor unrest in the late-nineteenth and early-twentieth centuries provoked nearly unanimous condemnation from the generals, who believed union activity interfered with national economic development, and strikes represented intolerable disorder.[35]

Short fell in step with his fellow generals in terms of love of country and service, but he did not join them lockstep in every attitude. He did not hold the cynical view of human nature widely associated with the military profession. He agreed with other generals that the war of 1914–18 would not be the last but differed with them on the reason. Subsequent wars would not result from a defect in human nature but the behavior of sincere though intolerant peoples acting on their own definitions of high moral principle. On occasion, Short disagreed with national and Army policies. He did not like to see the Army court-martial Billy Mitchell in 1925 because he thought that both civilian national leadership and the War Department general staff should have recognized and begun to develop the military potential of aircraft without waiting for the air power demonstrations and insubordination of one officer. Nor did he like to see the Army used to evict the Bonus Marchers from Washington in 1932.[36]

Despite his birth into a comfortable and locally prominent family and his attainment of high rank in the Army, Walter Short never developed the arrogance and elitist attitudes which many journalists, novelists, and motion picture directors have conditioned the public to expect in military leaders. Although relieved of an up-by-the-bootstraps struggle in his own life, Short went out of his way to assist talented young people not as fortunate. William Jay Smith, who later became a distinguished poet and literary critic, benefited from the general's encouragement and generosity at a key point in his life. A classmate of Dean Short's at Cleveland High School in St. Louis in the mid-1930s, Smith wrote an outstanding academic record. Teachers urged him to go to college but the modest income of his father made further education dependent on a scholarship. To complete his application, the aspiring scholar needed the support of someone widely respected. When he learned of Smith's financial need, Short rose from a sickbed and wrote the letter of recommendation which won the young man his scholarship. While the award took care of tuition expenses, it left unsolved the problem of acquiring a wardrobe suitable for campus. Short again assisted the talented young man, this time with an offer of several suits he no longer needed. What made Short's letter of recommendation and offer of old suits so unusual was the fact that Smith's father served as an enlisted man in the 6th Infantry band. Such expressions of generosity rarely bridged the chasm then separating officers and enlisted men as well as their families.[37]

Short's list of admirable people reveals a willingness to appreciate the efforts of those who take different paths to worthy goals, a cast of mind that led him to innovations of his own. He admired William T. Sherman, who as commanding general of the Army in the mid-1870s moved his headquarters from Washington to St. Louis to escape political meddlers in the capital. He admired Gen. George Crook for his humane treatment of tribes during the Indian Wars when virtually every other senior Army officer was calling for more brutality to open western lands for settlers. He admired Theodore Roosevelt for encouraging his secretary of war to reform the Army after the Spanish-American War. He admired Gen. John J. Pershing for his effective leadership of the American Expeditionary Force in the World War. And at a time of strict racial segregation, he respected two black officers he came in contact with, Charles P. Young and Benjamin O. Davis. Young, only the third black graduate of West Point, in 1889, distinguished himself in both military and diplomatic assignments in a thirty-one-year career, and Davis, who, like Short, was commissioned in the 1902 expansion, became in 1940 the Army's first black general.[38]

When applying his own policies and innovations, Short displayed no concern for public relations or reputation, in striking contrast to the two lightning rod personalities of his Army generation, Billy Mitchell and Douglas MacArthur. Instead of a loud voice, confrontational stance, or dramatic manner, Short relied on careful reason and professional demonstration. The best example of his method before he rose to general officer rank is the quiet revolution in machine-gun tactics he helped to bring about during the World War. He observed established practices, drew up a plan he thought avoided French and British mistakes, and then tested it under field conditions. Following further refinements based on combat experience, Short's machine-gun tactics were published after the war and accepted as Army doctrine for three decades. The general continued his innovating ways after his promotion, and because of higher rank his ideas received wider dissemination.

Walter Short's library reflected a nineteenth-century education and a deep involvement in twentieth century problems. Many feet of shelf space were taken up with the classics of American and European literature, carefully read in his youth and occasionally reread in later years. Popular novels won little of his time, and the pacifist views widely published in the 1920s and 1930s he dismissed as too far removed from reality to be taken seriously. Works added as he rose in his profession indicate a developing interest in relating his military

preparation to changing world conditions. Short enjoyed biographies and campaign histories from several nations and periods. Personal accounts by Great
War commanders especially interested him, and he purchased and read carefully General Pershing's two-volume *My Experiences in the World War.* He was
also interested in studies of international relations, and kept a copy of Richard
Stockton's *Inevitable War,* a book published in 1932 which predicted the continuation of armed conflict. As America's role in the world became more closely
linked with other countries and their problems, so did Short become more
aware of the Army's changing role. Although better read than most of his
peers, he shared with them an orientation toward the practical rather than the
theoretical. He knew that the way to devise and test tactical concepts was to
get into the field with a body of troops rather than consult Clausewitz or draw
diagrams at a desk.[39]

WHEN HERBERT HOOVER became president in March 1929, the third consecutive Republican in the White House, he had every intention of continuing his
predecessors' policy of curtailing expenditures and balancing the federal budget
as a matter of principle. Only four months after taking office, the president ordered a review of all military activities to discover ways to reduce War Department spending. The review, conducted by the Army general staff, made clear
that even with the current regular force of only 139,000 officers and men, the
variety of budgetary demands on the War Department in the post–World War I
environment—for the Air Corps buildup; support of the National Guard, Organized Reserve Corps, Reserve Officers' Training Corps, and Citizens' Military Training Camps; and a minimal weapons and equipment development
effort—were such that a reduction of military spending could not be achieved
with the cooperation of Army leadership. In early 1930, the president and his
secretary of war settled on the more realistic goal of stabilizing the military
budget. But the modest relaxation of budgetary constraints on the military did
not signal an end to belt tightening in the War Department. The search for sav-
ings had already cost the Army the suspension of large-scale annual maneuvers, as well as the amendment or cancellation of thirty-four procurement and
supply projects, including the ten-year rearmament program for antiaircraft
artillery, tractor replacement, a mechanized cavalry regiment, the 75-mm how-
itzer, the seven-year motor vehicle replacement program, the 81-mm mortar,
the 37-mm antitank gun, augmentation of war reserves, the 4.2-inch chemical
mortar, and the semiautomatic rifle.[40]

In the absence of a foreign military challenge or a reordering of domestic priorities, a stable military budget might have been maintained for a number of years. However, with the Hoover administration barely seven months in office, a catastrophic economic collapse forced abandonment of the hope of a budgetary stability. After gaining congressional approval for a series of economy acts, the president forced spending reductions on the military. Beginning 1 July 1932, Lieutenant Colonel Short and his fellow Army officers saw their pay reduced by 8.3 percent. Enlisted men were spared financial penalty from their commander in chief. Nine months later, at the end of Hoover's term in office, the pay cut deepened to 15 percent and now included enlisted personnel. During the Hoover administration, the military portion of the War Department budget was reduced from a high of $347 million in fiscal 1931 to $305 million two years later. Its budget bruised by the commander in chief's insistence on the smallest and cheapest land force, and its morale rocked by pay cuts, the Army went on to receive a black eye from pacifists, reform liberals, and labor unions for routing from their Washington encampment the Bonus Army of unemployed veterans in the summer of 1932.[41]

President Franklin D. Roosevelt's first year in office brought no budgetary relief to the War Department. The military appropriation was slashed by another $28 million from the last Hoover budget, which pushed Army expenditures nearly as low as they were in the mid-1920s and forced the cancellation of field training, including target practice, flight training, reequipment programs, and research and development. But the new president also acted to raise morale, initiating a graduated rollback of the economy acts, reducing the Army pay cut to 10 percent effective 1 February 1934, further reducing it to 5 percent five months later (1 July 1934), and eliminating it altogether on 1 April 1935.[42]

The restoration of pay was a relief to all in uniform but along with it came a new and unwelcome mission. The Hoover administration had briefly considered using the Army in a number of relief programs for the unemployed and their families, but strong opposition voiced by the chief of staff, Gen. Douglas MacArthur, and the general staff caused officials to set aside the idea. President Roosevelt, however, viewed the leadership and organizational skills of the Army as easily transferable to projects mobilizing large numbers of people, and he ordered the chief of staff to help carry out a new relief program, the Civilian Conservation Corps. Authorized by the Congress just days after the new president was sworn in, the CCC mobilized unemployed young men and able-bodied veterans in reforestation and other public works projects. Planners initially envisioned the enrollment of some 250,000 men in about thirteen hundred camps throughout the nation. MacArthur and the general staff grumbled about damage to military efficiency and readiness but prepared to divert 3,000 officers to the program. The initial mobilization, completed by 1 July, required the assignment of 3,109 regular Army officers, 532 regular Navy and Marine Corps officers, and 1,774 reserve officers. The president expanded the CCC in its second year, forcing the general staff to add 5,176 enlisted men to the contingent of officers at the growing number of camps. Alarmed at the diversion of personnel, especially officers, the general staff moved to return them to military duties by activating more than 9,000 reserve officers to staff the camps by the summer of 1935.[43]

While senior officers tried to limit the effects of the CCC on the Army, many civilians, including the secretary of war, found much to like about the program. Members of Congress came to see it as an effective, if short-term, answer to unemployment in their districts, and requested the opening of additional camps. Others lauded the program for providing gainful employment to men who might turn to crime to feed their families, and for exposing urban youth to a wholesome outdoors lifestyle. After four years in operation, the program was reauthorized by Congress in 1937 for another three years and eventually enrolled more than 3.3 million men in a growing variety of public works projects at a maximum of 2,109 camps. Although the CCC remained a War Department mission for the rest of the decade, senior officers never embraced it, with many viewing it as another experiment revealing the leftist tendencies of the New Deal. When the program brought the Army criticism from liberals and pacifists, who denounced the disciplinary standards and educational program in the camps as evidence of militarism, senior officers felt their worst fears justified. The best they could say about the CCC was that it had provided a refresher course to reserve officers and a mobilization exercise to supply and transportation specialists in the War Department.[44]

Short's career pattern was unaffected by the Civilian Conservation Corps but in the early 1930s he was in Washington and witnessed at close range the series of trying experiences and unrelieved criticism to which the Army was subjected in those years. On duty with the Bureau of Insular Affairs in the War Department, again in civilian clothes, Short saw the struggle of the chief of staff and the general staff to stave off new budget cuts harden into an annual clash of mounting antagonism with Congress and the White House, leaving many career soldiers feeling at best underappreciated and at worst like freeloaders on the taxpayers. With relations between soldiers and policy makers more grating than at any time since the end of the world war, the Army was given a mission which turned out to be a public relations debacle. In the summer of 1932, more than twenty-five thousand World War I veterans gathered in Washington to demand early payment of a bonus promised for their wartime service. President Hoover considered the self-styled Bonus Army nothing more than Communist-inspired rabble and ordered General MacArthur to expel them from the capital. The job required cavalry charges with sabers and tear gas and took the lives of six veterans. For its loyal response to the commander in chief's order, the Army was denounced by pacifists, reform liberals, and veterans' organizations. Along with thousands of others working and living in Washington, Short may have gotten a whiff of the tear gas used to drive the veterans from the streets of the capital, and he almost certainly saw the smoke rising above Anacostia Flats when the troops set fire to the demonstrators' tents and shelters.

Two years later, critics of the military found new ammunition, this time on Capitol Hill. Late in 1934, the leadership of the U.S. Senate appointed a special committee to investigate the munitions industry. Despite Democratic Party dominance of both houses of Congress, committee members chose Republican Gerald P. Nye, an isolationist from North Dakota, to chair the panel. Nye and his committee made sensational revelations about corporate and military "merchants of death" bribing politicians, sharing patents, collecting huge profits and evading taxes, even lobbying for declarations of war. At one point Nye's committee accepted the accusation that General MacArthur had acted as a virtual arms dealer during a recent official trip to Turkey. Nye kept his investigation alive by turning to the issue of American entry into the 1914–18 war, and revealed with practiced sensation that a cabal of diplomats and Jewish bankers had hoodwinked the U.S. government into joining the French and British on European battlefields in 1917.[45]

The Nye committee fueled, and in turn fed on, the traditional suspicion of the American people for foreign interventions as well as current concern about the increasing belligerence of Hitler's Nazi regime in Germany. The committee hearings raised enough alarm about the danger of American intervention in a new European war that the Congress passed the Neutrality Act of 1935, which prohibited the sale of arms to belligerents. President Roosevelt opposed the Nye committee and the isolationist cause it championed but, well aware of the depth of public feeling on the issue, made a show of cooperating with the senator and his colleagues, and in August 1935 he signed the Neutrality Act into law.

Continued funding restrictions and now diversions of uniformed personnel from military activities occasioned by the Great Depression as well as a resurgence of antimilitarism took a heavy toll on the Army and posed formidable obstacles to an effective mobilization if a serious threat developed. The American people were more fortunate than they knew that amid these discouraging conditions a handful of dedicated specialists in and out of uniform continued to develop technologies emergent during the 1914–18 war despite official neglect and, in some cases, public indifference. After planning and leading air operations in France, Brig. Gen. William "Billy" Mitchell pressed for expanded aircraft missions in Army doctrine and urged establishment of an independent American air force. Finding no enthusiasm for his ideas among postwar Army brass, Mitchell staged bombing demonstrations of battleships and long-distance flights that attracted wide attention and prodded Army leadership on air power development to the point of insubordination. Mitchell's methods ended in the personal tragedy of a court-martial, but his efforts contributed to the creation of a semiautonomous air arm within the Army in 1935. Tanks attracted even more attention than airplanes when they were first used on the western front by the British in 1916. Samuel D. Rockenbach and George S. Patton trained and led the first American armored units in France but watched in frustration when the new specialty was subordinated to the infantry, and force development funding dried up soon after the armistice. American armor advocates could only watch from afar as other armies developed the potential of tanks in the 1920s and 1930s. Finally, spurred by the menace of the German blitzkrieg, the War Department built upon the pioneering work of Rockenbach, Patton, and, later, Adna R. Chaffee and established the U.S. Army armored force in 1940.

Another remarkable veteran of the Great War, William F. Friedman, was just as determined as others to develop his specialty but labored in near anonymity. A quiet and unassuming genius, Friedman specialized in signals intelligence, a field gaining importance as nations and armies increased their reliance on wireless communication. Friedman described his work with a new term, "cryptology," which involved both the design of codes and ciphers to safeguard the messages of one's own government and the solution and translation of codes and ciphers transmitted by adversaries.

In 1929, the War Department formed the Signals Intelligence Service and chose Friedman to lead the new agency. Denied staff development funding, Friedman recruited half a dozen civilians and trained them on his own time and without compensation. Despite minimal funding through most of the 1930s

—for eight consecutive years the SIS budget was frozen at seventeen thousand dollars—the tiny cell of cryptanalysts persevered to give the nation a remarkable demonstration of technical skill and personal fortitude. In 1938, Friedman and his assistants took on the daunting task of deciphering the large volume of secret messages of an increasingly belligerent Japan. While the Office of Naval Intelligence concentrated on Imperial Navy codes, the Signals Intelligence Service tackled the Japanese diplomatic code called Purple. Intelligence insiders soon gave the code name Magic to Friedman's assault on Purple. In August 1940, after two years of the most tedious, concentrated labor, Friedman's magicians cracked Purple, and in so doing made the most important contribution to national security in the field of intelligence to that date.[46]

Within his specialty Walter Short, too, was an innovator. When he joined the Infantry School as assistant commandant in the summer of 1936, Short got the chance to resume work on an idea he had been toying with for nearly two decades. As a machine-gun trainer in the mud of the western front, he had seen the need for a motorized weapons and ammunition carrier rugged enough to operate over rough terrain. All research and testing for the infantry, both doctrinal and material, was conducted at Fort Benning, so this was the ideal place to try out new theories and gadgets. In a fortuitous coincidence, the U.S. Congress had begun increasing the annual appropriation for the Army just as Short arrived at the Infantry School, so now he and others had the funding to transform concepts and sketches into prototypes for testing.

In November, Short called to his office Robert G. Howie, a forty-six-year-old captain and tank instructor, and directed him to design and build a vehicle capable of transporting two men, a .30-caliber machine gun and tripod, and a quantity of ammunition, a load totaling about 750 pounds. Short told Howie that the vehicle should present a low profile and be light enough for four men to lift it over small obstacles and small enough to fit in the bed of the one-and-a-half-ton truck then in standard use by machine-gun units. The vehicle need not be particularly fast—a speed of ten miles per hour was sufficient—but it should be easy to operate and maintain. Finally, the vehicle should be commercially available, or at least capable of minor modification to desired specifications. To fund the project, Short made available to Howie the sum of five hundred dollars.[47]

Howie set out on his unique mission by gathering expertise and advice. He chose as assistant a noncommissioned officer who knew his way around a machine shop, M.Sgt. M. C. Wiley, then traveled to Chicago and Detroit to meet with owners and drivers of midget race cars. Back at Fort Benning, Howie and Wiley ordered parts from automotive catalogs and picked over the post salvage yard. Within a month they had put together a vehicle that seemed to embody the desired characteristics, and one of extremely varied parentage. Powered by a rear-mounted 13-horsepower Austin engine, the machine-gun carrier also had a motorcycle drive train and brakes, a mixed Ford-Austin steering assembly controlled by an airplane-style stick, and wheels and tires from farm tractors. A channel steel frame fabricated by Howie and Wiley held everything together. The carrier was 124 inches long, 62 inches wide, and 33 inches high, and it weighed 1,015 pounds without a load and a crew of two. Its maximum speed was twenty-eight miles per hour, and it could climb a forty-five-degree slope on dry, solid ground. The driver, propped on his elbows, held the steering stick in one hand and shifted among the five forward and one reverse gears with his feet.[48]

After a wait of several months, Short and Howie won a field trial of their hybrid vehicle. In February 1938, three evaluators loaded the carrier with over seven hundred pounds of machine-gun equipment and ammunition, then drove it over troop and tank trails, up hills, and through streams and mud holes. The machine made its way through any type of underbrush and up most hills as long as traction was maintained. On soft ground, however, the rear wheels quickly dug ruts as deep as the ground clearance of just over seven inches, and the vehicle bottomed out on its frame. The test team soon found more problems. The carrier lost mobility in mud and loose soil or sand, it was not sturdy enough for extended cross country use, and it was not commercially available, the last an important consideration when the War Department lacked the authority to demand that corporate production respond to military need. Because of those shortcomings the Infantry Board declined to pursue development of the vehicle. However, the board found some value in the machine, noting that it proved that equipment incorporating features necessary for battlefield use could be built from commercially available parts. Thus, in the event of military mobilization, the Howie carrier could be used to demonstrate to commercial manufacturers the feasibility of adapting their production to military needs.[49]

BY THE TIME his machine-gun carrier was tested, Short was no longer at the Infantry School. In December 1936, only five months after reporting to Fort Benning, he was promoted out of the assistant commandant's billet. As a new brigadier general, he took up a series of important commands in the famed 1st

Division. The first American division organized for service on the western front and the first to see combat, the 1st Division came out of the war as the pride of the Army's field forces. Headquartered in New York City, the 1st participated in so many civic and sports events that it quickly became the most visible unit in the postwar Army.

Short's move to the 1st Division coincided with the emergence of the Army from the shadows of budgetary neglect. The armaments programs and conquests of Germany, Italy, and Japan prodded the Roosevelt administration into modernizing and expanding the nation's small and obsolescent land force. Congressional appropriations jumped, skeleton units filled out, and the troops turned in old equipment for new. In the late 1930s, War Department annual expenditures approached $700 million, more than double the lean budgets of the 1920s, and the Army increased its manpower from 138,000 in 1935 to 188,000 four years later.[50]

Short began his time with the 1st Division far from the bright lights of New York City. In February 1937, he reported to Fort Ontario, on the shores of Lake Ontario near Oswego, and took command of the division's 2d Infantry Brigade. Like other major unit commanders at the time, Short kept a wary eye on the increasingly aggressive posturing of Hitler and the German Army as he trained his brigade. Off post, however, he could betray no unease or raise any alarms. The official attitude of the day was neutrality, as enacted by the Congress two years before, and local commanders were expected to balance time spent on military duties by cultivating good relations with nearby communities. That meant addressing Rotarians and lending the prestige of the uniform to public events. While heading the 2d Brigade, Short served as guest of honor at the Apple Blossom Festival in Brockport and Youngstown and crowned the festival queen.[51]

In the summer of 1938, Short received orders to Fort Wadsworth in New York City to head the 1st Division's other infantry brigade. He spent a little more than a year with 1st Brigade on Staten Island, then, in October 1939, rode the ferry across the Verrazano Narrows to Brooklyn to assume command of the entire 1st Division at Fort Hamilton. Now a genuine VIP, Short got a blizzard of invitations to the most glittering events in the city, among them dinner with the Crown Prince and Princess of Sweden at the tercentenary of New Sweden, and a place in the reception line for Britain's King George VI and Queen Elizabeth at the World's Fair. The division commander's perks included a chauffeured car equipped with a siren and granted unlimited speed and precedence over all traffic except ambulances. He also found satisfaction in the growth and early career decisions of his son. After two years at Johns Hopkins University, Dean was accepted with the U.S. Military Academy class of 1942.[52]

But all was not pomp and perks for an army general in the late 1930s. To division commanders like Walter Short, the president's military modernization program meant they could start to remedy the critical lack of higher-level field leadership. Two decades after the World War, the Army had no officers experienced in handling large units in combat. While no amount of money could recreate combat conditions against a determined enemy, increased appropriations allowed the Army to conduct more frequent maneuvers involving larger units. Short's chance to polish leadership skills came in the summer of 1939. The First Army maneuvers brought together Regular Army and National Guard units from nine northeastern states in the largest peacetime military concentration in American history. For two weeks, fifty-two thousand troops tested new weapons, equipment, and tactics near Plattsburg, New York. Short commanded the "Provisional Corps," consisting of his own 1st Division, two National Guard divisions, two separate brigades, and numerous support units. Termed "Blue" force for the maneuver, Short's corps went against Brig. Gen. Maxwell Murray's four-division "Black" force. A mechanized attack by Short's Blue troops highlighted the maneuver. The Plattsburg exercise did much to advance Army modernization. The infantrymen got a new rifle, the M-1 semi-automatic, trucks demonstrated their superiority over horses in positioning artillery, and the commanders involved gained valuable experience in the fast-paced mechanized tactics introduced by the German Army.[53]

After these maneuvers Short received an honor and a shock. From First Army headquarters came a certificate of commendation for his handling of Provisional Corps at Plattsburg. Then, with everyone back in garrison, stunning news from Europe interrupted the training routine. The German Army had invaded Poland. General Short called a meeting and told his staff that another world war appeared imminent and the United States might soon be in it.[54]

The War Department scheduled more maneuvers in 1940, each larger than the last, and each an attempt to devise tactics against the new German blitzkrieg style of warfare. On 1 March, Short was promoted to major general. Within days the chief of staff, Gen. George C. Marshall, jumped him over twenty others with more seniority to command IV Corps, a multidivision force drawn from eight states and headquartered in Atlanta. The next month, in the first field test of his new command, Short took IV Corps to Fort Benning and divided it into

"Red" and "Blue" forces. His Blue troops practiced defending against a blitzkrieg attack by Red forces across the Chattahoochee River, the same type of defense the Danes and Norwegians had failed to maintain against German invaders just five days before the maneuvers began. In May, Short's IV Corps took part in the Third Army maneuvers along the Sabine River between Texas and Louisiana, a massive exercise involving seventy thousand troops and hundreds of tanks and trucks. This time the script set Short against an old friend, Walter Krueger and his IX Corps. The umpires decided IV Corps won the battle, and Short won praise from observers as one of the few American commanders who understood the fast-paced and far-ranging tactics of mechanized warfare. Among those impressed with Short's performance was the retired Lt. Gen. Robert L. Bullard, who had commanded the U.S. Second Army in the World War.[55]

Short and Krueger carried on their mock war against the backdrop of the real thing. While American troops tramped through farmers' fields in Louisiana, German armies overran the Low Countries and broke through the Maginot Line. French defenses crumbled, and the British retreated to the beaches of Dunkirk. With the fall of France in June, American rearmament accelerated from the cautious to the frantic. General Marshall spent much time explaining Army needs to congressional committees but new Axis conquests quickly rendered his projections obsolete. At one point, Secretary of War Henry Stimson and Marshall were adding supplementary appropriations requests to budget proposals still being debated in Congress. The final appropriation for fiscal 1941 came to nearly $3 billion. By mid-1940, Army manpower topped 266,000, and Marshall's planners envisioned a total strength of four million men.[56]

General Short remained in the forefront of these changes. In September, two weeks after Congress enacted the first peacetime draft law in American history, he bade farewell to 1st Division and IV Corps, and took command of the new I Corps at Fort Jackson, South Carolina. The new corps commander settled into his new office, got a headquarters staff functioning and put a training schedule into effect. On Christmas Eve he got a telephone call that changed everything. General Marshall had decided to send him to Hawaii to lead the Army's largest overseas command. Marshall's decision came as a complete surprise, but Short began packing. After checking on his modest stock portfolio—fifteen shares of Bohn Aluminum and one hundred shares of Remington Arms—he went to Washington for briefings about Hawaii.[57]

At the War Department, Short mentioned to General Marshall that if the

Hawaiian assignment represented nothing more than a routine rotation of commanders, he would prefer duty within the continental United States because of his father-in-law's questionable health. Marshall dismissed Short's demure without giving his reason for either changing commanders in Hawaii or taking Short from I Corps after only three months. The Shorts boarded a train to visit relatives in the St. Louis area and Oklahoma City, then headed west to meet a 31 January sailing date from San Francisco.[58]

5

The Seriousness of This Situation

ABOARD THE GRACEFUL *MATSONIA*, STEAMING WEST THROUGH PACIFIC SWELLS, Walter Short had plenty of time to think about the command that awaited him. Judging from his habits of mind and reputation, he thought about his new assignment in terms neither dramatic nor mundane. He saw the defense of Hawaii as a duty, and a dangerous one, but not as perilous as the Philippines, the place everyone expected the Japanese to strike if they were foolish enough to attack American forces. The closest he came to dramatic interpretation was to call Hawaii a "hot spot," as he described it to relatives a few days before his departure. Like every other general officer in the Army at the time, Short was well aware of the vulnerability of island bases to air attack, but he did not yet have enough information to judge the dimensions of danger Hawaii faced. Swamped with the problems of rapid expansion of the Army, General Marshall had not had enough time to give a detailed briefing on the situation in the mid-Pacific. Short would just have to wait until he could meet the outgoing commander at Fort Shafter. He probably also wondered why Marshall had chosen him to command the Hawaiian Department, but here he had even less to go on than a hurried briefing. No doubt his well-deserved reputation as an expert trainer had something to do with it, but beyond that he could only guess, for his old friend had not provided any details.[1]

Short's selection for the Hawaiian Department was part of Marshall's solution to the problem of interservice rivalry. When the Army and Navy were small and separated by geography and different missions—the Army policing settlers and Indians across frontier expanses, the Navy patrolling coastlines—interservice rivalry rarely surfaced. But after 1898, the extension of American authority to distant possessions forced the Army and Navy into joint operations and raised questions of primary interest and jurisdiction. In the Caribbean and the Pacific, Army and Navy officers struggled with issues such as the seaward extent of a coast artillery commander's authority and the landward reach of an admiral's command when his ships were in port. The development of military aviation raised anew the issue of jurisdiction. Before a serious effort to distinguish responsibilities above coastlines and ports could be made, both services built up separate air arms and staked out missions. The disruptive potential of interservice rivalry remained unresolved.

The latest outbreak of Army-Navy contention had occurred in the Panama Canal area in the summer of 1940. General Marshall wanted to test defenses in the Pacific outposts he considered most vulnerable to Japanese attack, Hawaii and Panama. On 17 June, he ordered the two Army outpost commanders to put their forces on alert and inform their naval counterparts. The alert in Hawaii went off without incident. But in Panama, Army headquarters passed along the alert in the form of a directive rather than rewording it as a request. Navy authorities in the Caribbean took offense at what they saw as a breach of interservice protocol and protested to Washington. General Marshall and the chief of naval operations had to intervene to restore cooperation in the canal area.[2]

The outbreak of interservice animosity in Panama weighed heavily on General Marshall as he chose commanders to manage Army expansion. Surveying other areas of cooperative command—the Philippines, Hawaii, and Alaska—he felt confident that no flare-ups would hamper American rearmament, since local commanders had solved issues among themselves for several years. But at the end of the year delicate interservice relations were upset. The Navy made a change in Hawaii. In October 1940, the Pacific Fleet commander, Adm. J. O. Richardson, had been too pointed in protesting at the White House the transfer of the fleet base to Hawaii from San Diego. President Roosevelt ordered a change in command.[3]

The Navy shakeup in Hawaii forced the Army to consider a change. The incumbent Hawaiian Department commander, Lt. Gen. Charles D. Herron, had only a few months to serve before retirement. Rather than leave Herron to establish a working relationship with a new admiral shortly before his own relief and then expect a successor to repeat the process, Marshall preferred to appoint someone who, like the incoming Navy commander, could look forward to a tour of several years in Hawaii. More important was the character of the new Pacific Fleet commander. Adm. Husband E. Kimmel had been chosen over a large number of senior officers. His relative youth and, alarming to those aware of it, his reputation for gruffness, could not be ignored in maintaining Army-Navy cooperation in Hawaii. When Marshall applied the usual criteria of experience and availability to the Army's senior generals he came up with Walter Krueger. But Krueger was known to be inflexible and overly sensitive to criticism, and Marshall kept looking. He needed a diplomat to deal with the Navy and civilian Hawaii, as well as a proven trainer to whip into shape the fast-growing Army garrison in the islands. Walter Short scored high in both areas, and Marshall picked up his telephone.[4]

On 5 February 1941, as the *Matsonia* edged into its berth at Honolulu, a formation of Army bombers roared overhead in salute to the incoming department commander. Since General Short had worn civilian clothes throughout the voyage, most of his fellow passengers were unaware of him or the reason for the flyover. But when white-gloved MPs cordoned off part of the pier, a uniformed band struck up a series of flourishes, and a sedan with flags snapping on the fenders pulled up to the gangplank, the story buzzed through the crowd. The Army was changing commanders in the "Paradise of the Pacific." As young Hawaiian girls swung leis over his head and flash cameras popped, Short greeted General Herron, an old acquaintance from their days in France in 1918. The pile of flowers around his neck only emphasized Short's slight build, and provided family and associates with an unusually relaxed view of a man whose personal warmth rarely showed through photographs. Briefings and ceremonies filled the next two days, with everything reaching a colorful climax on 7 February at the change of command ceremony. On the parade ground at Fort Shafter, Herron passed the department colors to his successor. The generals then took the salute of their troops as color guards from every unit on the islands marched over lush lawn bordered by Royal palms bobbing in the warm Pacific breeze. Later, in front of department headquarters, a beaming Isabel pinned on her husband's third star. The slim infantry officer appeared almost broad-shouldered under the gleaming symbols of his new responsibility.[5]

A son of the Illinois prairie had now become one of only six lieutenant generals in the United States Army, and the folks back in Fillmore had to be proud. No one would have been surprised to see the new three-star take a day or two off to bathe in the pomp and fluff of reviews and receptions or try out the Fort Shafter golf course. But that was not Walter Short's style. Although his first full duty day fell on a Saturday, he made it a work day, meeting and evaluating subordinates, taking a look at the command he had until now seen only through the bland language and statistics of Army reports.

IN THE YEARS BEFORE General Short took over, much had been done to make the Hawaiian Islands a bastion of American power in the Pacific. A natural stepping stone between California and the Philippines, Hawaii, with its large sheltered port at Pearl Harbor, was an ideal coaling station for the new steam-powered Navy of the late nineteenth century. And wherever the Navy built a major base, the Army went to protect it. By 1913 the War Department had enough troops in the islands to establish a new regional command, the Hawaiian Department. When the Naval Limitation Treaty of 1922 prohibited new military construction west of Hawaii, the fleet base at Pearl Harbor and its Army defenses took on new importance. The Army posted more troops to the islands, and organized them into a new tactical unit, the Hawaiian Division, in 1921. Army engineers dug coast artillery gun pits at the mouth of Pearl Harbor, and horse-drawn graders leveled the land nearby for roads and airfields. Army manpower stabilized at just over thirteen thousand until the next buildup began in 1936. At the end of the 1930s, the Hawaiian Department numbered nearly twenty-two thousand officers and men. By 1938, the Navy had spent about $75 million on the development of Pearl Harbor, and the Army more than twice as much on installations to protect it.[6]

On the day General Short took command of the Hawaiian Department, the chief of staff addressed a letter to him. General Marshall wanted to make sure his new man in Hawaii began with a clear understanding of his mission and of the nature of the situation. Sensitive to interservice relations, Marshall asked Adm. Harold R. Stark, the chief of naval operations, about the Navy's new man in the islands, then passed along his findings to Short. On the organization charts, the Hawaiian Department commander shared authority with the commandant of the Fourteenth Naval District, Rear Adm. Claude C. Bloch. But because Bloch was more an administrator than a tactical commander, Short would have a closer working relationship with the commander in chief of the Pacific Fleet, Admiral Kimmel. Two years younger than Short,

Kimmel had risen rapidly to his four-star position. He had been in office only one week when Short arrived at Fort Shafter.[7]

Marshall wrote that Kimmel "was very direct, even brusque and undiplomatic in his approach to problems," but he was also "at heart a very kindly man." However, the chief of staff believed there would be ample opportunity to reason with the admiral, for Kimmel was also "entirely responsive to plain speaking on the part of the other fellow if there is frankness and logic in the presentation." Marshall also passed along Kimmels's view that the Army did not have enough aircraft and antiaircraft artillery to protect Pearl Harbor, and he directed Short to make the admiral aware of the Army's materiel problems: "Kimmel does not realize . . . that we are tragically lacking in this material throughout the Army, and that Hawaii is on a far better basis than any other command in the Army. . . . You should make clear to Admiral Kimmel that we are doing everything that is humanly possible to build up the Army defenses of the Naval overseas installations, but we cannot perform a miracle." The chief of staff promised the situation would soon improve, however, since he had arranged to ship thirty-one P-36 planes to Hawaii in ten days and fifty P-40Bs by the middle of March.[8]

The most important part of the chief of staff's letter concerned the mission of the Hawaiian Department and the risks the Army faced in the mid-Pacific. "The fullest protection for the fleet is *the* rather than *a* major consideration for us, there can be little question about that," he wrote. Near the end of his letter, Marshall gave his views of the challenges he saw facing Short's command: "The risk of sabotage and the risk involved in a surprise raid by Air and by submarine constitute the real perils of the situation. Frankly, I do not see any landing threat in the Hawaiian Islands so long as we have air superiority." The concern about sabotage was an old one to soldiers in Hawaii, fueled by assumptions derived from the racial composition of the Territorial population. Although several nonwhite groups lived in the islands, the Japanese, with 37 percent of the total of 423,000, dominated. Army intelligence officers and the FBI in Honolulu spent much time and effort on the sabotage fear, compiling and updating lists of hundreds of Japanese viewed as security risks as well as smaller numbers of Germans and Italians. The War Department subordinated the risk of direct attack by Japanese naval forces to that of sabotage because Japan's aircraft carriers were believed not to have the range necessary for a trans-Pacific raid, and if they tried to extend range by underway refueling, they would be detected by U.S. Navy air and sea patrols. The possibility of attack by submarine raised concern because the improved Japanese I-class boats built since 1937 were not only the largest submarines in the world but were believed capable of the great cruising range necessary to threaten the U.S. Pacific Fleet.[9]

In a lengthy reply of 19 February, Short listed the priorities of his command as he saw them. First on his list of eight items was "Cooperation with the Navy." The second to seventh items concerned either construction or weapons needed —aircraft revetments and other bombproof barriers, and roads and trails across and around Oahu; improved antiaircraft and coastal artillery guns, and search-lights—and last was more engineer troops to complete the construction projects. Obviously sharing Marshall's concern for Army-Navy relations, Short soon met with Bloch and Kimmel, appointed Army members to interservice committees, and began work on a new policy on defense against air attack.[10]

General Short's first accomplishment came in the area of his greatest concern, relations with the Navy. On 21 March, he and Admiral Bloch signed a joint air operations agreement to facilitate coordination of Army and Navy air units in emergencies. If the two commanders recognized an imminent attack, each would make his aircraft available to the other depending on the type of action considered necessary. In the case of joint air attacks on enemy ships, the Navy would command. In the case of joint defensive air operations "over and in the immediate vicinity of Oahu," the Army would command. In addition, the Navy would command when it requested Army aircraft to either complete long-range patrolling or protect friendly ships.[11]

Another agreement seemed to settle the delicate issue of interservice cooperation in Hawaii. The Joint Coastal Frontier Defense Plan, signed 11 April 1941, provided, among other things, that "the method of coordination will be by mutual cooperation" and that the Navy would provide distant reconnaissance around the islands. Army and Navy officers also drew up estimates of enemy action which, in the case of air action, ended with an embarrassing admission:

> It appears possible that . . . an Orange [Japanese] fast raiding force might arrive in Hawaiian waters with no prior warning from our intelligence service. . . .
>
> The aircraft at present available in Hawaii are inadequate to maintain for any extended period. . . . A patrol extensive enough to insure that an air attack from an Orange carrier cannot arrive over Oahu as a complete surprise. . . .
>
> It appears that the most likely and dangerous form of attack on Oahu would be an air attack. It is believed that at present such an attack would most likely be launched from one or more carriers which would probably approach inside of three hundred miles. . . .

In a dawn attack there is a high probability that it could be delivered as a complete surprise in spite of any patrols we might be using and that it would find us in a condition of readiness under which pursuit would be slow to start.[12]

Thus, from an early date the leadership in Hawaii knew it did not have the means to prevent the type of attack it considered most likely. Nevertheless, General Short set out to build his command into the strongest bastion possible for the Pacific Fleet and its base at Pearl Harbor.

Short won a second achievement in his early months in Hawaii, this one outside the military establishment. With the loyalty of more than one-third of the civil population in doubt and the islands requiring importation of most necessities, cooperation between the garrison and civil population in times of emergency was essential. Invited to address the Hawaii Chamber of Commerce on Army Day, 6 April, Short used the occasion to outline his emergency preparation program. The general called for production and storage of food, organization of medical professionals, formation of a police reserve and planning of evacuation routes and shelters. Led by Territorial Governor Joseph B. Poindexter, Mayor Lester Petrie of Honolulu, and managers of the Big Five combines dominating the economy, Hawaii responded with enthusiasm. Residents stocked canned goods in their homes, and farmers set aside a portion of pineapple acreage for vegetable cultivation. Medical personnel formed surgical teams and designated buildings to be used as aid stations. Volunteers formed auxiliary police and fire units to prevent sabotage. Honolulu and territorial officials designated shelters and evacuation camps. Soon after his Army Day speech, Short appeared before the Territorial Senate to speak in support of a Mobilization Day bill, which would grant him as department commander martial law powers and the governor broad executive authority in case of emergency. The legislators soon passed the bill. The only hitch in the preparedness effort developed when the Bureau of the Budget refused to authorize $3.4 million for the food storage program.[13]

Not all of General Short's efforts turned out as well as his dealings with the Navy and the civilian community. Less than a month after his arrival in Hawaii, he began asking the War Department for more personnel, new anti-aircraft batteries, and funds for a variety of construction projects. As the months passed, however, he found a growing number of his requests either inadequately answered or simply set aside indefinitely. In February, he requested $1,565,600 to build protective bunkers for aircraft; seven months later, the War Department answered that $1,358,000 would be made available for this purpose on about 1 January 1942. Also in February, he requested $1,370,000 to build or improve military roads, rail lines, and trails; he received only $350,000 for this purpose. Between early April and mid-May, Short asked for funds to improve or construct ten airfields. The War Department changed one of the sites requested for a new airfield, which pushed Short into a four-month wrangle with the Navy, also interested in the substitute location. Even after the interservice negotiation ended satisfactorily, the Hawaiian Department received no funds for airfield work. By the end of the first week in December, Short had requested a total of $22,953,697 for all projects but still had received only the $350,000 for roads and trails improvements, an appropriation of barely 1.5 percent.[14]

Short encountered still another problem with Washington when he tried to improve his defense against air attack. Since the 1914–18 war, technical improvements in military aviation and the advent of the aircraft carrier had dramatically increased the destructive power and range of aircraft. These developments rendered island outposts like Hawaii increasingly vulnerable to air attack, and Short wanted the best defense available. In the late 1930s, the War and Navy Departments had begun development of radar detection devices. In October 1940, the Army installed in Panama its first field radar set, and in tests it detected an approaching airplane 118 miles away. Impressed, Short ordered a dozen radar sets and began choosing locations on high ground.[15]

Like every other major commander, Short knew that requisition delays and priority down-gradings came with the office. The Army never had enough people, equipment, or money to satisfy everyone, especially in a period of rapid expansion. But when, in March, he discovered the National Park Service opposed his request for a mountaintop radar site because construction would ruin a scenic view, his irritation spiked somewhere above simmering Mauna Loa. He immediately radioed the adjutant general and wrote General Marshall that "the seriousness of this situation has not yet been appreciated. . . . I believe all quibbling over details should be stopped at once." Marshall shared Short's anger about the priority on scenery and immediately telephoned his demand for action to the Park Service.[16]

Most of Short's problems with scarce resources in the first half of 1941 were caused by events in Europe the previous year. The Roosevelt administration believed it had in the Pacific a solid foundation for viable defense with three major outposts under development in Alaska, Hawaii, and the Panama Canal zone. But in the Atlantic, the United States had no outer defense barrier. The fall of France in June 1940 added urgency to the situation, not only because the large and aggressive German navy could threaten American shipping and the Atlantic coast but also because of Berlin's interest in using its expatriates in South America to exert influence in the region. To close the defense gap in the Atlantic, the United States concluded the destroyers-for-bases deal with the British in September 1940. In exchange for obsolete warships, the United States received ninety-nine-year leases to sites on eight Atlantic and Caribbean islands: Newfoundland, Bermuda, Jamaica, St. Lucia, Trinidad, British Guiana, Antigua, and the Bahamas. Constructing barracks, antiaircraft batteries, and airfields and building up garrisons for these new outposts continued throughout 1941, reducing the amount of men, weapons, equipment, and money available to the Hawaiian Department. The competition for resources intensified when Congress approved the president's Lend-Lease proposal one month after Short took over in Hawaii. Now the Army would have to share American production with nations already fighting the Axis powers.[17]

In the summer of 1941, an event in Asia pulled American attention back to the Pacific but, paradoxically, did not alleviate resources shortages in Hawaii. In late 1940 and the early months of 1941, the Hawaiian Department enjoyed first priority for reinforcement among the major overseas commands. But when the Japanese occupied French Indochina in July, the War Department gave the Philippines a higher priority than Hawaii. This meant, of course, that in the latter half of 1941 Short would have more difficulty getting the men and equipment he needed, even those already approved by the War Department.[18]

Whenever possible, Short refused to wait on the bureaucracy and acted on his own. He used infantry units as engineer troops and built four airfields with materials intended for the Works Progress Administration. He also directed his district engineer to complete without funding a gasoline storage facility and five-thousand-foot runway at Bellows Field. And by diverting men and materiel from other missions, he completed eighty-five aircraft bunkers at Wheeler Field. Relaxed reporting procedures on these projects protected him from War Department vetoes.[19]

Short also strengthened his command by relying on the good relations he had established with Admiral Kimmel and by reorganizing and redeploying his own troop units. He arranged with the Navy for joint use of all airfields in the islands during training exercises. He arranged for the extension of Navy runways to accommodate Army heavy bombers. He offered the outer reaches of his command more security than any of his predecessors when he sent battalions of the 299th Infantry, the Hawaii National Guard unit, to garrison the islands of Hawaii, Kauai, Maui, and Molokai. He also acted against the worst eventuality his command could face, a hostile landing on the shores of Oahu. The command included one infantry division, an unnumbered unit known as the Hawaiian Division. A World War I–style "square" division of four regiments, the Hawaiian Division would be spread too thin if deployed around the entire shoreline of Oahu. The apparent solution, a centrally located force that could respond in any direction to an invasion, foundered on the geography of Oahu, which divided the island into northern and southern sectors, and the square division's lack of maneuverability. Short solved the problem by winning authority to reorganize the unit into two "triangular" divisions of three regiments each. Assigned one defense sector each, the units became the 24th and 25th Divisions in the Army order of battle.[20]

On another occasion, Short's improvisation got him in trouble with his own air officers and General Marshall. Constantly on the lookout for more manpower, like any commander, Short discovered that during periods of full-alert status or department-wide maneuvers nearly half of his seventy-two hundred airmen had nothing to do. It seemed neither tactically sound nor morally right that certain components of the command would not share the burden of defense, so in July Short directed infantry training for Hawaiian Air Force enlisted men. General Marshall tactfully advised reconsideration. Short wrote the chief of staff his justification for the policy and concluded with a pointed statement: "If it is not desired to train Air Corps men for their own protection and for the final defense of the air fields I would like to be so advised." Short's controversial policy died without notice in October when he received more ground units, and the Hawaiian Air Force returned to its own missions.[21]

Very few of the problems General Short faced in Hawaii could be solved with a conference or letter to Washington. To make any progress in strengthening his command, Short and his staff had to repeatedly remind the chief of staff of critical needs in personnel, equipment, and funds. Air defense in particular demanded extraordinary time and persistence from the department commander and his staff. Short made very clear the importance he attached to the issue when he wrote General Marshall in March: "I feel that the question of Antiaircraft Defense against air attack is the most serious problem that we have to face." He got off to a good start on the issue when he found the Navy receptive to his interest in coordinating joint defense plans for the islands. The agreements Short reached with Bloch and Kimmel on air defense and other issues brought high praise from Marshall. "It is evident," he wrote, "that you have been on the job, and I know that the Navy is delighted to have such generous cooperation. . . . It is most gratifying to hear you say that everything is going along extremely well."[22]

But effective air defense of Hawaii involved more than signing pieces of paper. Short arrived in Hawaii with a well-founded anxiety about air attacks on island outposts. Only three months before he took over, the Royal Air Force gave the world a stunning demonstration of the vulnerability of ships in harbor to air attack. On 11 November 1940, twenty-seven aircraft from the carrier HMS *Illustrious* struck the Italian fleet in the assumed safe harbor of Taranto in southern Italy. British dive bombers disabled three Italian battleships and two cruisers and sank two other ships. At a cost of only two aircraft lost, the British put half the Italian battle fleet out of action for six months.[23]

The air raid on Taranto commanded the attention of Army and Navy leaders in Washington, and they immediately reviewed the defenses of Pearl Harbor and other outlying fleet bases. Short recognized that the whole issue of air defense involved several separate problems and required a multifaceted solution. As he wrote Marshall in March, "One of the first projects which I investigated in this department was the Aircraft Warning Service which I believe is vital to the defense of these islands." When operational, the warning system Short envisioned would perform three functions: detect the approach of enemy aircraft, alert coast artillery batteries and pursuit squadrons, and control antiaircraft fire and the movement of pursuit planes to oppose enemy aircraft.[24]

The key to effective defense against air attack was early detection. In the days when the greatest danger to island outposts came at the slow pace of a naval task force, local commanders had plenty of time to alert their defenses, from the first sighting of smoke on the horizon until the ships reached bombardment range. But when the aircraft carrier freed pilots from airfields on land, outpost commanders lost the early warning given by ships' smoke, for attacking aircraft could swoop into bombing and strafing runs before defending gunners could get to battle stations or even learn of approaching danger.

The best hope for early detection lay with the new technology of radar. Despite the experimental state of radar in 1941, Short saw great promise in the new technology and pressed the War Department for six fixed and six mobile sets. By December he had received six mobile sets and components for three fixed sets. But only five mobile sets were in operation, site construction for the fixed sets was not yet complete, and no operators had arrived. Short had no choice but to use the sets to train operators among Signal Corpsmen already in the department until the new devices could contribute to a warning system.[25]

In the absence of a functioning radar system, only ships and planes could detect approaching aircraft and surface ships. Here Short had some help, for by joint agreement the Navy conducted distant reconnaissance around the islands. But having the Navy look over the horizon did not relieve the Hawaiian Department of all offshore responsibility. Close-in reconnaissance remained an Army mission, and this Short and his air commander, Maj. Gen. Frederick L. Martin, carried out as best they could under severe limitations in personnel and equipment. Martin exercised the only option available, combining resources and missions whenever possible. Thus, training flights became at the same time reconnaissance flights.[26]

Both Short's and the Navy's plans for sea and air reconnaissance fell victim to the shifts in strategic emphasis carried out by policymakers in Washington during 1941. In April, General Marshall had his staff prepare for Secretary of War Henry Stimson an estimate of the situation in the Pacific that would justify the diversion of men, armaments, and production from Hawaii to development of the eight Caribbean sites acquired under the destroyers-for-bases agreement with the British. According to the estimate, "The island of Oahu, due to its fortification, its garrison, and its physical characteristics, is believed to be the strongest fortress in the world. It has been carefully fortified against naval attack and its antiaircraft defense is relatively complete." General Short never read this extremely optimistic assessment of his command's state of readiness. If he had, it likely would have provoked another pointed letter to Marshall.[27]

For the Navy in the Pacific, the shift in strategic emphasis meant a loss of one-quarter of the fleet to the Atlantic. The list of ships detached included one of three aircraft carriers and three battleships, four light cruisers, and seventeen destroyers. The loss of the aircraft carrier, cruisers, and destroyers in particular reduced the Navy's reconnaissance capability, for these ships and attached aircraft could keep under observation thousands of square miles of ocean.[28]

For the Hawaiian Department, the shift to the Atlantic meant a serious loss of reconnaissance, pursuit, and bombing aircraft. When Short took over in February, Marshall promised him thirty-five new B-17 bombers in April, but he received only twenty-one in May. Marshall diverted the other fourteen to the Atlantic, and later in the year sent nine more of Short's B-17s to the Philippines. Of the remaining twelve B-17s on hand in December, six supplied parts to keep the other six operational.[29]

The Hawaiian Air Force seemed well equipped with an impressive number of pursuit aircraft, 117 planes of various types, but all were obsolete. In late

February, thirty-one P-36s with pilots arrived by carrier from the West Coast, and by mid-April fifty-five of the latest pursuit plane, the P-40, had arrived. Despite their numbers these planes, because of their much shorter range, could not compensate for the loss of reconnaissance caused by Marshall's B-17 diversions. American aircraft production for the British also adversely affected the Hawaiian Department's ability to protect itself. A production sharing agreement reached in July 1940 gave the Royal Air Force higher priority for new aircraft than the U.S. Army or Navy.[30]

With his radar not yet functioning and ships and aircraft diverted to other commands, Short had to rely on antiaircraft artillery, the oldest method of air defense. But here again deficiencies and diversions dominated the story. The most recent revision of the Hawaiian defense project, a plan approved by the War Department in September, called for a formidable array of antiaircraft weaponry: 84 mobile and 26 fixed 3-inch guns to counter high-altitude bombers, and 144 of the newer 37-mm automatic weapons and 516 50-caliber machine guns to counter low-level aircraft. The reality in Hawaii, however, fell far short of these numbers. In the fall of 1941, the Hawaiian Department counted 60 mobile and 26 fixed 3-inch guns, only 20 of the 37-mm automatic weapons, and only 109 50-caliber machine guns. Other difficulties further reduced Hawaii's meager antiaircraft firepower. Short had his 37-mm weapons almost from his first day in the islands but he got no ammunition for them until 5 December, a wait of nearly ten months. Also, a shortage of machine-gun ammunition precluded practice firing sufficient to maintain basic readiness. A deployment problem with about half of the mobile 3-inch guns—they were assigned firing positions on private property, several miles from ammunition depots—would keep them out of action for hours in case of alert. Only the fixed 3-inch batteries, with ammunition at the firing positions, could respond to alerts quickly.[31]

While prodding Washington for more arms and equipment, Short got together with the Navy in May to test his defenses. The exercise assumed that attacking Japanese would send an air assault against the islands to knock out the Hawaiian Air Force, then follow up with an amphibious landing on several beaches. In the first, or air, phase the Navy sent one of its carriers to an undisclosed location to launch aircraft against Oahu. Army bombers under Navy direction with Navy patrol planes succeeded in locating and bombing the enemy force 250 miles at sea. In the second phase, Hawaiian Department troops constructed extensive field fortifications in anticipation of ground assaults and sabotage. In the third phase, one regiment took the role of an invasion force landing on five beaches, while other units had to locate the main landing force and, by a rapid motorized movement, concentrate to repel it. For this climactic battle on the beach, Air Corps personnel made available by the assumed destruction of the Hawaiian Air Force augmented ground units, a possibility Short prepared for with his controversial policy of having airmen undergo infantry training. The maneuver proved more successful than expected, and Short enthusiastically wrote Marshall, "I believe we learned more about the coordination of Army Air Force, Navy Air Force and Antiaircraft than we had during any previous exercise." He planned another exercise later in the year, but priorities imposed by Washington forced its postponement.[32]

The strength of any military operation, offensive or defensive, may be affected more by the ideas that govern its use than any deficiency of men or arms. Two assumptions widely shared by officials in Hawaii and Washington in 1941 threatened to undermine Short's defense of the Hawaiian Islands and the Pacific Fleet in port. The first concerned the U.S. Navy: the closer the fleet to its base at Pearl Harbor, the safer the islands because ships' firepower could augment that of the Hawaiian Department. Dating from 1935, the view appeared again in a War Plans Division estimate two years later: "If the Fleet is in the Pacific and free to act, Oahu will be . . . secure against any attacks that may be launched against it. It is only in the case that the Fleet is not present or free to act that the security of the Hawaiian Islands can be seriously threatened."[33]

The assumption about fleet firepower led too many officials in Washington to the comforting conclusion that shortages of personnel and armaments in the Hawaiian Department could be overcome simply by keeping the fleet in or near Pearl Harbor. As a result, Short's pleas for more men, aircraft, and radar lost much urgency along the forty-five-hundred-mile distance between Fort Shafter and Marshall's office. The assumption also misled officials about the objective of the Japanese. The Pacific Fleet, not the base at Pearl Harbor, posed the only serious challenge to Tokyo's interest in expanding control over the western and southern Pacific.

The second assumption rested on a faulty assessment of Japanese naval capability: the limited range of Imperial Navy capital ships made an attack on Hawaii highly unlikely. General Marshall expressed this assumption when he sought in the spring of 1941 to assure Secretary of War Stimson that the Hawaiian Department "could put up such a defense that the Japs wouldn't dare attack Hawaii, particularly such a long distance from home." Add to this technical assessment an exaggerated faith in the ability of the U.S. Navy to detect Japanese fleet movements and the disparaging views of Japanese physiology and psychology current in 1941—they were too near-sighted to fly airplanes with any skill and they could not plan complex operations—and the assumption contributes to a dangerous underestimation of an adversary.[34]

THOUGH NEVER ACCEPTABLE, deficiencies of men and arms are known and measurable, which at least enables a commander to make contingency plans to cover vulnerabilities. What a commander dreads is the invisible deficiency, the unidentified threat. In 1941, no one in the Hawaiian Department knew much more about Japan than what newspapers published. For information on his most likely adversary in the Pacific, Short depended completely on Washington, and for information on potential adversaries anywhere in the world, Washington depended on an intelligence-gathering system that had changed little since Short's tour in the Military Intelligence Division two decades before. At the center of the intelligence effort for both the Army and Navy stood the attachés assigned to each American embassy. But no matter how well-trained and perceptive, the attachés could not by themselves provide an adequate picture of a nation's military capability. They frequently had to augment their own professional interpretations with some decidedly mundane and amateurish sources: newspaper clippings, snatches of cocktail party conversations, and the impressionistic observations of businessmen, missionaries, and tourists.

In the latter months of 1940, the Army found a better source of information than its network of attachés. The Magic decrypting effort led by William F. Friedman and the Army Signals Intelligence Service broke the Japanese diplomatic code known as Purple and opened a window into decision making in Tokyo. Magic intercepts reached the desks of only ten officials: the president; the secretaries of state, war and navy; the Army chief of staff; the chief of naval operations; and the chiefs of Army and Navy intelligence and war plans divisions. Short had not even heard of Magic. Whatever he learned from Magic came couched in vague references such as "information from numerous sources."[35]

In the summer and fall of 1941, information reaching the Hawaiian Department, much of it from Magic, described an increasingly volatile international environment. Officials in Washington had reluctantly accepted the probability of a collision between Japanese aggression and American interests somewhere in the western Pacific. Beginning in July, secret messages sent to General Short reported political and diplomatic developments relating to

Japan, and attempted to assess their meaning for the Pacific balance of power. Anxiety in Washington rose dramatically when German forces invaded the Soviet Union on 22 June. In a message dated 8 July, the War Department sought to interpret the new direction of the war in Europe. In the wake of German aggression eastward, officials believed the Japanese government had adopted a policy "of watchful waiting involving probable aggressive action against maritime provinces of Russia if and when Siberian garrison has been materially reduced in strength and it becomes evident that Germany will win a decisive victory in European Russia."[36]

The authors of the same message went on to speculate about other areas of Japanese interest: "Opinion is that Jap activity in the south will be for the present confined to seizure and development of naval, army and air bases in Indo China although an advance against the British and Dutch cannot be entirely ruled out." The rest of the message reported developments that seemed to promise a continuation of Japanese aggression but with no indication of where the blow might fall: "They have ordered all Jap vessels in US Atlantic ports to be west of Panama Canal by first August. Movement of Jap shipping from Japan has been suspended and additional merchant vessels are being requisitioned."[37]

Two weeks later, Short watched with surprise the next Japanese assault: not north against Soviet territory, as Washington expected, but south against French Indochina. No intent to confuse or mislead perverted the work of any official in Washington. The authors of messages like that of 8 July struggled conscientiously to predict the actions of volatile dictators and unstable cabinets. Estimates of Axis moves resulted from collaboration between the War Plans Division, under Brig. Gen. Leonard T. Gerow, the War Department G-2 (Intelligence) Section, under Brig. Gen. Sherman Miles, and General Marshall. Using Magic and other sources of information, the three officers interpreted recent events and discussed a spectrum of likely Japanese actions. When Marshall approved an estimate, it went, encoded and classified, to commanders in need of it. The 8 July message and several that followed revealed the depressing truth that a sincere effort to interpret information in Washington did not always translate into reliable guidance or clear understanding elsewhere.

The next critical message also came in July and reported the U.S. government's response to the Japanese occupation of French Indochina. A joint message from Admiral Stark and General Marshall, dated the twenty-fifth, announced that on the following day President Roosevelt would freeze all Japanese assets in the United States and call the Philippine militia to federal service. The message included a vague warning of possible Japanese response to the president's actions. Marshall and Stark wrote that they "do not anticipate immediate hostile reaction by Japan through the use of military means but you are furnished this information in order that you may take appropriate precautionary measures against possible eventualities."[38]

Short responded by putting the Hawaiian Department on full alert for more than a week. To prevent alarm among civilians, he had his chief of staff announce to reporters a maneuver period. After twelve days, Short called off the alert but left a twenty-four-hour guard at military and utility installations, bridges, and the Honolulu waterfront.[39]

Tension in the Pacific remained frozen at this new level for eleven weeks as other issues distracted the Army and official Washington. In July, the War Department became concerned about the approaching expiration of federal service for National Guard divisions, reserve officers, and draftees called the year before. Unless Congress extended the call-up beyond the original twelve-month term, all National Guard divisions would return to their home states, and entire Regular Army regiments of reserve officers and draftees would melt back into civilian life. Marshall appealed to the White House, and the president prodded Congress. In August the Senate, by the comfortable margin of 45 to 30, and the House, by the narrowest margin possible, 203 to 202, approved extension of federal service to thirty months for draftees, National Guardsmen, and Reserve officers, and to four and a half years for Regular Army volunteers. In Hawaii, Short breathed a little easier at the temporary stabilization of his personnel situation.[40]

On 17 September, the War Department revised its list of dangers facing the Hawaiian Department. After conferring with Miles and Gerow, Marshall ranked from most to least probable the forms of attack Short should consider within Japanese capabilities:

1. Submarine—torpedo and mine;
2. Sabotage;
3. Disguised merchant ship attack by blocking channels, by mines, or by air or surface craft;
4. Air raids, carrier based;
5. Surface ship raids;
6. Major combined attack in the absence of the U.S. Fleet.

Seven months earlier, as Short began his tour in the islands, Marshall had identified fewer dangers facing the Pacific outpost:

1. Sabotage;
2. Surprise raid by air;
3. Surprise raid by submarine.

The two lists show obvious differences and similarities. Twice as long as
the earlier list, the September revision conveys greater appreciation for Japanese
operational sophistication, with its references to disguised ships, mines, and
combined arms attack. But the danger of air raid has lessened in Marshall's
thinking, probably reflecting his view of limited Japanese carrier range expressed to Stimson in the spring. The high priority given sabotage by the chief
of staff in both lists certainly reinforced Short's own awareness of the possibility,
a perception already sharpened by the heavy proportion of Japanese in the
Hawaiian population.[41]

A third distraction from Army modernization arose in September. As
American military production increased through the summer and fall of 1941,
the opinion grew that the United States could best contribute to the defeat of the
Axis by arming and equipping other nations rather than building up a large army
of its own, and thus could reduce the U.S. Army from its current 1.6 million–
man size. The War Department strongly opposed any force reduction while the
Axis powers continued their aggressive behavior, preferring instead a balanced
buildup of military production and training. The movement to reduce the Army
proved unexpectedly attractive to the president, who, despite vigorous argument against the plan by Marshall and two assistant secretaries of war, directed
the writing of plans to deactivate some Army units. The chief of staff dutifully
drew up a schedule for deactivation of the National Guard's eighteen infantry
divisions beginning in February 1942.[42]

The succession of critical messages resumed with the resignation of the
Japanese cabinet in mid-October. On the sixteenth, the Navy Department attempted to predict the outcome of the political crisis in Japan with a message
to Kimmel, who forwarded it to Short. "The resignation of the Japanese Cabinet has created a grave situation," the message began. After noting the two political choices facing Japan, reappointment of the same cabinet or selection of
a new one, the Navy expected increasing anti-American sentiment in Tokyo.
And despite the Japanese move into Indochina in July, the Navy still could fore-

see aggression to the north: "Hostilities between Japan and Russia are a strong possibility." But other targets could not be discounted. "Since the US and Britain are held responsible for her present desperate situation there is also a possibility that Japan may attack these two powers." In conclusion, Stark directed Kimmel to "take due precautions including such preparatory deployment as will not disclose strategic intention nor constitute provocative actions against Japan."[43]

Four days later, Short received the War Department's corresponding message on the Japanese political situation. On 18 October, a new and strongly anti-American and anti-British cabinet had come to power, with Gen. Hideki Tojo of the Imperial Army as prime minister: "Following War Dept estimate of Japanese situation for your information. Tension between United States and Japan remains strained but no repeat no abrupt change in Japanese foreign policy appears imminent." These two October messages contrast markedly in two respects. Four times longer than the Army radiogram, the Navy message contains much more speculation about future Japanese actions and their implications for American forces in the Pacific. While such speculation by itself is of questionable value to a commander, it serves to keep him apprised of current thinking at a distant headquarters.[44]

More disturbing, and confusing to recipients, the two messages convey much different degrees of urgency. The reference to a "grave situation" in the Navy message makes clear to Kimmel how Washington wants him to view developments in Japan. But the War Department message tells Short that he should expect nothing worse than a continuation of the status quo. The contrast showed how differently two groups of intelligence specialists could view the same situation, and reflected a lack of interservice coordination that could leave dangerous gaps in the American defense perimeter.

For the next five weeks, Short received no critical messages, but during this period an important exercise took place and another serious distraction intervened. On 14 November, Short tested his Aircraft Warning Service with a simulated air attack on Oahu. The new radar sets detected planes taking off from a carrier eighty miles at sea. Pursuit planes rose to intercept only six minutes after receipt of the alert and found the attacking bombers thirty miles from Pearl Harbor. Short and his air officers believed the Aircraft Warning Service had performed very well for a new system still lacking key components. To his continuing irritation, six of the twelve radar sets he needed still lay crated on West Coast docks awaiting shipment.[45]

In Washington, and unknown to Short, another reexamination of strategy had taken place. Like the shift from a Pacific to an Atlantic emphasis in the spring, this one would have a significant impact on the condition of the Hawaiian Department. Since early 1939 War Department planners had viewed General MacArthur's command in the Philippines, with its ten thousand American regulars and twelve thousand Filipino Scouts, as an expendable obstacle in the path of Japanese aggression. At best, the island garrison would delay the Japanese while an Army-Navy expeditionary force gathered on the West Coast and in Hawaii. But in the summer and fall of 1941, after Japan joined the Axis and Germany invaded the Soviet Union, the Americans reassessed their Pacific priorities and assigned the Philippines new strategic importance. War and Navy Department planners came to believe that if sufficiently reinforced, the big island group could serve as a meaningful deterrent to Japan. Accordingly, in early November the War Department decided to grant the Philippines higher priority than the Hawaiian Department for reinforcement. Personnel and equipment earmarked for Short's command, and some for the British, went to MacArthur. The list included 6,264 men, 116 aircraft, 40 105-mm howitzers, 48 75-mm guns, 123 30-caliber machine guns, a small number of 1916-model 37-mm guns, and 15,000 land mines. In addition to tolerating these diversions, Short had to train air crews to fly new B-17 bombers to MacArthur. Short salvaged minimal satisfaction from this latest reduction of his combat power when Marshall let him keep his large-caliber antiaircraft artillery and his precious radar sets.[46]

These diversions were easier for planners in Washington to direct than for unit commanders in Hawaii to accept. The former could look at their personnel statistics and see that Short's command was growing steadily through 1941. In the summer, the Hawaiian Department went over the thirty-five-thousand-man mark, and by the end of November it approached forty-three thousand. But the strength reports gave no indication of the efficiency of men reporting to Hawaii, a detail Short and his staff noticed with increasing dismay. As more new men arrived, especially those called by the new Selective Service system, they showed less knowledge of the skills in which they were supposedly trained. A few questions revealed the reason for declining proficiency. Many had not completed courses of military occupational specialty after basic training, and, to the shock of unit commanders, some had not even completed the thirteen-week basic training cycle before being rushed to Hawaii. To remedy the situation, Short had to institute his own training program, which drew experienced men from their usual duties and postponed the day when new arrivals would contribute to department efficiency.[47]

The flow of critical messages resumed in late November. On the twenty-fourth, Stark sent a top secret estimate to Kimmel. Marshall agreed with the Navy analysis, and requested it be shown to Short. During the previous week a special envoy, Saburo Kurusu, had joined the Japanese ambassador in Washington for negotiations with Roosevelt and Secretary of State Cordell Hull. The Japanese wanted the United States to lift the strategic materials embargo and assets freeze imposed when they occupied Indochina. The Americans wanted Japan to get out of Indochina and halt aggression everywhere. Marshall and Stark informed their commanders in Hawaii that the chances of success in these negotiations were "very doubtful." Because of the discouraging prospects, Marshall and Stark believed that "a surprise aggressive movement in any direction, including an attack on the Philippines or Guam is a possibility."[48]

On the morning of 27 November, Short met for three hours with Kimmel in the admiral's office to discuss a joint War and Navy Department plan to reinforce Wake and Midway Islands as forward support bases for American retaliation in case of Japanese attack. In the course of this discussion, Kimmel asked his war plans officer, Capt. Charles E. McMorris, what he thought were the chances of a surprise attack on Hawaii. The captain answered, "None." No one disagreed.[49]

On the afternoon of the twenty-seventh, Short received another message from General Marshall:

> No. 472. Negotiations with the Japanese appear to be terminated to all practical purposes with only the barest possibilities that the Japanese Government might come back and offer to continue. Japanese future action unpredictable but hostile action possible at any moment. If hostilities cannot, repeat cannot, be avoided the United States desires that Japan commit the first overt act. This policy should not, repeat not, be construed as restricting you to a course of action that might jeopardize your defense. Prior to hostile Japanese action, you are directed to undertake such reconnaissance and other measures as you deem necessary but these measures should be carried out so as not, repeat not, to alarm civil population or disclose intent. Report measures taken. Should hostilities occur, you will carry out the tasks assigned in Rainbow Five so far as they pertain to Japan. Limit dissemination of this highly secret information to minimum essential officers.[50]

On the same day, Kimmel received a message:

> This dispatch is to be considered a war warning. Negotiations with Japan looking toward stabilization of conditions in the Pacific have ceased and an

aggressive move by Japan is expected within the next few days. The number and equipment of Japanese troops and the organization of naval task forces indicates an amphibious expedition against either the Philippines, Thai or Kra peninsula, or possibly Borneo. Execute an appropriate defensive deployment preparatory to carrying out the tasks assigned in WPL 46. Inform district and army authorities. A similar warning is being sent by War Department. Spenavo inform British. Continental districts Guam Samoa directed take appropriate measures against sabotage.[51]

These two messages repeat the pattern of previous classified communications. In the manner of intelligence estimates, they report on recent events and speculate on Japanese action that might follow. Of greater significance, they also, like the two October messages, reflect separate Army and Navy analyses and convey differing degrees of urgency. The Army message has a detached, ambiguous tone to it, with terms like "appears to be," "unpredictable," and "possible." The Navy message conveys a sharply contrasting tone. There is nothing detached or ambiguous about either the first sentence, which commands attention as no other wording can, or the clear directive to carry out "an appropriate defensive deployment." Short read the Navy message several hours after it arrived at Kimmel's headquarters.[52]

The 27 November message determined the condition of the Hawaiian Department in the following weeks and initiated a series of misunderstandings and mishandled communications between Washington and Hawaii. With Marshall out of town on an inspection trip, the War Plans Division chief, Leonard Gerow, tried to write as clearly as possible for outpost commanders. But because of a number of War Department policies and one of his own decisions, confusion replaced clarity. The planned buildup on Wake and Midway Islands, in addition to the recent personnel, weapons, and equipment diversions to the Philippines, seemed clear indication that Washington expected the Japanese to strike in the western Pacific, far from Hawaii. The cumulative effect of these developments caused officers in Hawaii to think of other areas when they read messages about possible hostilities, a tendency shared by officials in Washington.[53]

General Gerow contributed to the confusion when he wrote the 27 November message. The main message of that date went out as Radio No. 472, addressed directly to Short. In its original form, No. 472 contained a reminder of the danger of sabotage. After discussions with General Miles, head of War Department intelligence, Gerow removed the reference to sabotage. Because sabotage warnings fell within the mission definition of intelligence rather than Gerow's war plans function, Miles wrote a separate message on the subject, Radio No. 473, addressed to Short's intelligence assistant, Lt. Col. Kendall J. Fielder: "Japanese negotiations have come to practical stalemate. Hostilities may ensue. Subversive activities may be expected. Inform commanding general and Chief of Staff only." Unfortunately for all concerned, Gerow and Miles sent the two messages the same day.[54]

The 27 November message confused readers in another way as well. Each positive suggestion of directive carried with it a negative qualifier. Gerow directed Short to prepare for Japanese hostilities, but noted that "this policy should not, repeat not, be construed as restricting you to a course of action that might jeopardize your defense." WPD also directed the Hawaiian Department to undertake "reconnaissance and other measures" but "not to alarm the civil population or disclose intent." Finally, Gerow directed Short to "limit the dissemination of this highly secret information to minimum essential officers." This pairing of positive directives and negative qualifiers earned the message a nickname that would embarrass the War Department for years: the "Do-Don't" message.

Short studied the message word for word with his chief of staff, Col. Walter C. Phillips. As Short later explained, "The avoidance of war was paramount and the greatest fear of the War Department was that some international incident might occur in Hawaii and be regarded by Japan as an overt act." After some discussion, Short put into effect his Alert No. 1 and activated the Aircraft Warning Service, with the six radar sets manned from 4:00 to 7:00 AM daily. The command policy changes Short had made in Hawaii included institution of a three-alert system to replace his predecessor's single all-out alert. The new Alert No. 1 specified "a defense against sabotage and uprisings within the islands, with no threat from without." Alert No. 2 provided for defense against air, surface, and submarine attack, plus all measures contained in Alert No. 1. Alert No. 3 required "occupation of all field positions by all units, prepared for maximum defense" against all manner of attack, including hostile landing on the shores of Oahu.[55]

In deciding to put his command on Alert No. 1, Short considered several things. He believed the Navy reliable in its assumption of distant reconnaissance, with two or three task forces always at sea. He thus felt confident that if danger approached, the Navy would give warning in time for him to put his command on a higher alert status. From conferences with the Navy he believed

Japanese warships were either in home waters or supporting operations in the Indochina area, and he knew the Japanese did not have a land-based plane that could reach Hawaii. Additionally, the flexibility of his three-alert system allowed him to continue the various activities essential to his growing command, especially the training of aircraft mechanics and radar operators for his own use, and the training of bomber crews for the Philippines reinforcement, as well as the construction of roads, antiaircraft artillery positions and radar sites. The specific order "not to alarm the civil population" as well influenced Short's thinking. With many antiaircraft artillery pieces assigned to positions on private property, moving the guns to these sites would have provoked civilian protest.[56]

Short also considered his predecessor's experience with alerts. When the Hawaiian Department went on full alert in June 1940, it did so on General Marshall's order. Now in late 1941, Short felt that if Marshall, who had access to much more information than he, wanted the command on a full alert status, he would have ordered it himself. Finally, the possibility of sabotage figured prominently in Short's mind, as it did in the minds of War Plans Division members. As Marshall and Gerow had reminded Short in the second message of 27 November, "Subversive activities may be expected." Alert No. 1 best addressed the possibility of sabotage, with its provision for a large number of guards at public utility sites and military installations, especially airfields. Alert No. 1 also called for the concentration of aircraft in tight bunches in the middle of runways, a tactic which put them out of reach of saboteurs on the ground but made them a tempting target for enemy pilots.[57]

After ordering Alert No. 1, Short discussed the new situation with Major Generals Martin and Henry T. Burgin, his air force and coast artillery commanders, respectively. Following this conference, he radioed the War Department: "Reurad four seven two 27th Report Department alerted to prevent sabotage. Liaison with the Navy." Short then sent the 27 November message by secure courier to Kimmel's headquarters.[58]

When Short's reply to message 472 reached the War Plans Division it became the subject of the worst case of mishandled information in this critical year. Short prefaced his reply with a notation making clear which message it related to: "Reurad four seven two 27th," an abbreviation for "Reference your radio number 472 of November 27th." Despite this clear reference indicator, Gerow somehow thought Short's reply related to message 473. As Gerow later explained, "I must confess that in reading that message I tied it in my mind with a message that had been sent by G-2, and as a reply to their message and not a reply to this other message. It was not checked against the number, which should have been done either by myself or someone in my division." As a result of this oversight, after 27 November, no one in Washington acted to put the Hawaiian Department on a higher state of alert. At Fort Shafter, Short took the silence from Washington as approval of his decision for Alert No. 1.[59]

On 28 November, Short met with Kimmel for the second time in two days. They discussed the messages each had received the day before, as well as the possibility of an air attack on Hawaii and the effect on their defenses of the proposed reinforcement of Wake and Midway islands.[60] On the same day, Short received a message from Washington which seemed to confirm his choice of the antisabotage alert: "Critical situation demands that all precautions be taken immediately against subversive activities within field of investigative responsibility of War Department. Also desired that you initiate all additional measures necessary to provide for protection . . . against sabotage, . . . subversive propaganda and . . . espionage . . . , avoiding unnecessary publicity and alarm."[61]

Here was the second message in two days warning of the danger of sabotage. These warnings, combined with the high priority given the possibility of sabotage and subversive activities in messages going back to Short's first day in Hawaii, underlined the deep concern of officials in Washington with the issue. No one in the War Department, least of all Marshall and Gerow, could have been surprised that Short concentrated on defending against sabotage after so frequently warning him about it.

In response to the message of the twenty-eighth, Short radioed that "full precautions are being taken against subversive activities within the field of investigative responsibility of the War Department." He went on to describe at length his security arrangements for critical sites like power plants and bridges, as well as legislative provisions for martial law. On the twenty-ninth, Short received another message about the preparation of forward support bases in the central Pacific. The War Department had just assumed responsibility for the defense of Christmas and Canton Islands and directed Short to form base defense units for deployment to them, still another diversion of the Hawaiian Department's combat power. From the twenty-ninth to 7 December, Short received no more messages concerning Japanese intentions or American preparations for possible hostilities.[62]

Considered together, the critical messages sent to Short both informed and misled him about Japanese intentions and preparations. The messages accurately conveyed the rise in tension between Japan and the United States during 1941. This deterioration of relations greatly worried officials in Washington, who knew the Army and Navy needed more time to prepare for war in the western Pacific. As Marshall and Stark told the president in November, American strength in the Philippines would not reach the point of posing a threat to Japan until February or March 1942. The need for more time caused Marshall and Gerow to repeatedly caution Short not to provoke Japan. When the critical messages went beyond reporting international tension to describing the most likely Japanese move in the immediate future, they became so speculative as to border on the misleading. Despite the great value of the Magic intercept effort, it never found a transmission detailing when and where hostile action would occur because the Japanese never sent such a message. In the absence of so clear a transmission, Gerow's War Plans Division had to speculate about targets. But the wide geographical range of the speculation diluted its value—from the Soviet Maritime Provinces north of Japan to the Dutch East Indies and Thailand, three thousand miles south.[63]

The most troublesome aspect of the messages was the vastly different sense of urgency conveyed by the Army and Navy when they addressed the same issues. The difference first appeared clearly in the October messages and became most pronounced in those of 27 November. When Short read "Negotiations with the Japanese appear to be terminated" and Kimmel read "This dispatch is to be considered a war warning," they had to wonder which service overstated and which understated the situation. The disparity in urgency made extremely difficult the planning of a coordinated response in Hawaii.

FAR ACROSS THE PACIFIC from Short's Fort Shafter office, at a cold and remote bay on the northern extreme of the empire, the Imperial Japanese Navy quietly completed momentous preparations. In mid-November a task force had begun assembling in the gray waters of Hitokappu Bay. The flotilla included thirty combatant ships arrayed around six aircraft carriers, the warships sustained by four service vessels. Early on the morning of the twenty-sixth, the signal to weigh anchor passed from ship to ship and the task force headed for the open sea. As the ships plowed into heavy Pacific swells, strict radio silence went into effect.[64]

Unknown to the Japanese, American problems in combat intelligence would help to preserve the secrecy of the Pearl Harbor strike force. The Japanese changed their ship call signs twice, on 1 November and 1 December, and sent false messages about their aircraft carriers late in the year. These switches and feints caused U.S. Navy signals intercept teams in Hawaii to lose track of

Japan's carriers. American intelligence officers placed the big ships either in port or moving south toward Indochina. Instead, the sword was falling eastward across the Pacific.[65]

During the first week of December, Short and members of his staff had four conferences with either Kimmel, Bloch, or members of their staffs. These discussions centered on plans to reinforce garrisons on Wake, Midway, and Canton Islands. Recent movements of Japanese warships were not discussed.[66]

On 3 December, Kimmel and Bloch received word from Naval Intelligence in Washington that the Japanese Foreign Ministry had ordered key embassies and consulates, including Honolulu, to destroy all but one code system. A sure indication of hostile intent, this information sparked among Navy officers in Hawaii neither a heightened sense of danger nor increased awareness of the value of interservice teamwork in the islands. Both Kimmel and Bloch failed to pass the latest information along to Short, Kimmel assuming the War Department would take care of its man in Hawaii.[67]

On 5 December, a lone Army B-24 arrived from the mainland on the first leg of a secret mission to photograph Japanese activity on the islands of Truk and Jaluit in the Caroline and Marshall groups. Short's airmen refueled and armed the plane before sending it off the same day.[68] On the morning of 6 December, Short's staff got together for the usual Saturday conference, department chief of staff Colonel Phillips presiding. The assistant intelligence officer, Lt. Col. George W. Bicknell, told the staff that Japanese consulate personnel had been spotted burning documents. Bicknell considered the consulate's action ominous given the current tension in the Pacific, but the information provoked no discussion.[69]

Rising international tension and the burning of papers at a consulate made not the slightest change in routines outside the gates of Pearl Harbor and Fort Shafter. As Short's staff meeting broke up, several thousand people gathered in Honolulu to watch a college football game. In shirt-sleeve weather, a crowd dotted with Army and Navy uniforms watched the University of Hawaii defeat Willamette University by a score of 20 to 6.[70]

In a typical week for General and Mrs. Short, social events on and off post took them out of their quarters three or four evenings. Saturday, 6 December, followed the pattern of after-hours obligations, with the Shorts scheduled as guests of honor at a charity dinner-dance at Schofield Barracks. Insistent knocking at the front door interrupted their preparations. Answering, Short found his two intelligence officers, Kendall Fielder and George Bicknell, with a strange message they wanted the general to see immediately. Three days earlier, the FBI had intercepted a lengthy telephone call from a Japanese newspaperman in Tokyo to Mrs. Motokazu Mori, wife of a Honolulu dentist on the bureau's suspect list for many months. The FBI had completed its translation of the conversation earlier in the day and, not understanding it completely but finding in it possible references to the military situation in the islands, decided to share it with the Hawaiian Department. The Mori message contained some clear questions and statements ("Are airplanes flying daily?"), some questions that seemed to be coded ("What kind of flowers are in bloom in Hawaii at present?"), and a vague reference to the Pacific Fleet. Mrs. Mori answered that "lots" of planes fly over the islands and the hibiscus and poinsettia were in bloom, but declined to say anything about the fleet. Short and his intelligence officers pored over the message phrase by phrase. All agreed it looked suspicious but none could say just what it meant. The trio ended the unscheduled conference, and Short and Fielder joined their wives for the drive to Schofield Barracks.[71]

Besides all the after-hours obligations the Hawaiian Department commander and his lady had to fulfill—from an endless succession of receptions, luncheons, and banquets to interviews, charity balls, and beauty contests—the Shorts had to give attention to domestic issues as well. With a college-age son in the family—Cadet Walter Dean Short would graduate from West Point in June 1942—the Shorts still heard youthful demands on parental largesse. For several months Dean had been dropping hints to his father about what a necessity a car had become in the America of 1941, and it was certainly not too early to start thinking about how the new second lieutenant would get to his first duty station after graduation, and no, the fact that a car could dramatically improve a young man's social life had nothing whatever to do with the issue. Father finally relented, and late in the year Dean won the promise of a new car. In the same letter, the general informed his son that his mother would sail from Hawaii on Monday, 8 December to spend a few weeks in Oklahoma City.[72]

At Schofield Barracks, the Shorts enjoyed the Saturday night dinner-dance and an amateur performance entitled Ann Etzler's Cabaret. They then observed still another obligation of their position, leaving social events early so the younger set would not feel inhibited by the presence of high rank. On the way back to Fort Shafter, the general's driver took a road overlooking Pearl Harbor. Viewing the Pacific Fleet with deck lights ablaze, Short commented idly, "What a target that would make!"[73] That night the general slept soundly, confident of the Navy's distant reconnaissance.

AT 7:45 THE NEXT MORNING, the Shorts sat down to breakfast in their palm-shaded home. An early riser, even on a Sunday, the general had been up and about more than an hour. As he worked his way through toast, coffee, and the newspaper, he thought about nothing heavier than the round of golf he and Admiral Kimmel would share later in the morning. At 7:57, Short began hearing the roar of aircraft engines followed by explosions. They seemed louder that the usual practice bomb runs. He had no air training scheduled for this Sunday, so the Navy must have something going, he thought. But when the explosions continued, he walked out on his back porch to have a look.[74]

Next door, Colonel Phillips also heard the explosions but continued shaving. Not until his frantic wife made him take the phone she had just answered did he turn from the mirror. On the line was Lt. Col. James Mollison, chief of staff of the Hawaiian Air Force, yelling that bombs were falling at Hickam Field, only a mile from Pearl Harbor. Phillips asked his friend if he were drunk but, hearing the bombs through the receiver, accepted the incredible news and went into action. He bounded out of his house and across the lawn and hollered the news through General Short's screen door. Struck by the half-shaved, half-dressed appearance of his chief of staff, Short accepted everything he heard and told Phillips to put the department on Alert No. 3, the highest state of battle readiness. Short then ran as fast as a sixty-one year-old man could to his office, where he ordered his staff to move to the underground command post in Aliamanu Crater.[75]

For the rest of the morning, Short took messages in his office describing the air raid on Pearl Harbor, four miles away. Each new piece of information deepened the disaster. His antisabotage alert had given the Japanese a target at each airfield they could hardly believe. The American planes stood wingtip to wingtip on the runways, and the attackers took full advantage. In less than two hours they destroyed or damaged more than half of the Hawaiian Air Force and extensively damaged eight airfields. Worst of all, 683 of Short's troops had become casualties, 232 of them killed.[76]

Short also had to read bitterly terse updates from the Navy on ships sunk or damaged, ships the Hawaiian Department was charged to protect. The Pacific Fleet lost the heart of its battle line. All eight battleships were disabled by bombs or torpedoes, and most burned for hours, delaying rescue attempts.

Early in the afternoon, Short moved to his Aliamanu Crater command post. Under solid rock, he continued monitoring the depressing situation above. At 2:58, the adjutant general's office at Fort Shafter logged in a message from

General Marshall in Washington. In the confusion at department headquarters, more than an hour passed before someone carried the message down the hall to the chief of staff's office. Finally, sometime after four, Colonel Phillips read the message and took action to get its content to General Short. He picked up the phone connected to the crater and, when the general came on the line, read him the radiogram: "L529 7th [December] Japanese are presenting at 1:00 PM Eastern Standard Time today what amounts to an ultimatum also they are under orders to destroy their code machine immediately. Just what significance the hour set may have we do not know but be on alert accordingly. Inform naval authorities of this communication. Marshall."[77]

Listening in the dank crater, Short grew angrier by the second. With much of his staff standing by in stunned silence, the general swore like a sergeant for the first time in decades. After the general slammed the phone down, Phillips studied the dispatch notations on the piece of paper. The War Department message center had sent this extremely important warning by the slower commercial method of Western Union to San Francisco and RCA from the West Coast to Honolulu. If it had gone out by the faster method of scrambler telephone from the chief of staff's office, it would have arrived about an hour before the attack, giving Short enough time to put his command on a higher alert status. Instead, it had taken ten hours and thirty-eight minutes to go from Marshall's desk to Short's and arrived more than seven hours after the Japanese attack began.[78]

For the rest of the day, Short waited in his crater for the seaborne invasion he knew his troops could defeat. False reports of enemy troop ships approaching the shores of Oahu kept tension high at the radios. Forty-three thousand troops at battle stations on hills and beaches stroked rifle triggers and stared at the horizon. But the Japanese never came.

Walter Short's parents, Hiram and Sarah Short.
Courtesy Mrs. Sam Lewis

Captain and Isabel Short with their son Dean, Camp Grant, Illinois, about 1921.
Courtesy Mrs. Sam Lewis

Colonel Short at the end of World War I, just before reverting to the rank of captain, about 1919.
NARA

Colonel Short reviews the 6th Infantry at Jefferson Barracks, Missouri, about 1935.
NARA

Gen. George C. Marshall, Army chief of staff (*right*), reviews IV Corps maneuvers with General Short on an overflight of Fort Benning, Georgia, April 1940.
NARA

Isabel Short pins on her husband's third star at Fort Shafter, Hawaii, February 1941.
NARA

Lieutenant General Short (*center*) assumes command of the Hawaiian Department from Lt. Gen. Charles D. Herron (*left*) in ceremonies at Fort Shafter, Hawaii, 7 February 1941.
Walter Short Collection, Hoover Institution Archives

General Short (*right*) greets his predecessor, Lt. Gen. Charles D. Herron, at the dock in Honolulu, February 1941.
Walter Short Collection, Hoover Institution Archives

Lord Louis Mountbatten (*center*) calls on General Short (*left*) and Adm. Husband E. Kimmel, U.S. Pacific Fleet commander.
Walter Short Collection, Hoover Institution Archives

General and Mrs. Short relax in their quarters at Fort Shafter.
Walter Short Collection, Hoover Institution Archives

Dean Short (*right*) and his bride Emily visit his parents in Dallas, Texas, during the younger couple's honeymoon, September 1944.
Walter Short Collection, Hoover Institution Archives

Former lieutenant general Walter C. Short prepares to testify before the joint congressional hearing into the Pearl Harbor attack, January 1946.
NARA

6

The Glare of Investigation

B Y NOON, THE JAPANESE PLANES HAD TOUCHED DOWN ON THEIR AIRCRAFT carriers and the task force was steaming back toward friendly waters. Even if Short had been able to see the enemy ships escaping westward, he would have been unwise to believe it. He had to assume the worst, that the enemy would come back with more air attacks and then an invasion force. The general was as determined as his troops that the Japanese would not catch the Hawaiian Department by surprise twice. If they came back, they would face millions of rounds of fire from every Army weapon on the islands, and if they somehow got through that, forty-three thousand bayonets. For the rest of that bright and terrible Sunday, the troops continued frantic preparations for a decisive battle, distributing ammunition to every gun pit and foxhole on Oahu, digging new fighting positions in pineapple fields, gardens, and lawns without worrying about who owned the property.

The first thing Short learned during the battle was that he could not see much from inside a cave. Radio and hand-carried messages were no substitute for experienced eyes. When it appeared the attackers would not return, at least for several hours, he moved his headquarters out of the dank crater. Back at Fort Shafter, Short found still another problem. His men were shooting at almost everything that moved on or over the islands. Every soldier in the department was keyed up, suspicious of everything, and itching for a fight. Many civilians called in "sightings" of Japanese submarines, aircraft carriers, and dive bombers—even an entire invasion force. Too many soldiers and gun crews added their own sightings to the hysteria, and soon they were firing at clouds, shadows, rumors, and friendly planes trying to land on Oahu. In addition to his many other pressing concerns—caring for the wounded, deploying troops and distributing ammunition, evacuating military wives and children, and keeping the roads open for emergency vehicles—Short had to divert men from important duties to stop the waste of ammunition. Night brought even more shadows to mistake for enemy ships and invading troops. The indiscriminate shooting continued until the morning of the ninth, and rumors of renewed Japanese attack flew around the islands for weeks.[1]

With commanders at all levels working to calm trigger-happy troops, Short turned to other problems. He conferred with Governor Poindexter and put martial law into effect the afternoon of the seventh. He directed his staff to assist the FBI in rounding up confirmed and suspected enemy agents. By the next day, 482 Japanese, Germans, and Italians were in custody and on their way to incarceration on Sand Island. All available Hawaiian Air Force men and department engineers were put to work clearing the devastated Hickam, Wheeler, and Bellows air fields and getting repair shops and runways back into operation to salvage damaged aircraft and prepare for the arrival of replacement planes and equipment from the mainland. One piece of good news arrived while Short's command picked itself up from defeat. All funds requested for defensive improvements in Hawaii were released. It took a stunning defeat to gain Washington's approval for all the projects Short had long believed necessary for successful defense of the Pacific Fleet and the islands.[2]

By the ninth, everyone in the department headquarters agreed the Japanese would not attempt an invasion and occupation of the Hawaiian Islands. On that day, Short received a message from the War Department that hinted at the start of a new battle for him: "Please advise immediately exact time of receipt of our number five two nine repeat five two nine December seven at Honolulu exact time described message transmitted by Signal Corps staff and by what staff officer received."[3]

Beneath the literal intent of the message, to establish the effectiveness of communications, lay the sinister possibility that Marshall and Gerow, or their loyalists, were making preparations to shift blame for the disaster away from

Washington if it became necessary. Short quickly responded with the truth, and it stopped for the moment any self-serving thoughts in the War Department: "Delivered Honolulu via RCA seven thirty three morning seventh stop. Received signal office Fort Shafter eleven forty five morning seventh. This time approximate but within five minutes. Deciphered message received by Adjutant General Hawaiian Department two fifty eight afternoon."[4]

For the next week, Short and his troops continued preparations for war. When it became apparent that the Japanese had left the central Pacific entirely and were thus in no position to either invade Hawaii or attack the American mainland, the Hawaiian Department staff added political concerns to its military duties. Short needed no one to tell him that Washington was intensely interested in his version of the attack. While his field units worked on airfields, roads, and defensive positions, he put several subordinates to work on a report for the War Department. The completed document, titled "Report of the Battle of Oahu," was sent to General Marshall on 12 December and briefly summarized the attack and detailed the Army response to it.[5]

Short admitted the complete surprise achieved by the Japanese—"I could scarcely believe it," he declared—and recognized the deadly skill demonstrated by his adversary: "The attack had been thoroughly planned and was almost faultlessly executed." He also addressed a stunning coincidence which worked to the advantage of the Japanese. Attacking aircraft approached Oahu from the north at about the same time a flight of B-17 bombers originating in California was expected from the same direction. The assumption by radar observers that the approaching planes were American prevented dissemination of a warning while the Japanese were still more than one hundred miles from Pearl Harbor. Short went on to note high morale among his troops and described their state of training as the best in many years. He also implored Washington once more to send the troops and equipment he had been requesting for months.[6]

The War Department moved just as fast as Short in the first days after the attack. Marshall chose Short's successor, Maj. Gen. Herbert A. Dargue, and directed a War Plans Division officer, Col. Charles W. Bundy, to accompany Dargue to Hawaii for a personal assessment of the situation. In a tragedy that almost seemed an extension of Japan's success just days before, the plane carrying the two officers crashed in California, killing all aboard.[7]

Investigation of the Navy's performance on 7 December resulted from interest at the highest level. As a former assistant secretary of the Navy, President Roosevelt was personally stung by the extensive defeat inflicted on his beloved sea service. He ordered Secretary of the Navy Frank Knox to Hawaii to see the damage and interview key officers. Knox arrived on 11 December and went directly to Kimmel's headquarters. Short appeared later and spoke with the secretary for about two hours, describing the situation in the islands before the attack and conveying his suspicion of the local Japanese community. The next morning Knox went to Fort Shafter, where Short arranged a complete briefing for him. Using large situation maps and charts, he gave an overview of his command's capabilities and plans, then called on every staff and large-unit commander to detail his area of responsibility. Knox listened intently, asked questions, mostly about air defenses, and ended his investigation with a tour of Short's command post.[8]

In his hotel room and on the long flight back to Washington, Knox mulled over the information provided by Short and Kimmel. The secretary was greatly bothered by his finding that despite contingency plans that looked impressive on paper, both the Army and Navy had been caught unprepared. There could be no excuses, no equivocation about so obvious a defeat. And so when Knox took his report to the White House on the morning of 14 December, the president read: "The Japanese air attack on the island of Oahu on December 7th was a complete surprise to both the Army and Navy. Its initial success, which included almost all the damage done, was due to a lack of a state of readiness against such an air attack, by both branches of the service. This statement was made by me to both General Short and Admiral Kimmel, and both agreed that it was entirely true."[9]

Knox recognized that one of Short's problems was a lack of antiaircraft artillery, and he excused the general from any responsibility for it. "There is a dangerous shortage of guns of this [antiaircraft] type on the island," he wrote. "This is through no fault of the Army Commander who had pressed consistently for these guns." But from the lack of awareness that an attack on Hawaii was possible, Knox excused no one: "There was evident in both Army and Navy only a very slight feeling of apprehension of any attack at all, and neither Army nor Navy were in a position of readiness because of this feeling."[10]

While the Navy secretary completed his investigation, the president kept a short list of options to himself. Since the outpost of Hawaii was a joint Army-Navy command, the touchy issue of interservice rivalry lay just beneath the surface of events affecting the island base, threatening to compromise future American military action. From Roosevelt's point of view the worst eventuality would be to launch a war effort with the two services blaming each other for the disaster. That possibility could become reality if Knox found that one service had clearly contributed more to the Japanese success than the other. Fortunately for the nation, Knox found fault with both the Army and Navy, so Roosevelt proceeded with the least awkward of his options: heads from both services would roll. On 16 December, the War and Navy Departments made a joint announcement regarding personnel changes in Hawaii. The Army relieved Short and Frederick L. Martin, Short's air force commander. The Navy relieved Kimmel. The next day, without ceremony, Short turned over his command to an Army Air Corps officer, Lt. Gen. Delos C. Emmons.[11]

To an officer with a spotless record, relief under any circumstances comes as a shock. The term "relief" itself carries all the implications—incompetence, malfeasance, failure—a proud and highly motivated individual in any field views as anathema. Worst of all, the administrative act of relief leaves one vulnerable to the legal act of court-martial and its most dreaded finding, dereliction of duty. Short was aware of the possibility of his relief, he had said as much to at least one staff officer and his aide on the afternoon of the attack, but when he read the terse radio message from Washington it set off an earthquake beneath his professional demeanor. Nearly four decades of superior service was virtually nullified in a little more than two hours. Now he had to adjust to the unthinkable, and he had to do it alone. Mrs. Short had returned to the West Coast on the first available ship with several hundred Army and Navy wives and children.[12]

SHORT HAD LITTLE TIME to ponder his relief, for President Roosevelt immediately set in motion the second phase of his Pearl Harbor investigation. The Knox report had filled the need for a quick after-action view of the disaster. Its author knew that both the Congress and the public would demand a more extensive examination of the event to answer the many questions and rumors swirling around the country. The day after Knox returned from Hawaii he and Stimson discussed the membership of an investigative body the president had called for. In an effort to project impartiality throughout its work, the group would include an equal number of Army and Navy members and be presided over by a civilian of unquestioned reputation. Chosen to head the inquiry was Associate Supreme Court Justice Owen J. Roberts.

Selection of uniformed members proved more difficult. The needs for prestige and objectivity were obvious. The Army named Frank B. McCoy, a retired major general much respected in and out of the service. The Navy put forth William H. Standley, who had served as chief of naval operations in the mid-1930s. The character of the attack on Pearl Harbor called for additional qualifications. Because Oahu had been hit from the air, the Roberts inquiry needed some high-ranking expertise in air operations. But since the airplane was still a relatively new weapon in 1941, there were few generals and admirals who had spent more than a few years in the specialty and who were available as the nation suddenly found itself involved in a major war. The Navy offered Joseph M. Reeves, a retired rear admiral who at the age of fifty-three had changed specialties and gone to flight school. The Army came up with a surprising choice for its air representative, Joseph T. McNarney. Marshall considered McNarney the best candidate for the inquiry despite the facts that he had no major command experience, had been a brigadier general only eight months, and was unknown outside the Army. He was the only member of the Roberts panel still on active duty. In age the membership spanned more than two decades, from Standley's sixty-nine years to McNarney's forty-eight.[13]

The Roberts commission began its work in Washington on 18 December by taking testimony from Marshall, Gerow, Stark, and several other officers in both Army and Navy war plans and intelligence offices. Despite the presence of a Supreme Court justice at its head, the commission allowed its proceedings to be guided by some strange ground rules. For two days the panel accepted unsworn testimony, and recorded it in nonverbatim form. These practices amounted to an invitation to disavow testimony if events or evidence uncovered later proved embarrassing to Washington. Witnesses, too, had to deal with some troubling limitations. Short could not have counsel, could not be present while others testified, could not cross-examine witnesses, and could not read the transcript of commission sessions.[14]

The orientation of early sessions raised the issue of objectivity. Roberts himself was interested almost exclusively in whether or not Washington had given commanders in Hawaii adequate warning. This was certainly a valid concern of anyone looking into the Pearl Harbor disaster, but when pursued at the expense of another potentially profitable body of evidence—Roberts knew of Magic but did not consider its use critical to his work—it raised the suspicion that the commission had been convened to shift blame from Washington to Hawaii. Not surprisingly, all witnesses in Washington testified that they had given adequate warning to Hawaii.[15]

Struck low by his relief, Short stayed in Hawaii and turned to preparations for the Roberts commission. After five days of reading documents and writing notes, he had a refreshed memory and an opening statement. He was determined to give his interrogators as complete a picture as possible of his tenure in Hawaii, but he harbored a deep suspicion about their objectivity. With the commission en route to Hawaii, he predicted its judgment to his aide: "They're going to find me guilty!"[16]

Justice Roberts opened the Hawaiian sessions of his investigation at Fort Shafter on Monday morning, 22 December. The entire day was spent in a detailed review of Army and Navy defensive plans for the islands and the workings of the Aircraft Warning Service. The next morning Short waited in the headquarters building to testify as the first major witness from the scene of the attack. In the hall, the general spotted his former counterintelligence officer, George Bicknell, also scheduled to testify. It was Bicknell who had reported to the department staff meeting the morning of 6 December the burning of documents at the Japanese consulate and who had brought to the general's quarters later the same day the mysterious Mori message. Short took the opportunity to recognize the younger officer for his suspicions about Japanese intentions, suspicions horribly justified the next morning. "Well, Bicknell," he said, "I want you to know that whatever happens, you were right and I was wrong."[17]

Justice Roberts opened the questioning of Short by asking if any influence had been used by anyone to get the Hawaiian assignment for him, how many alerts had been ordered in Hawaii in response to warnings from Washington, and whether the Navy had shared important information with him. The general replied that no influence had been used on his behalf, he had ordered alerts twice following communications from Washington, and the Navy had shared everything important. Roberts then invited Short to proceed with his statement.[18]

Short's statement, consisting of fifty typed pages and a thick folder of documents, revealed his strategy. He believed he should be judged on all of his activities throughout the ten months of his command tenure in Hawaii, not only on decisions he made in the days immediately preceding the attack. In presenting his views, the general read the complete text of critical messages he had received from Washington and explained the interpretation and response he made to each. He detailed the problems he had encountered while improving Army defenses in the islands. He gave a nearly minute-by-minute account of his command's activities the day of the attack. He explained his success in awakening the local civilian leadership to its vulnerability and ended by reading a highly favorable letter of support from civic leaders.[19]

The heart of Short's argument was that he had made the right decisions about alerts and every other aspect of Hawaiian defense, considering the information and level of support he had received from Washington. If higher authorities had wanted a more complete defense of the islands, they should have sent him more troops, money, equipment, and information. Short hammered Marshall's staff for failing to get the crucial one o'clock message to him before the attack began. His voice slowing in emphasis, he told the commission, "They had *every great duty* to get that information to me as rapidly as possible."[20]

Short got rough handling from the two admirals and one of the generals on the commission. Neither Reeves nor McNarney liked his choice of Alert No. 1 in response to the 27 November message. The admiral was bothered by the fact that Short's alert did not put reconnaissance planes in the air nor did it provide for the manning of antiaircraft batteries. Short answered that if planes had been in the air as part of a dawn security patrol they would have been back on the ground by 7:00 AM, an hour before the attack began. As for the antiaircraft batteries, they would have been manned with ammunition at the ready if the War Department's warning of 7 December had not arrived seven hours after the attack began.[21]

McNarney turned out to be the hatchet man of the Roberts commission. The young general walked Short through two messages from Washington and the Hawaiian Department standing operating procedure, then asked if Alert No. 1 satisfied requirements directed in those documents. The heavy innuendo in his questions made obvious his view that Short's decision making left much to be desired. McNarney began in a direct but professional tone and Short responded in like manner despite the interrogator's insistence on making the witness repeat explanations from his opening statement. But as McNarney became more pointed, Short had to resort to different techniques, either interrupting and forcing a repeat of the question or making McNarney listen to a longer development of context before giving an answer. The sparring took time, but it allowed Short to make clear that he was not going to be bullied into supporting anyone's preconceptions about what had happened in the months and weeks before the attack.[22]

Unable to badger Short into a damaging statement, McNarney tried to get other witnesses to say the general had been negligent or even disobedient. A month after Short testified, McNarney asked Leonard Gerow if Short was guilty of disobedience of orders for not initiating aerial reconnaissance upon receipt of the 27 November message. Gerow responded that Short already had reconnaissance in effect. McNarney kept after Gerow but could get no more than agreement to the hypothetical situation that if no reconnaissance were in effect in Hawaii, it would have been a failure to obey orders.[23]

From the beginning of the attack on Pearl Harbor a deep anger had smoldered throughout the Navy over the failure of the Army to protect the Pacific Fleet. Surprisingly, the rage came close to flaring into the open only once during Short's testimony. In the last hour of the general's daylong appearance, Admiral Standley asked about the purpose of a naval base. Short replied that it is "to provide facilities to which the Navy can go for servicing the ships and for repairing them and for supplying them." Standley then asked who was responsible for protecting ships in port, knowing that the language of the Hawaiian Department commander's mission made it an Army job. Short replied, "It would be everybody's responsibility." Stunned, Standley could only say, "The what? Whose?" Short calmly explained that he expected ships in port to augment Army defenses by putting their antiaircraft batteries on alert and placing Marine Corps batteries ashore under Army control. Standley tried again to maneuver Short into admitting failure: "Is it your concept . . . of this base that the Navy is to go out and stay out? Or . . . is the base to be used as a place of rest, a haven where the Navy can go in and be protected? What is your belief?" Short answered with a fact of modern military life: "I don't believe, under modern conditions of aviation, that there is any restricted area where it will ever be safe for the Navy to go in and huddle."[24]

Standley brushed off Short's answer and kept pounding the Army on its mission in Hawaii. "Well, but that is afterthought. Now, what has been the concept of this base from the beginning of time?" Now Short changed tactics. If the admirals were going to use the commission sessions to attack the Army, he would reply in kind until they got back to the facts of the situation. He decided to bring up an issue as sensitive to the Navy as the subject of fleet protection was to the Army: President Roosevelt's decision over Navy protest to base the Pacific Fleet at Pearl Harbor instead of San Diego. "I think the Navy has been perfectly conscious in the last two or three years," he declared, "that this was too restricted an area for the fleet. . . . I am implying that it would be practically impossible to protect the ships in such a restricted area against a serious attack. . . . They would be bound to suffer losses."[25]

Frustrated that he could not hang Short on the issue of service mission, Standley followed the witness into the question of base suitability. He asked if Short had ever discussed with Kimmel how many ships the Navy would bring into Pearl Harbor at any one time. The general said he had not. With no other line of questioning to pursue for the moment, Standley abruptly informed Justice Roberts he had no further questions. Short had avoided Standley's trap, but the two admirals on the commission and the thousands of others in the fleet were far from mollified. After testifying for five and a half hours, Short was excused with a warning and an order. He was not to discuss anything he had said or heard during the session, and he was to stay in Hawaii in case the commission wanted to question him further. The general sat on his hopes and his hands for fifteen days, and spent the most subdued Christmas and New Year's since he was in France in 1917–18.[26]

On 8 January, Short was called back. Roberts showed him a Japanese message, not deciphered until after the attack, requesting information on the movements of Pacific Fleet ships, and asked him what effect the message would have had if he had seen it before the attack. Short replied, "I think that I would have been very suspicious that a raid might take place." Pursuing the hypothetical, Roberts asked the same about the one o'clock message of 7 December. Short answered, "I would have gone immediately to either—to at least an alert against an air attack, and I probably would have gone against a complete attack, because it looked so significant." Roberts followed up: "What was in that message that would have stirred you up?" The general, drawing on his military intelligence experience to interpret enemy intent, said, "The thing that would have affected me . . . was the fact that they had ordered their code machines destroyed, because to us that means just one thing: that they are going into an entirely new phase and that they want to be perfectly sure that the code will not be broken for a minimum of time, say of three or four days. That would have been extremely significant to me, the code machine, much more significant than just the ultimatum."[27]

The major confrontation of Short's second appearance occurred when Standley resumed his attack on the Army, first about the workings of the interceptor command, still incomplete on 7 December, and then about the Navy's long-range patrolling. All he got out of Short were repetitions of his opening statement that not all radar equipment had arrived by the day of the attack and the Navy had not given him details of its distant reconnaissance procedures. After fifty-five minutes, Short was released by the commission and scheduled his return to the mainland.[28]

During his testimony, Short came across as conscientious, attentive to a vast range of detail, in command of the technical aspects of his position, and consistently faithful to his oath of office and his own high standards of integrity. On the few occasions he did not have an answer, he admitted it. When he

THE GLARE OF INVESTIGATION

thought he had made a mistake, such as in not going to a full alert upon receipt of the 27 November message, he said so. He made a sincere effort to help the commission understand the problems he had faced during his ten-month command, so sincere that he inadvertently compromised part of his own testimony. In his first hour before the commission, he said of the Navy's role in helping him protect Pearl Harbor, "The question of just how the total reconnaissance was carried out was never known by me." After thereby calling into question Army-Navy cooperation in Hawaii, he went on to praise repeatedly his relations with the Navy.[29]

Despite a few bright spots in his testimony, as when he refused to be bullied by McNarney and escaped Standley's trap, Short's performance before the Roberts commission was not particularly impressive. He was noticeably nervous, understandable in one who suspected he was being set up as a scapegoat. But his efforts to reword and repeat his own explanations invited the suspicion that he was not as knowledgeable as he should have been about certain aspects of his duties in Hawaii. At one point in his testimony, Short revealed a way of thinking which commission members found unconvincing. He took the Army's dispatch of unarmed B-24s to Hawaii, the machine guns removed to gain cargo-carrying capacity, as indication that the War Department considered a Japanese attack extremely unlikely: "They considered that the hazard of carrying the extra weight between the mainland and Honolulu was greater than the possibility of a Japanese attack." Here he was stretching an implication further than anyone in Washington had intended. Short also confused commission members on occasion, especially when explaining the intricacies of the Aircraft Warning Service. He used terms like "interceptor command" and "information center" without making clear their different functions, and he did not differentiate clearly between how the system was designed to function and how it actually worked the morning of the attack. Finally, Short's presentation of a letter of support signed by prominent Hawaiian civilians appeared irrelevant and self-serving.[30]

Justice Roberts made a sincere effort to conduct an exhaustive and fair investigation. He and his commissioners called 127 witnesses, collected 1,862 typed pages of testimony, and compiled a small mountain of documentation. Some of the evidence gave Short badly needed support, as, for example, when Leonard Gerow admitted that he and his War Plans Division in Washington had mismatched the general's replies to the 27 and 28 November messages and then failed to follow up on the first. The general's revelation that no one had told him about code-burning at the Japanese consulate just before the attack also helped. Inevitably, however, not everything uncovered strengthened Short's tenuous position. McNarney maneuvered him into admitting that interservice rivalry had interfered with the defenses of Hawaii. Asked if he thought he should have had more detailed information on the areas covered by Navy reconnaissance ships and planes, Short answered, "I did not feel that it was my business to try to tell Admiral Kimmel how he would conduct his reconnaissance. I think he would have resented it very much."[31]

As the Roberts investigation continued, a number of problems developed. One was time. The president, Congress, and the nation were anxious to read the commission's answer to the question of who was to blame for the disaster. The commission's study was never intended to be exhaustive, and members had to restrict the witness list to personnel in or closest to centers of authority. Another problem turned out to be the chairman himself. The record makes clear that Justice Roberts followed closely the testimony of each witness, but his lack of military experience made it difficult for him to understand much of what was said. "I am very much in difficulty because of my lack of knowledge of military procedure," he admitted. Repeatedly, sessions had to be interrupted while a witness or member put statements in layman's terms, as, for example, when Short had to explain that "pursuit ship" referred to a type of aircraft, not a warship. Roberts also had to devote valuable time to a rumor rampant in the United States since the attack. The justice asked witnesses if they had observed or been part of an amount of drinking the night of 6 December sufficient to impair judgment or fighting ability the next morning. Answers were uniformly negative.[32]

The Roberts commission questioned its last witness in Hawaii on 9 January, then returned to the mainland to hold closing sessions and write its report. Short and his aide, Capt. Louis W. Truman, reserved seats on a 12 January Pan American Clipper flight, and that day a small group of his former staff members escorted him to the airport. On the West Coast he found a small army of reporters. To their insistent questions he declined comment. His country was at war now, and any personal crusade for vindication would have to wait, no matter how good a story it would make. Short spent his first night on the mainland at the Presidio of San Francisco. While there, he received a telegram authorizing him to proceed to Oklahoma City and await further orders. There he rejoined his wife at her parents' home and settled into an uneasy wait for information about his future.[33]

On Sunday, 25 January, word came. The Roberts commission report appeared in newspapers across the nation. When Short found it, his eyes jumped

THE GLARE OF INVESTIGATION

down the column-inches of small type, rifling through words and paragraphs for anything resembling a verdict, something that would either allow him to continue the career he loved or sink him forever. He reached Conclusion 10, and read, "The order for Alert No. 1 of the Army command in Hawaii was not adequate to meet the emergency envisaged in the warning messages."[34]

Conclusion 17 was much worse: "In the light of the warnings and directions to take appropriate action, transmitted to both commanders between November 27 and December 7, and the obligation under the system of coordination then in effect for joint cooperative action on their part, it was a dereliction of duty on the part of each of them not to consult and confer with the other respecting the meaning and intent of the warnings, and the appropriate measures of defense required by the imminence of hostilities."[35] Dereliction of duty. The most detested phrase to a career soldier was directed at him. Instead of being praised as the outgunned and undermanned commander who had absorbed the first attack of the Japanese and then struck back, Short was vilified as the incompetent who had helped make the attack successful. Four years later, he described his jumbled emotions for the public record: "When I read the findings of the Roberts Commission . . . I was completely dumbfounded. To be accused of dereliction of duty after almost forty years of loyal and competent service was beyond my comprehension."[36]

Making Short's pain worse was the fact that he had to read the judgment against him in the public press, at the same time it was being read up and down Main Street from coast to coast. And no sooner had the country read it than the reporters were on the phone asking for a statement. To all he gave the same answer: "Not a word."[37]

As soon as the reporters were off the line, he called General Marshall in Washington. Thinking first of the country and the war effort, he asked if he should retire. Marshall told him that since he had not had time to examine the Roberts commission report, Short should "stand pat but if it becomes necessary I will use this conversation as authority." Short said he put his fate entirely in Marshall's hands, having complete faith in the judgment and loyalty of his friend of nearly four decades. After he hung up, Short decided Marshall should have more than a phone conversation to base action on, so he wrote the authorization prescribed by the adjutant general: "I hereby submit my request for retirement after more than thirty-nine years service, effective upon a date to be determined by the War Department."[38]

With his request, Short enclosed a personal letter in which he thanked Marshall for his advice and expressed his preference to "remain on the active list and take whatever assignment you think it necessary to give me." He also took the opportunity to underline his view that the arrival in Hawaii of twelve unarmed B-17s during the attack indicated War Department approval of his antisabotage alert. Finally, he reminded Marshall that he had not been shown three Navy messages sent to Kimmel only days before the attack relating to the destruction of Japanese codes. Short sent his request for retirement and the letter, which he considered "a purely personal matter between two old friends," in the confidence that Marshall would see that Short's interests were respected in any eventuality. But with the coming of war to American territory, old friendships were not high on the chief of staff's list of priorities.[39]

When he ended his phone conversation with Short on Sunday, Marshall had probably not yet decided whether to accept his old friend's request for retirement or give him another assignment. But by the next day he had made a decision. In a memo to the secretary of war he wrote, "I am now of the opinion that we should accept General Short's application for retirement today and to do this quietly without any publicity at the moment." Henry Stimson needed no suggestion from anyone on what to do about Short. His view had been fixed within days of the attack. As the secretary later told a congressional committee, Short's preparation of the Hawaiian Department to repel sabotage "betrayed a misconception of his real duty which was almost beyond belief."[40]

For the next three weeks advice and memos flew back and forth among Roosevelt, Stimson, Knox, Marshall, the attorney general, and the Army judge advocate general. The question was not whether to retire Short; Roosevelt and Stimson were already determined to have him out. The question was how to get him out so he could not make any of three responses: interpret the government's acceptance of his retirement as condonation of his conduct of duty in Hawaii, which would obviously preclude a court-martial; demand a court-martial during wartime and thereby force revelation of much secret information, especially that derived from Magic; or later charge he had been persecuted by the government, then ride a wave of public sympathy to win vindication.[41]

Short left the government to its self-serving manipulations and wrote his son a letter that reveals much confidence about his ultimate reputation:

Feb. 8th [1942]
Dear Dean:
    From the papers and a talk with General Marshall it looks like I shall be retired and that the case will be closed in the next few days. I had hoped to remain on active duty but apparently that is the best the War Department can

do under the present political situation. The public does not have all of the facts and probably will not have until the war is over. I shall give you the complete picture when I see you. You may have guessed that I have a lot on my side if you have been reading the columnist. Mother and I are thinking of going to San Antonio for a month when the case is definitely closed, also to St. Louis for a few days.

Don't let all of this publicity about me worry you. Sometime in the future when the full facts can be made public I shall be exonerated.

Lots of love,

Dad.[42]

By mid-February, the legalistic wordsmithing had been completed, and on the seventeenth Short read his government's decision: "By direction of the President, Major General Walter C. Short (O-1621), United States Army, upon his own application, is retired from active service to take effect February 28, 1942, under the provisions of Section 1243, Revised Statutes, after more than 39 years' service and without condonation of any offense or prejudice to future disciplinary action."[43]

So the War Department was going to let him twist in the wind, neither guilty nor innocent but branded with the hated decision of the Roberts commission, "dereliction of duty." In return for trusting Marshall, the Army, and his government, Short got a sordid display of bureaucratic venality. But at least he was spared the embarrassment of reading about his forced retirement in the public press. This time the Army was considerate enough to send the letter by courier before telling the press corps.

With his career ended by others, Short could do nothing but sign the forms and wait for the paper mill to process him back to civilian life. He went to Fort Sam Houston, near San Antonio, Texas, for his retirement physical examination. This routine activity turned into an administrative wrangle with the War Department that affected the Shorts' standard of living. On 27 February, one day before the general's retirement would go into effect, examining physicians discovered a heart and lung condition which had to have developed over a period of years. Had the condition been known earlier, it would have justified his retirement by reason of physical disability. The examination results were of great interest to Short because different official reasons for retirement implied different benefits. If he could retire on physical disability he could have his pension tax free. But if the reason for retirement remained "upon his own application," his pension would be taxable income. Already faced with a 25 percent pay cut, from eight thousand dollars per year while on active duty to six thousand dollars per year, as well as loss of housing, subsistence, and personal expenses benefits, Short understandably acted to cut his losses. He requested retirement by reason of physical disability. The War Department, however, was not persuaded by the medical evidence, and turned down his request.[44]

For Walter Short, the Roberts commission triggered professional demise and personal tragedy. Three defeats—the "dereliction of duty" finding, forced retirement, and the denial of disability status—had fallen fast upon one another. For the president who ordered it into existence, however, the commission meant something completely different. In the days after the Japanese attack, Roosevelt faced a problem with his own people almost as dangerous as that presented by the Japanese. For years he had been calling upon his divided countrymen to assist peoples facing fascist aggression, only to receive the most grudging support. Suddenly he found himself at the head of a people united in humiliation and rage, a people clamoring to get into the war and exact revenge. If not handled carefully, public anger over the attack could turn into an exercise in retribution that would cripple the war effort.

In the weeks and months after the attack on Pearl Harbor, the American people were in no mood for a patient investigation of the workings of the nation's military bureaucracy. What everyone knew was that a major breakdown in the nation's security arrangements had occurred—in the idiom of the day, someone had fallen asleep at the switch—and people wanted to know who was responsible. They wanted names, and the fewer the better. So Roosevelt quickly appointed an investigative panel with the balance and prestige to command public respect and acceptance of its judgments. The president could then concentrate on rallying the nation for a united effort against foreign enemies. Things turned out just as the master politician in the White House expected. The investigation turned up two names the public could label villains, Short and Kimmel, and the people got on with the war effort.

As the nation geared up for war, it did so holding an impression that greatly compounded Short's problems. Despite the facts that the Roberts commission was not a court of law and had no authority to reach a verdict or pass a sentence, most Americans accepted the commission's finding of "dereliction of duty" against Short as an official judgment of guilt. That impression proved extremely persistent as the general planned his campaign to overcome it.

WITH THE PROBLEM of causation for the Pearl Harbor attack taken care of for the moment, Walter Short and millions of his fellow citizens might have expected that official attention would be turned on the other American outpost that received a devastating attack on 7 December. In the Philippines, the War and Navy Departments maintained ground, air, and sea forces with missions and organizations similar to those in Hawaii. Gen. Douglas MacArthur commanded the U.S. Army's Philippine Department, operating with the U.S. Navy's Asiatic Fleet according to the same "mutual cooperation" doctrine that governed Short and Kimmel in Hawaii. Although it had been the subject of frantic reinforcement since the previous September, the Philippine Department represented an even greater mismatch of resources to mission than the Hawaiian Department, having only about 10,600 American troops, organized into ground and air components, and 12,000 locally recruited Philippine Scouts. Only in air assets was the Philippine Department stronger than Short's command had been in December 1941, with 277 aircraft of all types on hand compared to 231 in Hawaii.[45]

Soon after Japanese planes made their last bombing runs over Pearl Harbor, MacArthur's staff in Manila received news of the air raid. Rather than preparing to defend against a similar attack on their own more vulnerable installations, MacArthur's command vacillated, making and then delaying plans to strike Japanese airfields on the island of Formosa, five hundred miles to the north. American aircraft had taken to the air at various times in the morning, either on alerts or reconnaissance missions, but when Japanese bombers appeared over the airfields shortly after noon, all were on the ground, refueling and waiting for a decision from MacArthur. Nine hours after they learned of the attack on Pearl Harbor, MacArthur and his command began to hear bombs exploding among their planes parked at Clark and Iba fields, and Zeros screaming into strafing runs against barracks, fuel tanks, and stunned troops. Within an hour, MacArthur's air force was destroyed. Three days later Japanese troops landed on the northwest coast of Luzon and began the drive south to Manila.

After his defeat, MacArthur received much different treatment than Short. Rather than being investigated, relieved, and retired in disgrace, MacArthur became a national hero. As Japanese forces pushed steadily southward through weak defenses, and Americans and Filipino troops fell back to the Bataan peninsula and the island of Corregidor, their commanding general took on the aura of a larger-than-life figure holding his ground in the face of hopeless odds. When the Navy ordered a task force to steam for the Philippines, the American people forgot a major reason for the unfolding debacle, MacArthur's loss of his air force on the ground, and prayed that the heroic general and his brave band of Americans and Filipinos could somehow hold out until relief arrived. On 11 March 1942, President Roosevelt ordered MacArthur to leave his troops and evacuate to Australia. On the twenty-sixth, in a ceremony in Melbourne, MacArthur was awarded the U.S. government's highest military decoration, the Medal of Honor. Back in the Philippines, his troops faced the humiliation of surrender, the horror of the Bataan Death March, and years of imprisonment and starvation.[46]

The stark difference in official responses to the two outpost defeats of 7 December 1941 demands explanation. The Japanese provided part of it. Short probably would have been spared the rage of his countrymen and the censure of his government if the Japanese had invaded Hawaii, which would have been much easier for them to occupy than the Philippines because of its smaller size and population. MacArthur's obvious failure was effectively shielded from intense scrutiny by the national rage directed at Short and Kimmel in Hawaii coupled with the Japanese decision to invade and occupy the Philippines. The concept of being saved by one's enemy is difficult to imagine and impossible to predict, but that is what happened to MacArthur.

The rest of the explanation lay with Franklin Roosevelt. Unlike Walter Short and every other Army general at the time, Douglas MacArthur had a political following. When Herbert Hoover chose MacArthur to be his Army chief of staff in 1930 he did more than reward a competent officer with a nice sunset assignment, and MacArthur returned more than the pro forma respect due a commander in chief. The charismatic general came to feel right at home with the Hoover administration. Except for the president's willingness to reduce the military budget, MacArthur shared most attitudes and approved most policies of Herbert Hoover, especially his business-first orientation and disdain for working people and immigrants with their socialistic ideas.

In 1932, the opportunity arose for the chief of staff to make a dramatic demonstration of loyalty to his commander in chief. That summer, thousands of unemployed World War veterans assembled in Washington to press for a bonus for their wartime service. The veterans only wanted help in feeding their families in the worsening economic depression, but Hoover and his chief of staff saw them as a mob under the influence of Communist agitators. MacArthur proved most willing to lead the forcible expulsion of the veterans.

The Roosevelt administration, however, was a different crowd to the elitist general. Like most of his fellow career soldiers in the early 1930s, MacArthur never did warm to the president's advisers or the New Deal legislation they pushed, which senior military leaders considered too leftist for the American people. Roosevelt was well aware of MacArthur's charismatic personality and formidable ambition, as well as the vulnerability of a democracy in periods of economic distress to the bombastic appeal of a demagogue. In Germany a democratic experiment had recently fallen to a dictator, and in the United States several individuals had already attracted sizable followings with simplistic solutions to widespread problems. On one occasion, shortly before he became president, Roosevelt had described MacArthur to an adviser as one of the two most dangerous men in America, the other being Huey Long of Louisiana. After he was in the White House, Roosevelt once told MacArthur to his face that he was the best military leader in the country but he would make "our worst politician." Now, eight years later, with American defenses in two major outposts shattered, the last thing President Roosevelt wanted after securing a declaration of war from the Congress was to have MacArthur in the United States offering free advice on the proper conduct of the war while under investigation for his failure in the Philippines and at the same time being courted by Republicans eager to avenge three presidential defeats in a row. The popular general was a political problem, not a military one, and had to be handled with great care.[47]

IN THE NORMAL COURSE of legal proceedings, military or civilian, the issuance of a judgment is followed by the opportunity of appeal. But there was nothing normal about the Pearl Harbor attack and the secret commission that looked into it, and traditional investigative and appellate processes were set aside. Added to the sting Short felt at the "dereliction of duty" finding, then, was the frustration of not knowing when he would have the chance to refute it. In the meantime, he had to do something with his life, and he preferred that it relate to the war effort. He got help from an unexpected source. One of the nation's, and the world's, foremost geniuses of business had watched the Roberts commission and forced retirement of Walter Short with great interest. Henry Ford wasted no admiration on either Franklin Roosevelt or the New Deal, which he saw as an assault on the freedom of American business managers. With Short forced out of the Army, Ford saw the opportunity to acquire an experienced manager and thumb his nose at Roosevelt in one stroke.[48]

No sooner was the ink on Short's retirement papers dry than Ford offered him a job. The general went to Detroit, met the father of the Model T, toured factories, and discussed a position. He was pleased to find that Ford had a plant in Dallas, close enough to Oklahoma City for occasional visits to his wife's parents. Wartime rationing of heating fuels gave added incentive to settle in a warm climate. Ford and Short agreed that the general would manage the traffic department of the Dallas plant, a position which required him to schedule delivery of new military vehicles to ports on both coasts for shipment to the various theaters of war. The job hardly compared to the major combat command Short knew he deserved but at least it was war-related. In preparation for his new life as a business executive, Short spent the spring and most of the summer at a Ford plant in the Detroit area.[49]

In May, the Shorts journeyed to West Point, New York, for son Dean's graduation with the Military Academy class of 1942. The event, the only joyful occasion they could foresee during the war years, gave them the chance to show off some parental pride and take a well-earned vacation trip at the same time. On the plain high above the Hudson River, the deep green carpet of the parade ground shone in the spring sun, and the Long Gray Line sparkled in braid, plumes, and brass. But with two Shorts in the audience and another in the graduating class, and General Marshall on the dais as guest of honor, a measure of tension hung in the air. At the presentation of degrees, the audience paid extra attention. As a staff officer read each graduate's name, a small patter of clapping from proud family and friends broke out. But when Dean's name was called, the audience erupted in enthusiastic applause, a spontaneous demonstration of support for the cadet's father. On the dais, General Marshall held his professional demeanor. In a gracious gesture after the ceremony, Marshall walked across the lawn and spoke to the Shorts briefly about their early service together. Nothing was said about Pearl Harbor or the handling of Short's retirement.[50]

Short completed his familiarization at Ford in the summer and went house hunting in Dallas. He found a two-story stone-finished home in the University Park section of the city. Now began a quiet, almost reclusive period in the Shorts' life together. Though eased somewhat by Henry Ford's quick offer of a job, Walter's transition from commanding general to private citizen was a challenge, one made more difficult by the sting of official censure. The attentions of an orderly, driver, and aide-de-camp, the assistance of dozens of efficient staff officers, and the whirl of training cycles, field maneuvers, troop reviews, and official receptions suddenly ended. Worst of all for a career soldier, he had to sit out the largest war in history, a war in which he knew he was qualified to play a major role. Walter started work in September and drove himself to the office every day. Isabel volunteered her services to the Dallas City-County Civilian Defense Council. In driving to area high schools to explain rationing schedules, she exceeded the gasoline ration and had to request additional coupons. Both Walter and Isabel liked to be outside, but their large corner lot was too much for them, so they hired two Southern Methodist University students to take care of the yard.[51]

Social life at 3141 Southwestern Boulevard narrowed dramatically for the new residents. Gone were commanding general's receptions for several hundred guests, replaced by infrequent dinner parties with two or three retired business executives and their wives. The Shorts went out so rarely that most neighbors did not know their names.[52]

In one respect, the Shorts' new life as retirees did not change. They still received a fairly heavy volume of mail. In nearly forty years of military life they had made hundreds of friends, many of whom passed along congratulations on promotions and kept them informed of changes of duty assignments as well as marriages and births. The attack on Pearl Harbor and Short's relief and retirement brought nearly one hundred letters and telegrams to the general. From old friends in uniform he received fewer letters than one would expect for an officer who had trained or served with most of those soon to become major unit commanders in the war. Quick to offer moral support was Robert L. Eichelberger, superintendent of the military academy at West Point for two of Dean Short's four years as a cadet. Eichelberger wrote, and at West Point called Dean to his office to express his concern. Short also heard from Frederick Martin, who had been his Hawaiian Air Force commander and a vigorous opponent of his plan to give infantry training to airmen. Martin blasted the Roberts commission report and forced retirement of Short as "unnecessarily cruel and inhuman," assuring the general of his "willingness and eagerness to help."[53]

Other letters came from family acquaintances in Illinois and Oklahoma, autograph seekers and outright cranks. Some ventured the view that the sole purpose of the Roberts commission had been to find scapegoats for the Japanese attack. Others offered conspiracy theories based on secret international or ethnic alliances to explain the events of 7 December 1941, and after. There were also a few threatening calls and letters but not enough to make Short consider hiring a bodyguard.[54]

Like millions of his fellow home-front citizens, Short followed the war in local newspapers. But unlike the millions, he knew well most leaders of the unfolding American campaigns and he had opinions about some of them that would never appear in War Department press releases. He heartily approved of the rise of his old friends Lesley McNair to head all Army ground forces and Robert Eichelberger to command Eighth Army. Somewhat surprising to him was the selection of Walter Krueger as Sixth Army commander, the same officer Short had decisively defeated in the 1940 Louisiana maneuvers. Short was confident he could perform well as a large-unit commander but, assuming he were sent to the Pacific, not so sure he could subordinate himself to Krueger's theater commander, Douglas MacArthur. Short had no doubts about the former chief of staff's formidable leadership ability, but he felt MacArthur's huge ego prevented him from becoming an even better commander.[55]

7

Toward Vindication

Despite the large number of people questioned and the wide publicity given its report, the Roberts commission failed to satisfy intense curiosity both in Congress and among the public about who was responsible for the Pearl Harbor disaster. There would have to be a more extensive investigation. But when? No one could predict when the war would end, and as long as it continued, the evidence that could prove the most important of all, the Magic intercepts, would remain unavailable. By late 1943, a legal technicality, the two-year statute of limitation on courts-martial, brought urgency to the issue. Secretary Stimson was determined that Short never have the opportunity to use the statute to frustrate exposure of what he considered incompetent conduct. In September, he dispatched a courier to Dallas with a waiver prepared for Short's signature. Confident of eventually winning vindication in open court, the general promptly signed the document.[1]

While submitting to Stimson's request, Short settled in his own mind the terms under which he would cooperate with a court-martial. If the War Department moved to try him during or after the war in a closed court to protect top secret information, he would plead the statute of limitation and refuse to cooperate. But if the War Department agreed to an open proceeding during which Short would have access to all relevant classified material, he would honor his waiver of the statute and cooperate.[2] Even with Short's signed waiver in his files, Stimson reserved an option in case a problem developed. Confiding to his diary, the secretary determined that "we could still punish him for conduct unbecoming a gentleman and dismiss him from the Army on that score."[3]

One astute senator was not satisfied with Stimson's tactics. Homer Ferguson, Republican of Michigan, did not see how the secretary of war or anyone else could know who was responsible for the defeat at Pearl Harbor without a complete investigation. Stimson had a waiver from the officer he believed most responsible for the disaster, but if a court-martial revealed shared responsibility, others could still use the statute of limitation defense. To avoid this possibility, Ferguson shepherded through Congress an extension of the limitation to six months after the end of the war.[4]

At the same time the statute of limitation issue arose, the Navy Department became concerned that the duration and campaigns of the war would dull memories and claim casualties among Pearl Harbor principals. Early in 1944, Secretary Knox named Adm. Thomas C. Hart, retired, to conduct a one-man investigation of the attack. Information Hart collected was to be held for the as-yet-unscheduled courts-martial of Short and Kimmel. Over a four-month period the admiral took statements from forty witnesses. But a gaping hole in the witness list denied him much credibility: Admiral Kimmel refused to participate.[5]

When he first learned of it, Short was willing to cooperate with the Hart inquiry, although he requested he not be contacted until April because his wife was to undergo surgery in March. In preparation, he retained retired Col. Allen J. Greer as counsel. Short was anxious to present his case before a body more objective and more attentive to his rights than the Roberts commission. But Kimmel's refusal to testify made clear to him that the collection of testimony by one man would never develop into a meaningful investigation, and he declined to meet Hart. Speculation that the War Department would appoint an officer to gather evidence from Army personnel died in the general disappointment over the inadequacies of the Hart inquiry. In June, Short revealed growing cynicism in a note to Kimmel. "I suppose we shall continue to be a political football until the election is over but do not anticipate any real action by the War and Navy Departments," he wrote.[6]

For once, Short's bitterness was unjustified, or at least premature. Unimpressed with clumsy attempts by the services to prepare for postwar legal proceedings, Senator Ferguson once again intervened to keep alive the search for answers to the Pearl Harbor mystery. In June, he introduced a resolution directing the War and Navy Departments to establish investigative boards. The president approved the resolution on the thirteenth, and the two service secretaries set about selecting members for their respective panels. The War Department chose three generals still on active duty for its Army Pearl Harbor Board. Only the president of the board, George Grunert, had been in uniform as long as Short. For its Court of Inquiry, the Navy tapped three long-experienced admirals, all beyond the retirement age.[7]

As the next round of investigations approached, Short was determined that he would not have to defend himself from the position of weakness the Roberts commission had imposed on him. This time there would be different ground rules, and they would recognize his constitutional rights. During the summer, he made six requests of the War Department: that he be furnished a copy of the full transcript of the Roberts commission investigation; that Brig. Gen. Theodore H. Green, Short's adjutant general in Hawaii, be detailed as his active duty counsel; that he be furnished copies of all testimony taken by the Army Pearl Harbor Board on a daily basis; that he be allowed to choose two members of the board; that he be granted access to all exhibits placed before the board; and that he be furnished copies of all synopses of testimony prepared by the board. Secretary Stimson granted only the first three requests.[8]

Despite partial success in amending the investigative ground rules, Short would still have to contend with some procedures carried over from the Roberts commission. Neither he nor his counsel could be present during the testimony of other witnesses, nor could he cross-examine witnesses. Both the Pearl Harbor Board and the Navy Court of Inquiry had to work around a major restriction on evidence. The imperative of wartime secrecy prevented use of, or even reference to, the Magic intercepts. And just over the horizon loomed the event which threatened to destroy the credibility of both inquiries. Nineteen forty-four was a presidential election year. If the investigations lasted too long, they might become pawns to political electioneering.[9]

Short was as concerned with strengthening his testimony as with making fair the rules under which he gave it. He remained convinced he had done a good job before the Roberts commission, despite that body's devastating judgment against him. He had confined his testimony to the facts as he knew them, and he had not engaged in any self-serving finger pointing. He also knew his testimony had been weak at several points and, overall, not convincing enough to answer all issues raised about his tenure in Hawaii. In retirement he had relived his actions before the attack and the explanations he had given after. Nagging questions remained. Why had Marshall sent the crucial one o'clock warning by the slowest method? How much information did the War Department have about Japan in the weeks before the attack? What did the coded phone call from a Japanese newspaperman in Tokyo to Mrs. Mori in Hawaii mean?

In the years and months since 7 December, Short had collected pieces of evidence that might be useful to him, pondered strategies to get more information out of Washington, and updated the list of witnesses he would submit to a future tribunal. He strongly suspected the War Department had had much more information about Japanese intentions than it told him in the messages of October and November 1941, and he was anxious to uncover some type of evidence that would confirm his suspicion. But the war made verification impossible. All officers directly connected with the attack except himself and Kimmel were involved in heavy wartime responsibilities at scattered points all over the globe. The inconvenience of distance was compounded by the possibility of death. Seven weeks after the D-day invasion of Fortress Europe, Short received a shocking demonstration of how the war might disrupt his attempt to win vindication. On 25 July, his friend of more than forty years, Lt. Gen. Lesley McNair, was killed while observing combat operations in France. McNair had no direct connection to the Pearl Harbor tragedy, but if even a three-star general could fall on the battlefield, no one who might be of help to Short could be considered available indefinitely. There was nothing to be gained by waiting in silence.

By the summer of 1944, Short believed he had enough evidence to put something on paper. He addressed two questions to Col. Otis K. Sadtler, who in 1941 headed the Military Branch of the Army Signal Corps, the agency charged with transmitting messages to outpost commanders. Short wanted to know why Marshall's one o'clock message of 7 December had been sent by the slowest method. The second issue was a bombshell, potentially damaging to Short if talked about too widely:

> I know that the Australian Government received information that Japanese carriers were headed for an attack on American possessions, probably Pearl Harbor. They received one message 72 hours before the attack and a second 24 hours before the attack. I would like to know if that information was communicated to the War Department.

Any information you may give me will be held strictly confidential. Also I would like for you to say nothing about my knowledge of the information received by the Australian Government as I am sure the War Department does not know I am in possession of that information.[10]

No record of a reply by Sadtler exists, but Short's questions indicate that he went into the Army and Navy investigations deeply skeptical of the War Department's assertion that it had done all it could to prepare him for the Japanese in 1941. With his Australian tip-off, Short thought he had a factual basis for believing authorities in Washington had withheld something from him.

The Pearl Harbor Board began its work on Monday morning, 7 August. The first witness was General Marshall, and for his convenience the board met in his office in the just-completed Pentagon building. No sooner had the board placed in the record the chief of staff's name, rank, organization, and station than Marshall asked for a closed, off-the-record session, during which he told the board about Magic and the importance of keeping it secret. When Short saw this gap in the record, which lasted nearly an hour, he knew Washington had something to hide. Back on the record, Marshall offered "I don't recall" and "I have no recollection" in response to so many questions that his testimony was of little value. While frustrating to all, the chief of staff's poor memory about events in 1941 did not necessarily indicate an attempt at deception, for he had been occupied exclusively for nearly three years with the details of fighting a multifront war with an army now numbering in the millions. Marshall was more certain about his correspondence with Short, copies of which he placed in the record.[11]

In Dallas, Short took a leave of absence and bought a train ticket for Washington. Henry Ford again offered help, this time with civilian counsel, but Short preferred his Judge Advocate General team of Green and Greer. Marshall arranged quarters at Fort Myer and an office and secretary in the Munitions Building, site of most board sessions. Short arrived at Union Station alone the morning of 9 August and walked unrecognized among hundreds of other travelers. To save him a second trip to Washington, the Navy scheduled him for an appearance before its investigation the day after the Pearl Harbor Board finished with him.[12]

Short began his testimony before the board as he had before the Roberts commission, with a lengthy statement. He also planned to rely on the same strategy. He wanted his interrogators to look at all aspects of his command in Hawaii, not only those policies and decisions contributing to the condition of the Hawaiian Department on 7 December 1941. Short even suggested, with the investigation barely begun, that the board find him not guilty: "I do not believe that I should be found guilty even of an error of judgement because I did not have the vision to foresee that the War Department would not notify me of a crisis in the least possible time and that the Navy with its large fleet in Hawaiian waters would not be able to carry out its mission of intercepting Japanese carriers, or at least detecting their presence in Hawaiian waters and informing me of the fact."[13]

For the most part, the board rejected Short's approach and pursued its own agenda. Members were unimpressed with his complaints of personnel, money, and equipment shortages in 1941; the construction he carried out on the Hawaiian and other islands; his popularity with civilians in Hawaii; and his presumption to suggest a finding of innocence. They wanted to know how he got along with the Navy, how he used his aircraft Warning Service, and why he chose Alert No. 1 in response to the 27 November message.[14]

In its early questioning of Short, the board seemed interested in going to war with the Navy. The general was given the opportunity to blame the Pearl Harbor disaster on Kimmel and his colleagues. Maj. Gen. Walter F. Frank asked if the Navy had been cooperative in Hawaii. "I felt that they played the game pretty well," Short answered without equivocation. "Really, I felt they played the game better than I had ever seen the Navy play the game."[15]

Frank set out the bait three more times, but Short would not bite. He came closest to openly criticizing the Navy when Frank asked if he might have had "misplaced confidence" in the effectiveness of naval protection. Short responded, "I had too much confidence." But when Frank asked if Short felt the Navy had withheld important information from him, the general declined to go further. "I don't believe that they purposely withheld anything from me that they thought really concerned me."[16]

Fortunately for the credibility of its investigation, the board abandoned the attempt to blame defeat on the Navy after two days. For Short and his former staff members, the questioning remained sharp, frequently loaded with insinuations of incompetence, if not guilt, and often delivered with scant regard for the courtesy which career officers, who also consider themselves gentlemen, typically observe. It was also maddeningly repetitious, even after General Grunert admonished his colleagues not to ask about issues covered in Short's opening statement. The board president soon disregarded his own policy. Much disturbed by Short's choice of Alert No. 1 in response to the 27 November message, Grunert asked if restrictions in the message—not to alarm civilians, not to disclose intent, not to show the message to any but his closest subordinates —caused him to feel he was not permitted to choose a higher level of alert. Short gave an answer so unmarked by interest in self-preservation as to make a defense attorney wince: "No, sir; I will say frankly that I did not believe, in view of all the information I had, that there would be an air attack there, so I didn't—I didn't want to go into Alert No. 2."[17]

Grunert asked what action was necessary to defend Hawaii, in view of Short's discounting the possibility of an air raid. "My judgement at the time," he replied, "was that while the hostilities might take place, the hostilities, in our case, would be in all probability sabotage, or possible uprisings; and I believe from the testimony of the Chief of Staff that he was thoroughly in accord with that opinion, himself."[18]

Reminded by the witness that the War Department had made no comment on the decision for Alert No. 1, Grunert asked if silence from Washington relieved Short of taking additional action. The general answered, "It led me to believe that the War Department was 100% in accord with my belief, that they approved definitely of what I was doing." A few minutes later, Grunert put the same question in different terminology. "It never occurred to you, though, to ask the War Department whether or not you should take additional measures?"

"I had reported," Short replied. "They gave me a directive to report the action taken. I reported exactly the action I had taken, and I figured if they did not approve, that they would come right back and say so, or if they wanted me to do more; and they did come right back, but it was just more sabotage, so I thought that they approved of what I was doing, but wanted to be 100% sure of the details."[19]

Grunert next moved the focus from sabotage to preparation for combat. "Did it ever occur to you that the warnings in this information necessitated taking a state of war readiness as compared with a state of internal security readiness?" he asked. Short answered that there were "two things involved":

> One was the information that I had from the Navy as to what they knew about naval ships; and, as I say, my confidence that they could prevent the carriers from getting through. The other was the insistence on the part of the War Department that the public must not be alarmed and that the intent must not be disclosed and that there must not be any provocative measures against Japan. I think if they had been convinced that something was absolutely imminent, the only thing they would be worried about

would be my getting one hundred per cent ready. They would not have cared whether I alarmed the public or what I did so long as I got ready in the least possible time to meet the situation. If they had been expecting an air attack they would have said, "Alert for an air attack at once." I do not think they would have taken any chances.[20]

Grunert disregarded the answer and the War Department's message when he soon asked why the Hawaiian Department did not prepare for any eventuality. Short explained, "If you had taken measures to meet any eventuality, you would have disregarded other parts of the message. They said, 'Do not alarm the public. Do not disclose intent. Do nothing provocative to Japan.'"[21]

Under this intense and repetitive questioning, Short continued to patiently but persistently recount his thinking in the ten days before the Japanese attack. Challenged on the limitations imposed by the War Department in the 27 November message, he explained how the transport of live ammunition through Honolulu would have raised in the public mind exactly the kind of questions and speculation Washington authorities did not want to deal with at the time. Grunert, at the point of exasperation, asked, "They knew that the army was kept over there to defend the island. Are they supposed to be impotent and not be trusted to take ammunition out? I cannot understand the psychology." General Short replied, "Taking live ammunition out, I think, in a period of strained relations like that, is a very different thing from moving it in maneuvers or on target practice that everybody has been accustomed to. . . . The papers were writing up the situation and they were writing scare headlines, and in combination it would have been just exactly what they told us not to do. They said not to alarm the public."[22]

For the third time, Grunert brought up the issue of Short's interpretation of the lack of follow-up from Washington to his decisions, and for the third time Short explained his reasoning. "Did you consider, having made this report and no reply having been received, that it absolved you against taking other measures?" Grunert asked. "I did," Short replied. "I thought they agreed with me a hundred percent. And there were other things that influenced me. I pointed out before certain planes coming in from the mainland without ammunition and with all guns cosmolined. I can see a definite argument that they did not consider any great danger in the situation."[23]

A change of interrogators brought a different line of questioning. General Frank tried a hypothetical approach, asking Short what he would have done had he received a message reading "War imminent. Act accordingly." Short answered, "I, in all probability, would have gone to Alert No. 3." Grunert jumped in to continue the hypothetical line. "What, short of a War Department order to do so, would have caused you to take Alert No. 2 or No. 3?"

"If they had radioed me that they considered there was danger of an air attack we would have been in Alert No. 2 in three minutes," Short said. "If they had wired me that they considered there was danger not only of an air attack but a possible attempt at landing, we would have been alerted just as fast, because we were so organized that all we had to do was to put Alert No. 2 in effect or Alert No. 3 in effect and there would be no delay and no confusion."[24]

Frank then changed his tack. Abandoning hypothetical questions for a patronizing manner, he led the witness through basic principles of officer responsibility going all the way back to Short's days as an Illinois Brigade cadet. Launching into a discourse on military education, Frank asked what kind of enemy action commanders are taught to prepare for. Short listened patiently and answered, "The worst." Frank came back with, "The worst. Now, can you tell me why that was not done in this instance?" Short reminded him who knew more about Japanese intentions in 1941:

> Everything indicated to me that the War Department did not believe that there was going to be anything more than sabotage; and, as I have explained, we had a very serious training proposition with the Air Corps particularly, that if we went into Alert No. 2 or 3 instead of No. 1 at the time that we couldn't meet the requirements on the Philippine ferrying business. Also the fact that they told me to report the action taken unquestionably had an influence because when I reported action taken and there was no comment that my action was too little or too much I was a hundred per cent convinced that they agreed with it. They had a lot more information than I had.[25]

Maj. Gen. Henry D. Russell took over the questioning and immediately got into a fruitless wrangle with Short about how many Navy task forces were at sea the week before the Japanese attack and whether they went east or west of the islands. Grunert mercifully stepped in and adjourned for the day.[26]

In a half-day session Saturday, the board touched superficially on a wide range of topics, including Japanese-American diplomatic relations, the Aircraft Warning Service, close and distant reconnaissance, command relations, and the Mori message, plus almost every subject raised the day before. The questioning remained repetitive but much less acrimonious. Only once did it appear a confrontation might develop. With perfect vision in hindsight, Grunert and Frank observed that if Hawaiian Department aircraft had been dispersed, the Japanese could not have destroyed so many of them. Why were the planes bunched on the runways? Once more Short explained that guarding dispersed planes would have taken men away from important training and construction. This Saturday session uncovered nothing of value to the investigation and brought out only one item of interest, Short's belief that unity of command would have been more effective than the cooperative arrangement he and Kimmel had had to contend with.[27]

Short's former chief of staff, Col. Walter C. Phillips, got much harsher treatment when he came before the board a week later. A Chinese language specialist since the 1920s, Phillips held a key position on Gen. Joseph W. Stilwell's staff in the China-India-Burma theater of operations when called to testify. The long trip from the CBI to Washington was poor preparation for the buzz saw he ran into. Early in his testimony, he tried to explain that the passage of time and his present duties had dulled his memory of events in 1941. Marshall had said the same during his testimony, but board members were in no mood to grant Phillips the same indulgence they had extended the chief of staff.[28]

The board raised with Phillips the same issues it had with Short. The questions came fast, and the board wanted specific names, dates, and places. Unable to get the details they wanted, interrogators expressed a surprising amount of snide commentary and sarcasm. When Phillips said he had brought no documents or notes to refresh his memory, Frank asked, "Have you any notes any place in the world, on this subject?" When Phillips said that both the Army and Navy were aware of the possibility of attack, Grunert demanded, "You had better tell me what you expected, and not talk for the rest." After listening to a response he thought too vague, Frank snapped, "You just will not answer that question, will you?" Not getting the answer he wanted, Frank expressed a judgment he was not qualified to make: "You weren't very positive as a chief of staff, were you?" The badgering of Phillips did nothing to assist the board and stands as the low point of its investigation, an unprofessional deviation from Secretary Stimson's purpose in convening the body.[29]

CALLED INTO EXISTENCE a few days after the Pearl Harbor Board, the Navy Court of Inquiry shared the same purpose, to investigate the Pearl Harbor disaster and make appropriate recommendations, but operated by different rules. Major witnesses at the Navy court were recognized as "interested parties" and granted more rights than those called by the Pearl Harbor Board. As an interested party, Short could attend all sessions, listen to all testimony, cross-examine, and have counsel with him even when not testifying.[30]

By directing the War and Navy Departments to conduct separate investigations, Congress seemed to open the door for each service to blame the Pearl Harbor defeat on the other, and this in the midst of a global war, when interservice cooperation was imperative. In the opening sessions of the Navy court, it looked as if an Army-Navy slugfest would develop. When the first witness, Adm. Harold R. Stark, was asked what he expected the Hawaiian Department to do in response to the 27 November message, he set aside all protocol:

> I expected the Army to utilize its warning system to the utmost. . . . I expected them to make ready a maximum number of planes possible. I expected them to man their antiaircraft defense. . . . I expected them to man their batteries. . . . I expected them to implement arrangements which they had with the Navy in joint agreements. I expected them to take some sabotage measures. In other words, I expected them to assume a maximum state of readiness in defense of Pearl Harbor. The defense of the Naval Base at Pearl Harbor was an Army responsibility. . . . In particular, I would have expected the Army to have ready their pursuit planes, some of them certainly in instant readiness, and full alertness with regard to others, to man these pursuit planes in the earliest possible time in emergency. These were the principal or certainly the primary weapon of defense against an air attack coming in from the sea.[31]

With such a strong pro-Navy statement at the beginning of their inquiry, the admirals had no need to resort to the heavy insinuation and sarcasm which the Army Pearl Harbor Board directed at some of its witnesses.

Short appeared before the Navy court on Monday morning, 14 August. The second witness to be called, he began by letting the admirals raise issues rather than by reading a statement, as he had before the Roberts commission and Pearl Harbor Board. Most of the questioning concerned interservice coordination and the Hawaiian Department's ability to defend Pearl Harbor and the fleet when in port. After walking Short through basic documents of Army-Navy joint operations on the Hawaiian frontier, the court asked if in 1941 he had had adequate weapons, equipment, and personnel to defend Pearl Harbor and the island of Oahu. In a lengthy answer, Short listed the paltry resources he had to carry out his mission: of 140 37-mm antiaircraft guns he wanted, he had 20; of 345 50-caliber machine guns needed, he had 180; of 24 90-mm guns ordered, he received none; and the shortage of coast artillerymen was so severe in 1941 that not even the inadequate number of harbor defense and anti-aircraft guns on hand could be manned at the same time. Of 180 B-17s, Short believed he needed to conduct an adequate air reconnaissance around the islands, he had twelve, only six of which were in flying condition. Of 200 pursuit planes needed, he had 105, only 80 operational. The Aircraft Warning Service was still in the early stages of development at the time of the attack. Of the twelve radar stations planned, six fixed and six mobile, only the mobile sets were in operation, and those for only three hours a day because of the shortage of qualified operators. Important components for the fixed sets were still on West Coast docks in December 1941.[32]

Turning from equipment shortages, the court asked, "The Commanding General of the Hawaiian Department was responsible for the defense of Pearl Harbor? Is that correct?" Short was not going to declare the Navy innocent at his expense, especially when an Army-Navy agreement backed him up. "Supported by the naval forces," he answered without hesitation. Asked what kind of naval support he had expected, Short listed long-range reconnaissance, interception of enemy ships approaching the Hawaiian Islands, Marine and Navy shore batteries, Marine aircraft and antiaircraft fire from ships in port.[33]

The rest of the questioning covered a variety of topics, superficially for the most part. The court let Short have his say about his understanding of messages received, his choice of alert status, his use of the incomplete Aircraft Warning Service, and his interpretation of War Department inaction days before the attack. The court also followed the lead of Justice Roberts in checking out a rumor still in circulation after two and a half years. The court asked if Short had seen any heavy drinking the night before the attack. The general had seen none and added, "I don't believe I saw more than two officers under the influence of drink during the whole time I was in Hawaii."[34]

In the last half hour of the daylong session, the admirals turned from the passive receipt of testimony to set a subtle trap. By comparing a Navy message sent to Kimmel on 3 December reporting the Japanese destruction of secret documents and code machines with Marshall's tardy one o'clock message of the seventh, they tried to establish that Short had had enough information four days before the attack to get his command on a higher alert and thereby better defend the base and fleet: "General, insofar as Washington is concerned, that dispatch [to Kimmel] gave the same information which you might have received from General Marshall by telephone on the morning of December 7?" But

Short's perception had not been dulled by five hours of testimony. He immediately reminded the admirals of the greater urgency of Marshall's message. "Oh, no. He [Marshall] said there had been an ultimatum delivered and ordered codes destroyed."[35]

After testifying some fifteen hours in four days, Short took a train back to Dallas. This time he was going back to more than a job and a quiet life. On leave earlier in the year, son Dean had met Emily Irby of Blackstone, Virginia, and an engagement soon followed. Now the Shorts could set aside official investigations and prepare for a September wedding.[36]

IN THEIR FIrst MONTH of existence, both the Pearl Harbor Board and Navy Court of Inquiry carried out their assigned tasks in a businesslike manner. All relevant witnesses set aside wartime duties for a few hours, and all cooperated as much as responsibilities and memories allowed. Neither investigation was paralyzed by the need to maintain the secrecy of Magic intelligence intercepts; both found a great deal of other information to collect and analyze. But from the early sessions of the Navy court, tension had been rising.

Kimmel provided the spark that exploded the generally sedate atmosphere of the investigations. Like Short, he had found someone willing to verify his suspicion. In the early weeks of 1942, Cdr. Laurence F. Safford, a Navy communications specialist, had heard through the service grapevine that Kimmel would soon be court-martialed. While rereading documents to refresh his memory for the expected trial, which would almost certainly call for his testimony, Safford found proof that vital information had not been sent to Pacific Fleet headquarters in 1941. He immediately informed Kimmel of his discovery. The admiral then won approval from the chief of naval operations for his counsel to make copies of forty-three Magic intercepts never sent to Hawaii. But an objection from Joseph McNarney, who had been an Army member of the Roberts commission, blocked delivery of the intercept copies to Kimmel. Rejection, however, only intensified the admiral's determination to bring the intercepts before the court.[37]

Even before the Navy court began calling witnesses, Kimmel was pushing for access to Magic intercepts. He faced a formidable bureaucratic barrier, for officials at the highest echelons of both the Army and Navy adamantly opposed even indirect mention of the sensitive intelligence effort while the war continued. Nevertheless, on 28 July Kimmel asked the judge advocate of the Navy court to allow introduction of Magic intercepts. The Navy responded with the classic bureaucratic tactic of passing Kimmel from one official to the next, each of whom found a reason to refuse the request and send him elsewhere. At one point, Navy officials even claimed to have lost Kimmel's letter of request, which only spurred the admiral to more vigorous prodding of the bureaucracy. On 7 August, with the court continuing its interrogation of Stark, Kimmel read into the record his request for Magic intercepts. The judge advocate of the court replied that the requested documents were not essential to the work of the court, but when the session resumed, Kimmel requested the intercepts four more times. The admirals refused four more times.[38]

Kimmel fought the Navy stonewall by taking his case to the Army, a risky move which opened him to the charge of disloyalty to his own service. At the end of his testimony before the Pearl Harbor Board on 25 August, he not only requested classified documents but also made some startling allegations:

> Since Pearl Harbor information has come to my knowledge that vital information in the hands of the War and Navy Departments was not supplied to responsible officers in Hawaii; in particular, that the War and Navy Departments knew that Japan had set a deadline of 25 November, later extended to 29 November for the signing of an agreement, after which they would take hostile steps against the United States; that on 26 November an ultimatum was delivered to Japan by the United States. . . . I am further certain that several days prior to 7 December, 1941, there was information in the War Department and the Navy Department that Japan would attack the United States and, very probably, that the attack would be directed against the fleet at Pearl Harbor, among other places; that there was information in the War and Navy Departments on 6 December, 1941, that the hour of attack was momentarily imminent, and that early on 7 December, 1941, the precise time of the attack was known. It was known at least three or probably four hours before the attack. All this information was denied to General Short and to me. . . . Had we been furnished this information as little as two or three hours before the attack, which was easily feasible and possible, much could have been done.[39]

Kimmel's statement makes clear that he had learned of an intercept which became known in the Pearl Harbor investigations as the "bomb plot message." In the fall of 1941, the Japanese had instructed their consular personnel in Honolulu to divide Pearl Harbor into several areas, like a target grid, and report types of ships anchored in each. The message clearly indicated a new orientation in Japanese interest in the U.S. Pacific Fleet, from task force movements outside Pearl Harbor to specific locations of ships in the harbor. Intercepted on 24 September and deciphered by 9 October, the message had been read and discussed by intelligence officers and top officials in both the War and Navy Departments. While everyone who read the message recognized the redirection of Japanese interest it conveyed, few deduced that information gained in response to it could be used to plan an air raid, and no one concluded that the message should be sent to commanders in Hawaii. The interest in warship locations, had it been known to Short, would have caused the general to think more in terms of defense against air attack than against sabotage.[40]

In search of substantiation for Kimmel's allegations, the Pearl Harbor Board broadened its inquiry to include the diplomatic background of the attack. Had the State Department somehow pushed Japan to attack? Secretary of State Cordell Hull and former ambassador to Japan Joseph Grew vigorously denied any provocation. Had naval intelligence intercepted the Japanese decision to go to war against the United States? Commander Safford told both the board and Navy court that he had received a coded message—"east wind rain"— which indicated Japan would attack American forces somewhere. But no documentation on the message could be found. While these lines of inquiry turned up nothing conclusive, the shift in focus from military commanders in Hawaii to civilian officials in Washington invited serious consideration of the core of Short's defense, his belief that the War Department had not given him enough information to mount a more effective defense.[41]

Three days after he brought his sensational allegations to the Pearl Harbor Board, Kimmel won a major victory. The Navy Department released the Magic intercepts. Until now, the board and the Navy court had been operating independently of each other, although they necessarily shared many witnesses. But the release of classified material to one investigation had to affect the other because the same material was the basis of warnings sent to both services in Hawaii in 1941. Within days, the Navy Department's action changed the rules of evidence for the Pearl Harbor Board. When he learned that members of the Navy Court of Inquiry were discussing Magic intercepts, General Marshall authorized the board to read and consider particular intercepts as they might become relevant to their investigation. While Marshall's action opened a crack in the solid wall of wartime secrecy around the Magic cryptanalysis effort, it did not result in any immediate benefit to Short, for he was still barred from seeing the intercepts. Nevertheless, Marshall's authorization and Kimmel's willingness to confront the Navy bureaucracy raised the possibility that coordinated action by the two disgraced officers might force a broader relaxation of the restrictions on Magic. Anxious to increase the pressure on the two service investigations, Kimmel contacted Short in Dallas and the general made another train reservation for the capital.[42]

Back in Washington, Short arranged a meeting with Kimmel. A discussion about intelligence not sent to Hawaii in 1941 soon turned to the Army chief of staff's behavior since the attack. Short listened in stunned silence as Kimmel characterized Marshall as an "enemy" engaged in a "doublecross" of his old friend. Short reeled. He was well aware of how a proud institution like the Army could strike back when it felt itself betrayed—he had been in Washington during the court-martial of Billy Mitchell there in 1925—but this was too much to comprehend. The personal aspect of his relationship with Marshall made it very difficult for Short to accept Kimmel's warning. The realization that a fellow officer he had respected for nearly forty years might not be defending him, might even be working against him, was as incomprehensible now as the sight of Japanese planes dive-bombing Pearl Harbor had been three years earlier. And there was more. Kimmel suspected Short's counsel, General Green, of working more for Marshall than Short and refused to let him see the Magic intercepts.[43]

Aroused by Kimmel's allegations about information withheld from Hawaii and stung by the possibility of Marshall's disloyalty, Short made his second appearance before the Pearl Harbor Board ready to fight. Taking most of the afternoon of 29 September, he listed in rapid succession the documents and statements he wanted Grunert and his colleagues to pursue. First, he entered into the record the affidavit of Sidney Graves, who heard the Australian minister in Washington say at a dinner party that his government had learned of a Japanese naval task force approaching American possessions twenty-four hours before the attack on Pearl Harbor. Short wanted to know why he had learned nothing of this Australian information before the attack. Grunert said the board was looking into the matter.[44]

Short then cited three statements or questions by officials alluding to the existence of secret information. The first was a question from the Roberts commission inquiry. Justice Roberts had asked a witness about the "east wind rain" coded message supposedly sent from Tokyo. To Short, the question was far more important than the answer, for it indicated that Roberts knew more than the general about intelligence gathering in 1941. The other two examples were Marshall's one o'clock message and Kimmel's stunning allegations to the board on 25 August. Short had to be circumspect in his interpretation of these three examples. If he said they proved the existence of Magic, the board could target him for breach of security, since he was not supposed to know about the supersecret intelligence source. So he gave a safely vague view of the statements. Referring to Kimmel's charge of withheld information, he said:

> I feel that Admiral Kimmel would not have made that statement unless he had factual data to corroborate it. I haven't had access to that data, and, from reading Admiral Kimmel's testimony, it does not appear that the Board has been furnished with it. I think it is absolutely essential that his factual data be considered by the Board, and that my counsel and I have access to what that was, because that is a tremendously important matter, to me, just as important to me as it was to Admiral Kimmel, to know what the information was that was denied us.[45]

Short dropped the professional restraint he had maintained thus far. He reminded the generals of the limitations they had placed on him. He also told them he was going over their heads to get more information, an act most career officers would consider unethical:

> Inasmuch as I was not given an opportunity before the Board to cross-examine witnesses, I had no opportunity to elicit from Admiral Kimmel the information to which he referred. I have written a letter, as of today, to the Secretary of War, asking that a search be made, that the Board be authorized to, and that my counsel be authorized, to make a search of War Department files for the information which pertained to all three of these; and that, if it is not to be found in the War Department files, that a demand be made on the Navy for the information with reference to these things.[46]

General Frank fairly spluttered, "General, are you putting the Board in the position of working for you?"

Short replied, "I am putting the Board in the position, I hope, where I feel that they should want to consider everything, that this should not be a one-sided investigation; but that here is something that is tremendously important from my point of view. I feel that they ought to be just as much interested in it as I."[47]

Frank renewed his challenge. "Have you found anything in the proceedings of this Board that has indicated to you that this Board has not tried to conduct an impartial proceeding?"[48]

Short repeated his intention and rejected Frank's questions:

No, I have not . . . but I feel that he [Kimmel] definitely would not have made that statement without . . . data to support it. If the Board has already considered all this, that's what I am after. . . . On the other hand, if they have considered it, and it has been off the record, . . . then I hope my letter to the Secretary of War will cause them to be made available to me. I do not know what the Board has had, off the record. . . . I do not think your statement is a fair one, that I am trying to have the Board work for me. I am really just hopeful that they will get everything before the Board that is necessary for a complete understanding of the case . . . but it seems to me that I have a perfect right to know the basis for things of that kind.[49]

In his letter to Stimson, Short pointed out that after examining the records of the Roberts commission and Pearl Harbor Board before his second appearance, "I fail to find a disclosure of certain vital information which high Washington officials appear to have had prior to December 7, 1941, of the imminence of an attack by the Japanese." He cited the question and statements of Roberts, Kimmel, and Marshall to show that "a knowledge of pertinent facts which are not later disclosed in the record is inferred." Short "urgently requested" that the secretary keep the Pearl Harbor Board in session until "all of the evidence concerning this matter is in the record" and, furthermore, that "my counsel be given access to all War Department records which would be pertinent to this matter."[50]

Shocked at Short's knowledge of Magic and his challenge for verification, board members mounted a clumsy attempt to throw their determined witness off the paper trail. The generals, of course, were aware that the Navy Department had released Magic intercepts to its Court of Inquiry. But board members did not interpret either that release or Marshall's authorization for them to read Magic as permission to share top secret information with witnesses. They were still determined to shield the intercepts from Short and to deflect any attempt to get at them. Grunert got into a time-wasting tête-à-tête with Short's counsel over whether he had to be sworn as a witness to do nothing more than read into the record a portion of the general's previous testimony. As president of the board, Grunert knew the answer—it was not necessary to swear Green—but still he threw out the roadblock.[51]

Grunert next resurrected the old rumor that key officers in Hawaii had been drunk the night before the attack. Then both Grunert and Russell repeated their earlier questions about the lack of long-distance reconnaissance. Russell went on to bring up another issue covered in Short's first appearance before the board, the limited hours of operation of the new radar sets. The general patiently repeated his earlier answers. But when Maj. Henry C. Clausen, assistant recorder of the board, again brought up the issue of distant reconnaissance, Short put enough fire in his response that Grunert had to step in to cool the combatants. "We will have no arguments. . . . There is no use arguing one way or another," he declared. That ended the questioning, and the board excused Short.[52]

Three days after he wrote the secretary of war, Short had an answer. In choosing between the rights of a witness and the need for wartime security, Stimson came down heavily in favor of the latter. Stimson agreed to release the Magic intercepts, but to Short's counsel only, not to the general himself. Green could examine the intercepts "in the presence of a member of the board. No copies of these exhibits, however, may be made." Thus Short appeared to win a partial victory, somebody on his side of the inquiry could now read relevant classified material, but attached conditions interfered with his client-counsel confidentiality and called into question his loyalty. Green could hardly make meaningful use of the intercepts without Short's knowledge. Stimson's decision made clear that there would be no complete and open hearing as long as the war continued.[53]

Short left Washington with mixed feelings about the Army Pearl Harbor Board and what it meant to him. He knew he had turned in a stronger performance than before the Roberts commission. He was more confident, certain of his facts, even demanding in his efforts to win release of top secret information. But at the same time, he had cause for concern. Congress had called both the Pearl Harbor Board and Navy court into being not only for the purpose of investigating facts relevant to the Pearl Harbor attack but also "to commence proceedings against such persons as the facts may justify." Short could not simply assume the board shared his conviction that blame for the Pearl Harbor disaster lay in Washington, nor could he influence any further the generals' deliberations. He would just have to await the board's report.[54]

IN WASHINGTON, the political temperature rose when the Navy Court of Inquiry and Pearl Harbor Board concluded their work on 19 and 20 October, respectively. With a presidential election only weeks away, much talk in the capital centered on the content and timing of release of the two reports. Republicans in Congress feared the president would seek votes by either a preelection release of reports favorable to Washington officials, and therefore unfavorable to

Short and Kimmel, or a postelection release of reports reaching the opposite conclusion. But the worst fears of Republicans did not come true, for the president let his generals and admirals conduct their investigations at their own pace.[55]

In its report, the Army Pearl Harbor Board wrote a stinging indictment of American diplomatic and military leadership in 1941. By so doing, the board spread responsibility for the Pearl Harbor defeat far beyond Short's headquarters in Hawaii. With no regard for reputations, the board named names and listed offenses. Secretary of State Cordell Hull was faulted for his counterproposal of 26 November 1941, which called upon Japan to remove its military forces from China, Indochina, and Manchuria. In the board's view, Hull's proposal "was used by the Japanese as the signal to begin the war by the attack on Pearl Harbor. To the extent that it hastened such attack it was in conflict with the efforts of the War and Navy Departments to gain time for preparations for war."[56]

The War Department also received sharp criticism. Although they declined to name Stimson, board members found fault with him for not keeping Short informed of the course of Japanese-American talks in November 1941 and for not upgrading his alert status.[57] The evidence supporting criticism of the War Department included surprising information about the authorship of messages sent to outposts in the weeks before the Japanese attacked. In questioning the secretary of war, the generals of the board heard Stimson describe himself as a mere messenger of the president. Unconvinced, the generals kept digging. They eventually discovered deep involvement by the secretary in the last critical messages sent to Short. It was Secretary Stimson, not any uniformed member of the War Plans Division, who added the fatal ambiguities to the "Do-Don't" message. In their draft of the 27 November message, Gerow and one of his subordinates, Col. Charles W. Bundy, had begun with the straightforward statement that negotiations with Japan had terminated. Stimson then changed the sentence by adding words and phrases to more than double the length and heavily qualify the tone of the Gerow-Bundy draft: "Negotiations with Japan *appear* to be terminated *to all practical purposes* with only the barest *possibilities that the Japanese Government might come back and offer to continue.*"[58] Short would find this discovery very useful as he continued his search for vindication.

General Marshall came in for the heaviest criticism of his otherwise exemplary career. He was charged with failing to keep Short "fully advised of the growing tenseness of the Japanese situation," failure to recommend to Short an alert status more appropriate than antisabotage, failure to get into Short's hands before the attack the critical one o'clock message, and failure to investigate the Hawaiian Department's state of readiness in the days after sending the 27 November message. Marshall's chief of war plans, Leonard Gerow, was censured for failure to send Short summaries of Magic intercepts, failure to clear up ambiguities in the "Do-Don't" message of the twenty-seventh, failure to realize that Short's reply to the "Do-Don't" message did not indicate a state of readiness for war, and failure to implement plans and agreements between the Army and Navy. Thus, the top echelon of the War Department was hit with more criticism than anyone could have imagined from officers in uniform who, it could be assumed, had a tempting incentive to avoid pointing out neglect in high places, especially by General Marshall: the chance for a wartime command.[59]

Listing mistakes by Washington officials did nothing to vindicate the former Hawaiian Department commander, however. In the board's view, Short failed to put his command on alert for war, failed to reach agreements with Navy officials in Hawaii for implementing joint defense plans, failed to inquire about the effectiveness of the Navy's distant reconnaissance, and failed to replace inefficient staff officers.[60]

As might be expected in wartime, when the highest degree of interservice cooperation was essential, neither investigative body dealt harshly with the other service in its report. The Navy court noted that the defense of Pearl Harbor was an Army responsibility and acknowledged Navy responsibility for distant reconnaissance but then went on to excuse the failure of Kimmel and Bloch to conduct such reconnaissance because of shortages of aircraft and crews. Like the Pearl Harbor Board, the Navy court decided Washington must share blame for the disaster, but the admirals censured only one official. As chief of naval operations, Adm. Harold R. Stark "failed to display the sound judgement expected of him in that he did not transmit to Admiral Kimmel . . . during the very critical period 26 November to 7 December, important information . . . regarding the Japanese situation." The Pearl Harbor Board report noted that distant reconnaissance from the Hawaiian Islands was a Navy responsibility. The generals went on to depart from their gentle treatment of the sea service by listing two failures of the Navy in Hawaii: to advise Short of a Japanese naval concentration in the Marshall Islands in late November and to inform him that an enemy submarine had been sunk near the entrance to Pearl Harbor an hour before the attack began. Neither report censured officers of the other service, and, oddly in view of the individual failings cited and the two service secretaries' charge to do so, neither recommended punishment for anyone.[61]

Alone among the Pearl Harbor investigations, the Pearl Harbor Board examined extensively Short's staff and subordinate commanders. Long experienced in Army ways, both written and customary, the generals of the board knew how a strong staff could help a commanding general accomplish his mission and how a weak staff could frustrate him. Ultimate responsibility for the performance of any unit rests with the commanding officer. But a capable staff can contribute much to a commander's decision making by detailing all threats he faces and presenting options to counter them. At the very least, a competent staff should always make the "old man," the commander, look good. The generals of the Pearl Harbor Board wanted to know if the key to the Hawaiian Department's unreadiness on 7 December 1941 lay with the staff. Had Short disregarded good advice from his staff, or had the staff failed to make him aware of the danger he faced?

The board found a number of disturbing features of Short's staff. For one, key players were still not settled in their posts late in the year. The chief of staff, Walter C. Phillips, did not officially assume his duties until 5 November, barely a month before the Japanese attacked. Additionally, all but one of the five principal staff assistants held at least two different posts, and one officer, Morrill W. Marston, held three during 1941. The generals of the board, like executives in any organization, suspected that the "musical chairs" character of the staff had detracted from the quality of advice Short had received.[62]

The board was even more disturbed about Phillips's performance in Hawaii. A pivotal figure in any command, the chief of staff is responsible for molding a staff into an effective team and presenting the commander with the best assessments and advice, no matter how unwelcome. When the board discovered that Short had decided on his antisabotage alert without consulting Phillips or other assistants, it suspected the chief of staff had not offered the analysis and options expected of him. Further questioning revealed that loyalty toward Short was not weakened by the lack of consultation because the staff officers almost to a man agreed with their general that a Japanese air attack was highly improbable, and both Short and Phillips knew the staff agreed on that issue before the 27 November message arrived. But questioning on other issues confirmed the generals' suspicion about Phillips's work, and they concluded that his selection as chief of staff "appears to have been a mistake."[63]

Ugly rumor made worse the board's judgment against the colonel. Years later, Phillips's widow was told that someone had placed in her husband's record of service a letter for future promotion boards. The letter supposedly contained the sentence "This officer is not to be promoted."[64]

In a press release of 1 December, Secretary Stimson gave his views of the Pearl Harbor Board's work. "On the recorded evidence, I agree with some but not all of the board's conclusions." What he did not agree with was criticism of himself, Marshall, and Gerow. But in the years since the attack, the secretary had become satisfied that "proper steps were taken to correct such inadequacies of either personnel or organization as were shown to exist either in the War Department or in the field at the time of the Pearl Harbor disaster." As for Short, Stimson felt the general's relief was "sufficient action" for "his errors of judgement." On the question of a court-martial for Short or anyone else, he stated, "My conclusion is that under all the circumstances the evidence now recorded does not warrant the institution of any further proceedings against any officer in the Army."[65]

The board gave Short an important boost in his effort to tell the nation his side of the Pearl Harbor story. The general was more impressive in his testimony, and the investigation itself was more comprehensive in scope and more professional in conduct. After watching his old friend George Marshall and the War Department decline to defend him against the "dereliction of duty" charge for nearly three years, Short knew he would have to fight his own battle. He still preferred to give a gentlemanly presentation of his views, but when the questioning became repetitious or pointed for no purpose, he responded forcefully. And this time not only the style but also the substance of his testimony was more convincing, for, taking up on Kimmel's lead, he made use of Magic intercepts verifying his contention that important information had been withheld by Washington officials.

Overall, the Pearl Harbor Board came closer than the Roberts commission to solving the mystery of Pearl Harbor. The single-service, active-duty membership of the board invited the suspicion that the War Department was interested in blaming the disaster on the Navy, or at least exonerating Washington officials, who could still influence the careers of board members. But led by the strong hand of General Grunert, the board proved unwilling to shield anyone from the bright light of investigation. As the board's report makes clear, not even Secretary Stimson was out of reach. While the conclusions against several War Department officials did not add up to exoneration of Short, they made clear that the state of preparedness in the Hawaiian Department on 7 December 1941 resulted from not the questionable analysis of one man but the decisions and oversights of several.

In Dallas, Short reacted to the Pearl Harbor Board's conclusions with subdued satisfaction for the present and confidence for the future. He told the press that when the full story of Pearl Harbor finally came out, he was "certain of complete vindication in the eyes of the American people."[66]

After the board submitted its report, Stimson appointed Maj. Henry C. Clausen to take additional testimony relating to classified information made available to the board. Clausen had served as assistant recorder of the board, and while interrogating for that body had clashed with Short. Suspecting that Clausen's real purpose was to get witnesses to change their testimony so as to exonerate War Department officials, Short refused to meet him.[67]

BACK IN DALLAS, Short resumed the quiet routines of a business executive. He took production reports and government requisitions from his In box, and put shipping schedules and rail manifests in his Out box. He met with Ford officials and talked on the phone with War Production Board bureaucrats in Washington. He drove home alone from the office, a distance that did not overstretch his gasoline ration. Occasionally the mail brought news clippings about Pearl Harbor that fellow University of Illinois alumni thought would be of interest. Short dutifully acknowledged all such offerings. Over dinner he listened to his wife tell of her volunteer work. Later, like millions of his fellow citizens, he settled into his favorite chair and read newspaper accounts of battle campaigns in progress.[68]

One feature of this quiet routine was different now. For the first time in three years Walter Short went through the motions of his stunted career with a measure of satisfaction. The Pearl Harbor Board had for the most part accepted his view of the Pearl Harbor disaster and lifted the deadening weight of the "dereliction of duty" charge from his life. But because of wartime censorship, the public could not yet read the secret documents on which his defense rested. As soon as the war ended, he could present his case to the nation and win back the respect of his countrymen. As soon as the war ended.

For the Shorts, as for millions of other Americans, there were dramas of triumph and loss that would not wait for the war to end. Between his father's two Army Pearl Harbor Board appearances, Dean Short took some leave and brought a daughter-in-law into the family. On 8 September, he married Emily

Irby in Blackstone, Virginia. The general met Emily after she and Dean had enjoyed the elder Shorts' wedding present, a Florida honeymoon trip.[69]

In the new year of 1945, the news from the European battle front became a source of personal pride for the Shorts. Serving with the 78th Infantry Division in Germany, son Dean was decorated for bravery in action. As Allied armies approached Berlin, the Shorts anxiously read the heavily censored newspaper accounts. Fortunately, all the news coming to 3141 Southwestern Boulevard gave cause for celebration. In the remaining months of the war, Dean received seven more awards for valor, including the Silver Star and Purple Heart.[70]

8

A Full and Complete Investigation

With the surrender of German armies in May 1945, millions of soldiers laid down their arms and began the long journey home. In Dallas, Texas, one soldier prepared to resume his war. Walter Short resigned from Ford Motor Company in the spring and reviewed his documents and defenses for the court-martial he had expected for years. The collapse of Japan could not be far off, and when it came, he would no longer be gagged by wartime censorship. All the documents would be available, and when the American people saw in open court all the information Washington had kept from him in Hawaii, they would demand that justice be done and the honor of Short's name restored. Even better, a court-martial would force the War Department to give a verdict rather than allow just another compilation of testimony he could neither hear nor refute.

But in the last months of the war, events that threatened to distract national attention from the investigation that might vindicate Short began to occur. The sudden death of President Roosevelt in April brought to the White House a man who, though determined to do right, was little prepared for the troubling issues now facing him. As Harry S. Truman struggled to learn one of the most difficult jobs in the world, international problems of great urgency and frustrating complexity came to his desk: Soviet-sponsored Communist subversion in several countries, independence movements against colonial powers, civil war in China, millions of displaced people in Europe and Asia, establishment of a Jewish state, organization of the United Nations, occupation policies for Germany and Japan, and economic aid for war-exhausted allies. At home the new president faced problems just as numerous and perplexing: demands to bring the GIs home faster, "reconversion" of the economy to peacetime production, strikes in key industries, inflation, demands for full employment, and the development and control of atomic energy.

Aside from the passage of four long years of war, the stark technological differences between 1941 and 1945 stood in passive discouragement of a major reconsideration of Pearl Harbor. In a world about to be made over by atomic energy, jet propulsion, television, and computers, investigation of an embarrassing incident in which prominent roles were played by propeller-driven airplanes, an antique radar system, and an old general from the horse-and-wagon Army seemed irrelevant.

Two weeks after war ended in the Pacific, President Truman revived interest in the Pearl Harbor attack. On 29 August, he called a press conference to release the reports of the Army Pearl Harbor Board and the Navy Court of Inquiry. Withheld from the reports were references to all still-sensitive Magic intercepts, but added to them was a memorandum by Henry Stimson in which the secretary of war expressed strong disagreement with Army Pearl Harbor Board findings against General Marshall. When the president immediately told reporters he endorsed Stimson's support for Marshall "wholeheartedly," he made clear that Short could assume neither assistance nor even sympathy from the new president in his search for vindication. Short might have to battle all over again the Roberts commission's "dereliction of duty" finding.[1]

In Dallas, reporters rushed to Short's home to get his reaction to the Pearl Harbor Board report. In a signed statement, the general ignored the president's support for Stimson and Marshall, and noted instead that the report shows "beyond question that there was available to the authorities in Washington, before the attack, critical information which was not disclosed to me." He ended his statement confidently, saying, "My conscience is clear."[2]

The next day, at another presidential press conference, Truman gave his opinion of who was responsible for the Pearl Harbor disaster: "I came to the conclusion that the whole thing is the result of the policy which the country itself pursued. The country was not ready for preparedness. Every time the

President made an effort to get a preparedness program through Congress, it was stifled. Whenever the President made a statement about the necessity of preparedness, he was vilified for doing it. I think the country is as much to blame as any individual in this final situation that developed in Pearl Harbor."[3]

With renewed interest in Pearl Harbor in the nation at large and the Congress—and among not a few Republicans, interest in embarrassing the Roosevelt-Truman administration—Senate majority leader Alben W. Barkley called for a congressional Pearl Harbor inquiry. In September, both houses of Congress approved Barkley's Senate Concurrent Resolution 27, which authorized a ten-member "Joint Committee on the Investigation of the Pearl Harbor Attack" to conduct "a full and complete investigation."[4]

As the majority party of the Seventy-ninth Congress, the Democrats appointed six of the ten joint committee members. In general, the Democrats chose experience and prestige, while the Republicans leaned toward prosecutorial expertise. One of the venerables of Capitol Hill would wield the committee gavel. Alben W. Barkley had come to Washington as a new representative from Kentucky in 1913 and moved to the Senate in 1927 without a break in service. Commanding great respect as Senate majority leader, Barkley at the same time enjoyed much popularity on both sides of the aisle, a trait that would enable him to mediate committee squabbles.

Senior even to the majority leader, Walter F. George was serving his fifth term as senator from Georgia when tapped for the joint committee. As a high-ranking member of the Foreign Relations and Civil Service committees and chairman of the Finance Committee, George exercised great authority in the Senate. But as a southerner uncomfortable with New Deal domestic policies, his enthusiastic defense of all aspects of the Roosevelt administration could not be assumed. Scott W. Lucas of Illinois carried the reputation of a New Dealer but, just beginning his second term, little of the prestige and authority that attach to seniority. Like Short a rural "downstater," Lucas would feel at home with the general's lack of guile and might sympathize with him as a country boy beset by government lawyers and War Department officials. Republicans Owen Brewster and Homer Ferguson completed the Senate side of the committee. A former state legislator, governor, and U.S. representative from Maine, Brewster had been in the Senate less than five years. Even newer to Capitol Hill, Ferguson had taken his seat less than three years before the joint committee convened. A former circuit judge in Detroit and surrounding Wayne County, Michigan, Ferguson had already shown intense interest in the Pearl Harbor story, sponsoring extensions of the statute of limitations that would allow Short and Kimmel courts-martial and more recently pushing for the joint congressional inquiry of which he was now a part.

The senior House selectee, and thus co-chairman of the committee, was Democrat Jere Cooper of Tennessee. In the House since 1929, Cooper brought to the Pearl Harbor investigation long legislative experience and knowledge of the Army and its ways, first acquired during World War I. J. Bayard Clark had won nine consecutive terms from a coastal North Carolina district. Representing a region with two major military installations, Fort Bragg and Pope Air Base, Clark might prove better qualified to participate in the investigation of a military event than his banking and lawmaking background would suggest. The youngest committee member at forty-two, John W. Murphy had represented his northeast Pennsylvania district less than three years by the time the committee was announced. But seven years as an assistant district attorney fit him for an investigative assignment. House Republicans Bertrand W. Gearhart and Frank B. Keefe rounded out the committee. In his sixth term from the agricultural district around Fresno, California, Gearhart had what appeared an appropriate experience to investigate an air raid: he had served as an Army Air Service officer in World War I. A former prosecuting attorney from Wisconsin in his fourth term, Keefe doubtless had the incisive interrogation skills that could make witnesses squirm and reporters scribble.[5]

At a superficial glance, the joint committee looked like any other on Capitol Hill, with its mix of seniority and inexperience, a quarter-century age spread, and prominent as well as gray personalities. But when viewed against the highly controversial event its members would look into, the committee displayed traits not so ordinary. Many observers might find it strange that among ten men chosen to investigate a military event only four had ever worn the uniform of their country, while six were experienced courtroom prosecutors. Not surprisingly, the numbers reflected a political strategy and its counter. The Republicans had lost four straight presidential elections, and with the nation still celebrating victory in the greatest war in history, there was not much to build a GOP renaissance on. Except Pearl Harbor. If the committee could uncover solid evidence that Roosevelt had somehow baited the Japanese into attacking Pearl Harbor, as some had charged, then perhaps large numbers of Democratic loyalists would be disgusted enough to vote Republican in 1948. A Republican prosecution of the late Roosevelt administration made much political sense, and if the three Southern Democrats on the panel, George, Cooper, and Clark, wanted to add some anti–New Deal venom, the Democratic majority might even be overturned. Committee Republicans, then, came poised for assault while Democrats braced for defense.

The joint committee membership was announced amid high hopes and pious pledges from congressional leaders of both parties for an inquiry free of partisan politics. But those hopes were quickly dashed as fierce political maneuvering began in both houses of Congress weeks before Chairman Barkley's gavel fell. Brewster led in the Senate with an attack on an executive order issued the month before the committee's first session. Concerned that the investigation might degenerate into a political witch-hunt and reveal material unrelated to Pearl Harbor but damaging to the national interest, President Truman in August had prohibited public release of information about the Magic cryptanalytic system. But having no desire to impede the investigation, Truman in October had exempted all intercepts and analyses relating to the Pearl Harbor attack, and directed the State, War, and Navy Departments to make such documents available to the committee. Nevertheless, Brewster charged that the executive order banned all discussion of Magic, and dropped hints about missing and destroyed files. Ferguson spoke in support but then entered into the record the complete texts of the executive order and the exception made for the investigation, texts which made clear the error of Brewster's charge. In the House, Gearhart and Keefe made a series of sensational charges of decoded messages pointing to the exact hour of the attack, witnesses coerced to change testimony, and cover-ups in Washington. None of the Republicans' charges was true but all gave reporters plenty to write about and raised interest in the investigation.[6]

In scheduling its witnesses, the committee put Short in a position that might allow him to overcome the rush of postwar problems drawing attention away from Pearl Harbor as well as the lack of presidential enthusiasm for another official investigation. The committee would begin by detailing the background of the attack as it appeared to the top officials of the State, War, and Navy Departments, then work its way down the national chain of command in 1941 to hear from Short and Kimmel. Thus, if members kept to a minimum the recalling of witnesses or the search for new testimony, Short and Kimmel might have the last word in the official record of Pearl Harbor investigations.

Chairman Barkley rapped his gavel on Thursday morning, 15 November 1945, and the marble-walled Senate Caucus Room, packed with hundreds of reporters, cameramen, and spectators, fell into a tense silence. Though not scheduled to testify for several weeks, Short was in the crowded chamber, and would take a taxi from the Fairfax Hotel to the hearings for almost every session. The committee began by having an Army and a Navy officer, Col. Bernard Thielen and Rear Adm. Thomas B. Inglis, read into the record a lengthy chronology of events, including Japanese diplomatic messages and descriptions of the dispositions and conditions of the Hawaiian Department, the Pacific Fleet, and the Fourteenth Naval District in the months before the attack. This recitation, and questioning by committee members, took most of four days, enough time to cool the excitement of some spectators and provoke shifting on sore feet and in hard chairs.[7]

The first witness to have personal knowledge of events leading up to the attack took a seat before the microphone on the afternoon of 19 November. Adm. J. O. Richardson had lost none of his burly command presence or combative nature in the five years since he had commanded the Pacific Fleet. Still smarting from his relief after a confrontation with the president over transfer of the fleet from San Diego to Pearl Harbor in 1940, Richardson disappointed no one listening for provocative statements. "Roosevelt Predicted Jap War, Kept Fleet Around Hawaii as 'Restraint,' Richardson Says," screamed the next morning's headline. Richardson's recounting of the October 1940 conversation with the president that led to his firing caused a sensation in the crowded caucus room. The next day the admiral kept the crowd on tiptoe by revealing that the president had suggested a blockade of Japan, an idea that caused Richardson to fear war in the Pacific before the U.S. Navy was ready. The next afternoon, Adm. William D. Leahy, the late president's naval aide, could not recall details of Richardson's talk with the president but expressed complete faith in the admiral. After hearing three days of testimony about a president flirting with war and an admiral counseling caution, Republican members of the committee might have begun to believe their anti-Roosevelt strategy would pay off.[8]

Even after the committee began taking testimony, political skirmishing over the purpose of the inquiry continued in the Senate. On 20 November, Senator James Tunnell (D-Del.) drew an analogy between the Japanese attack four years before and what he saw going on in the Senate Caucus Room now. Describing Republican members of the committee as "apologists for Japan" and the "kimono boys," Tunnell went on to accuse them of making a "sneak attack upon the grave of Franklin D. Roosevelt." Incensed Republicans rose to shout down the Delaware Democrat until one of their cooler heads took the floor. Leverett Saltonstall of Massachusetts censured Tunnell for violating senatorial courtesy, and the Democrat walked out of the chamber.[9]

The committee next examined the diplomatic background of the Pacific war. Former secretary of state Cordell Hull's health had deteriorated considerably during the war years, but he was very anxious to personally refute the judgment of the Army Pearl Harbor Board that by his diplomacy he had "touched the button that started the war" with Japan. Hull spent much of three days denying in the most forceful terms—the former cabinet officer repeatedly referred to the Japanese as "thugs" and "savages"—that his diplomacy had amounted to an ultimatum to Tokyo. Two of Hull's subordinates in 1941, former assistant secretary of state Sumner Welles and former ambassador to Japan Joseph Grew, spent three more days endorsing their former chief's diplomacy and testimony, though in more temperate terms.[10]

Turning to the uniformed services, the committee took a full month to examine Army and Navy war plans and policies of administering outposts and fleets, and keeping distant commands informed of critical developments. The appearance of Gen. George C. Marshall was the highlight of this phase of the inquiry and of the investigation to date. Fresh from the great victory he did so much to bring about, Marshall strode into the caucus room to a round of applause. But the end of the war four months earlier had not consigned him to an honor-filled retirement. He now carried the hopes of millions in a new role. Within days of Marshall's resignation as Army chief of staff, President Truman appointed him special envoy to China with the specific mission of negotiating a cease-fire in the civil war between the Nationalist government of Chiang Kai-shek and Communist revolutionaries led by Mao Tse-tung. Marshall came before the committee in an atmosphere of electric anticipation, since a plane was being held at a nearby airport to fly him to China as soon as the committee excused him.[11]

General Marshall had already put into the growing official record of Pearl Harbor investigations a number of views on Short's work in Hawaii, some of them complimentary, some not. He had made known in 1941 his gratification at Short's successful dealings with the Navy and the civilian community in Hawaii, as well as the defensive improvements he made in the islands. More recently, before the Navy Court of Inquiry in 1944, Marshall had given his estimate of Short's qualifications to command the Hawaiian Department with just three words: "Very superior officer." But Marshall had also expressed dissatisfaction with Short's inability to turn back the Japanese on 7 December 1941, despite the fact that the Hawaiian Department was at the time the strongest of all Army outposts. Less than a month after describing Short's superior ability to the Navy Court, Marshall told the Pearl Harbor Board repeatedly, four times in the same session, that the Hawaiian Department had had sufficient information, manpower, and weapons to defeat the kind of attack it received. Now everyone present wondered if Marshall would emphasize the complimentary or the critical views he expressed earlier.[12]

Watching intently as Marshall took a seat at the witness table and began answering questions, Short could be forgiven for harboring the faint hope that a friendship reaching back four decades would soften the disappointment Marshall had felt on learning of the Japanese attack. Short did not have long to wait to learn the tenor of Marshall's testimony. The former chief of staff was asked to recall his November 1941 estimate of the Hawaiian Department's ability to resist an air raid. "My own impression," he said, "was that the garrison was sufficiently established and equipped and organized to prevent a landing and to successfully resist an air attack and to defend the naval base."[13]

Two days later, Marshall added to the already considerable store of public respect he enjoyed when he admitted to a lapse in his supervision of the War Plans Division in 1941. Asked by Representative Gearhart why he had not acted to put the Hawaiian Department on a higher alert status during the week before the Japanese attack, Marshall said simply, "That was my opportunity to intervene and have a further check made and I did not take it. Just why I do not know." In the next few minutes Marshall made obvious his belief in the inadequacy of Short's alert against sabotage following dispatch of the 27 November message. Investing the "Do-Don't" message with more clarity than it had conveyed, the former chief of staff declared, "That was a command direction for alert against a state of war." Marshall went on to criticize not only Short but also Kimmel for misreading the situation they faced in the weeks before the Japanese struck: "They were both long experienced in the military considerations. They were men of mature judgements and they were men of high rank and they were in a position of great responsibility. They knew, certainly, why Hawaii was set up in the military way as it was. They knew the capacity of an enemy to do certain things under certain circumstances. We did not have to tell them that."[14] Sitting close to the witness table, Short and Kimmel betrayed no emotion upon hearing Marshall's testimony. But reporters present found Marshall a gold mine. Drawing a conclusion the former chief of staff did not state, editors in Washington summed up the day's testimony with a headline devastating to the former Hawaiian commanders: "Marshall Places Blame on Short, Kimmel / Pearl Harbor Chiefs Failed to Call Alert, He Declares."[15]

Following a Sunday recess, Marshall returned to a full day of questioning by only one member of the committee. Senator Ferguson had been among the earliest critics of the Roberts commission determination that all blame for American unpreparedness lay in Hawaii, and a constant voice in favor of a more comprehensive investigation. Less abrasive than Brewster, Gearhart, and Keefe, Ferguson stood a better chance than other committee Republicans of getting Marshall to make an admission damaging to Washington officials in 1941, and thus helpful to Short, without provoking a backlash from the general's many admirers. In dealing with the situation in the Pacific in 1941, Ferguson asked why the War Department expected Japan to attack in the southern, western, or northern Pacific but not Hawaii. Marshall admitted, "Because we did not anticipate a general attack on Hawaii." That was all Ferguson and Short got. Two days later, under questioning by Representative Keefe, Marshall repeated his headline-provoking charge of four days before, this time even more forcefully: "I feel that General Short was given a command instruction to put his command on the alert against a possible hostile attack by the Japanese. The command was not so alerted."[16]

Hearing repeated criticism of his actions in Hawaii, Short gave the committee counsel a list of questions he wanted asked of Marshall. But it did him no good. Even when under sharp questioning by Republicans trying to highlight oversights in Washington in 1941, Marshall managed to cite what he considered failures by Short. As Marshall left the chamber to another round of applause, Short realized he faced the formidable if not insurmountable challenge of building a credible case against one of the nation's most revered soldiers.[17]

The day after releasing Marshall, the committee had to deal with an organizational crisis. All but one member of the counsel's staff resigned. Chief Counsel William D. Mitchell had agreed to work without pay and with the understanding that the investigation would conclude by the deadline set by congressional leaders, 3 January 1946. But with testimony heard from only eight of sixty-eight scheduled witnesses by the middle of December, it had become obvious the committee would need several more months to complete its work. When Senator Barkley told reporters that as majority leader he should be devoting his time to the nation's postwar problems rather than a Pearl Harbor postmortem, and Senator George added that overlong cross-examination by minority members was confusing the issue, Republicans apparently got the message that they were in danger of losing one of the best political platforms they had found since before the war. It took only a brief executive session for the committee to agree on the formula that would keep the investigation on track: shorten the witness list, limit cross-examination, and set a new deadline. Both houses of Congress quickly granted a six-week extension, and Senator Barkley called the next witness.[18]

After holiday recesses and a week of testimony from Marshall's Navy counterpart in 1941, Adm. Harold R. Stark, the committee got down to the Hawaiian commanders' level, and called Admiral Kimmel on 15 January. The admiral took the same approach before the committee that he had taken with the Army and Navy inquiries in 1944, that Washington officials had withheld the vital information about Japanese diplomacy and forces that would have enabled him to meet his attackers with a more effective defense. In six days of testimony, Kimmel presented a mountain of documents and answered hundreds of questions with a strident confidence. He even offered the opinion that the 27 November message from Stark, beginning with the sentence "This dispatch is to be considered a war warning," did not constitute a war warning because it "did not state expressly or by implication that an attack in the Hawaiian area was imminent or probable."[19]

The committee, especially its Democratic members, showed much interest in Army-Navy relations during Kimmel's tenure at Pearl Harbor. The admiral tried mightily to downplay interservice misunderstanding and friction, the logical tactic to keep the committee's attention on errors in Washington. But since Kimmel was already on record in correspondence with Stark for criticizing Army defenses on Oahu, the picture of harmony was not easily drawn. He had no trouble praising Hawaiian Department leadership in 1941. Asked about relations with the Army, Kimmel cited joint agreements and volunteered an evaluation of his counterpart: "I found General Short a very likable gentleman, and subsequently a very able Army officer." But when Representative Murphy read several passages from Short's testimony to the Roberts commission, Kimmel had to admit disagreement with the general's understanding of Navy distant reconnaissance capability in 1941 and his brief response to Marshall's 27 November message.[20]

Throughout Kimmel's testimony, Short listened carefully from a seat near the witness chair, as he had since the opening session of the hearings. Whatever emotion he felt at the testimony he heard remained under control, for his serious professional expression never changed. He moved only to shift in his seat or whisper a comment to his military counsel, Brigadier General Green. But Kimmel's week with the committee gave Short a better idea of the treatment he could expect from a panel of politicians than the testimony of all the

Washington officials preceding the admiral. Republicans Ferguson and Keefe had been friendly toward the admiral, Democrats Cooper and Murphy clearly hostile.[21]

SHORT CAME BEFORE the committee better prepared than at previous inquiries but in frail health. For the first time, he had direct knowledge of top secret information from 1941, since he was allowed to read a folder of War Department messages two days before the investigation opened the previous November, and a selection of Magic intercepts when he came to testify on 22 January. To help him with this and other evidence, he now had a second attorney, Lt. Col. Randolph Karr, who joined him in mid-January. Short also came before the committee fully aware that this might be his last chance to win vindication. With this the fourth major Pearl Harbor investigation in four years, he could not expect the government to continue funding inquiries while urgent postwar problems demanded the attention of all officials. This time Short would have to be more convincing, and with access to formerly secret documentation, he should be able to support his charges of neglect and malfeasance in Washington in 1941.[22]

Short's ability to put up the determined defense he knew would be necessary had become questionable. In the year before the joint committee met, he had received painful reminders that he was well into the winter of his life. His sister Mary and brother Ulysses died, leaving only himself and one sister from among the six siblings. More recently, his own health broke, causing many to wonder if Father Time would cheat him out of his first chance to tell the public his side of the Pearl Harbor story. With the committee barely through its first month of work, Short suffered an attack of pneumonia and spent Christmas week in Walter Reed Army Hospital.[23]

At ten o'clock Tuesday morning, 22 January 1946, Short moved slowly to the witness table and took the seat in front of the microphone. In consideration of Short's health, Chairman Barkley offered to have someone read his opening statement. Buoyed by his wife, son, and daughter-in-law sitting nearby, he declined and pushed on toward what was for him the battle of a lifetime. The old general's appearance and voice evoked more sympathy than awe in his listeners, for he was obviously beyond the age of command presence. His suit hung loose, and he faced committee and camera with a pale complexion and sunken cheeks. He took his oath in a weak but determined voice, then arranged his papers beneath the microphone with drawn hands. The careful pronunciation, the upper range and slightly detached tone of the voice made him seem of an earlier age, a time when self-control and impeccable manners in any adversity conveyed more credibility than profanity and table-pounding. But the rage provoked by years of scorn burned hot. Politicians, reporters, and spectators hung on every word, every pause as the worn general praised the committee for its insistence on an open hearing, and then blasted its predecessors for their unjudicial treatment of him:

> Mr. Chairman, I want to thank you and the members of the committee for giving me, after four long years, the opportunity to tell my story of Pearl Harbor to the American public. I appeared before the Roberts Commission but was not permitted to hear the other witnesses nor given the privilege of cross-examination. I was not given the opportunity to read the evidence taken before the Roberts Commission until August 1944. I appeared before the Army Pearl Harbor board, but again was not permitted to hear the other witnesses nor given the privilege of cross-examination; however, I was furnished a copy of the hearings except for the part considered top secret. The Army board labeled certain evidence top secret and I was never permitted to see that until this committee was about to meet. Both boards took testimony off the record which has not been made available to me.[24]

Short continued with a lengthy statement summarizing his interpretations of events in 1941. His conclusions came next, the heart of which was his conviction that Washington had withheld vital information about the Japanese. The major part of his statement he presented as a list of numbered and labeled topics, such as "Agreements with Navy," "Alert plans," "Do-Don't message," "No magic to Hawaii," and so on. He apparently thought a round number would prove easy for his listeners to remember, so he shaped his topics to total one hundred. But those who read the statement closely noticed that some topics were duplicated, and the sequence skipped number 25. A marked improvement this time was his omission of the presumption he had floated to the Pearl Harbor Board, his view that investigators should not find him guilty "even of an error of judgement."[25]

The general's strongest charge came in paragraph 98, "Unjust War Department Treatment":

> I do not feel that I have been treated fairly or with justice by the War Department. I was singled out as an example, as the scapegoat for the disaster. My relatively small part in the transaction was not explained to the American people until this joint congressional committee forced the revelation of the facts. I fully appreciate the desire of the War Department to preserve the

secrecy of the source of the so-called magic, but I am sure that could have been done without any attempt to deceive the public by a false pretense that my judgement had been the sole factor causing the failure of the Army to fulfill its mission of defending the Navy at Pearl Harbor. I am sure that an honest confession by the War Department General Staff of their failure to anticipate the surprise raid would have been understood by the public, in the long run, and even at the time. Instead, they "passed the buck" to me, and I have kept my silence until the opportunity of this public forum was presented to me.[26]

Short took nearly four hours to read his statement. When he finished, he was exhausted, as he knew he would be. That morning he had asked Chairman Barkley if he could be excused at the conclusion of his statement because he was still weak from his hospitalization. As he stood and slowly walked out of the caucus room, the crowd gave him a warm ovation.[27] After Short had left the room, Barkley excused spectators and reporters for the day but held his colleagues for an executive session. Once again the committee had underestimated the time needed to complete its work. The members agreed that to speed the proceedings they would delete from the witness list twenty former members of Short's and Kimmel's staffs.[28]

On Wednesday morning, Associate Counsel Samuel H. Kaufman began examining Short. Kaufman's range of questioning predated the Pearl Harbor attack by decades; he invited the general to summarize his career from the day he was commissioned in 1902 to the day of his change of command ceremony on the Fort Shafter parade ground thirty-nine years later. For the next three hours, he asked Short what happened during his tour in the islands and what policies he put into effect. Kaufman's role in the hearings was only to suggest lines of questioning, and he was to leave controversial aspects of the story to committee members. From Short's point of view, Kaufman did more than point the way for the committee; he laid out a minefield. In dealing with several topics, he shaped a series of innocuous questions to elicit affirmative answers then followed with a potentially damaging query if answered in the affirmative.

Typical was his treatment of Short's duties as Hawaiian Department commander. Kaufman asked, "One of the principal duties of the Hawaiian Department was the protection of the fleet when the fleet was in the harbor? . . . And we might summarize the duties of the Hawaiian Department as follows: To protect the island from invasion of any kind, or an attack of any kind? . . . And the installations of the fleet while it was in the harbor? . . . And that particularly including the fuel supply around the harbor?"[29] To each of these questions, and to six more related queries, Short answered in the affirmative. Then Kaufman sprung his trap with the eleventh question in the series: "But with respect to a directive, the commander in the field had the responsibility of determining the manner of performing the directive issued to him?[30]

Short immediately backed away from the cliff edge and pointed his inquisitor in the direction he wanted to go. "Yes, sir; and the War Department also had the responsibility of furnishing him with the information available." This early stage of the Short-Kaufman joust gave committee members and spectators a vivid demonstration of how differently an Army officer and a civilian can view a military situation.[31]

Late in the morning, Kaufman got Short to make a rare criticism of the Navy. Asked why Kimmel did not know the Hawaiian Department was on an antisabotage alert rather than an all-out alert, Short said, "The only way I can account for that would be poor staff work on the part of the staff of the Fourteenth Naval District. . . . We had furnished them with ten copies of our staff operating procedure, which somebody in that naval staff certainly must have dug into and known what it meant. Why it did not get to Admiral Kimmel I do not know."[32]

Minutes later, Kaufman provoked a sharp correction from the witness. Attempting to summarize the basis of Short's defense, Kaufman said, "And your argument throughout your statement is that although in the first instance the error [antisabotage alert] was yours Washington should be partly responsible for not having corrected your error?" Short fired back, "I would say wholly responsible." Seeing he would not shake the general from his position, Kaufman turned to other issues until the chairman declared a recess at noon.[33]

In the afternoon, Kaufman concluded with a few questions about Short's aircraft warning service and his antiaircraft batteries. After some three hours of interrogation, counsel turned the witness over to committee members, who would question by seniority, Democrats first. Chairman Barkley warmed up with a few questions about Short's and Kimmel's assumptions of command in the islands and how they got along. Within minutes he brought the witness to the issue that concerned him most about Hawaiian Department leadership, the interpretation of secret messages from Washington.[34]

Barkley was bothered by Short's reading of the 27 November message, especially the sentence directing the general to "undertake such reconnaissance and other measures as you deem necessary." The chairman read the text of the message then gave his interpretation of it. "This is not a request. It is not an intimation. It is a direction. . . . In general broad terms, that doesn't mean to look out after sabotage, does it?"³⁵ The general, taking refuge in his joint agreement with the Navy and in General Marshall's previous testimony on that document, said, "No, sir; but long distance reconnaissance, by the agreement with the Navy, was definitely a Navy problem, and General Marshall agreed that under that construction all I had to do was to turn over my planes to the Navy if they were called for."³⁶

Short's reliance on documents and the testimony of others only irritated the chairman. Barkley continued hammering on what he saw as the general's insistence on taking minimal action upon receipt of a war warning: "The words are simple, there is no ambiguity about it. . . . Why didn't you in your reply to him say either that you had made the planes available to the Navy or you had not done so and why you had not done it, instead of just saying that you had taken steps against sabotage? . . . Why in your reply to General Marshall did you limit this to sabotage instead of saying something about reconnaissance, which is the only specific thing he mentioned in his direction to you?"³⁷

Short again tried to protect himself with paper. "I was directly obligated by the agreement with the Navy to furnish these planes," he said. "It had been approved by the Chief of Staff and the Chief of Naval Operations and it did not seem to me that it was necessary to reiterate that because they told me that—there was also a provision in that agreement that if the agreement were to be abrogated it would be in writing."³⁸ Barkley was unconvinced. With his prominent jaw jutting directly at the witness, the Kentuckian bored in on another weak spot in Short's armor, his coordination with Marshall in Washington: "Now it seems that after you received this message on the 27th you made no further effort, and so far as the naval end of it is concerned, they made no further effort to ascertain just what it was that Washington had in mind when they gave these instructions about reconnaissance and defensive deployments and all that language that has been used here in this hearing. What have you to say about that? That bothers me, General."³⁹

Short scrambled to regain his footing. For the third time in minutes, he took refuge behind the joint agreement with the Navy: "I believe that Admiral Kimmel felt full responsibility for the reconnaissance; I think he realized that it was his full duty." Just as quickly for the third time, Barkley brushed aside the joint agreement. He suggested the general had ignored Marshall's intent: "This direct instruction to you to institute reconnaissance was just idle words, it didn't mean anything so far as he was concerned, you think?"⁴⁰

Desperate to deflect one of the most skilled interrogators in Congress, Short referred the chairman to what he hoped no one could dispute, the wording of the 27 November message. "You will notice it says, 'Such reconnaissance as you may deem necessary.'" Barkley would have none of it. "No; that is not what it says," he snapped, and he read what he saw as the key part of the same sentence: "You are to take such reconnaissance and other measures." Short gave his honest interpretation of the wording, but the answer conveyed a patronizing tone the general could not have intended: "I think the 'deem necessary' applies to all. I don't think there is any question of it in reference to any part of it."[41]

Short got a welcome breather when Representative Murphy read into the record the general's Pearl Harbor Board testimony on his understanding of Navy reconnaissance. But Barkley soon returned to make clear that he was in no mood for a grammar lesson from the witness. He hammered on the lack of reconnaissance, now focusing on one day. "Do you know why, General, and can you tell the committee why it was that there was no reconnaissance on the 6th of December, the day before the attack?" he asked.[42]

"I believe, it is my impression that Admiral Kimmel was making a considerable reconnaissance," the general answered. Barkley took advantage of the speculation, and Short found himself defending the Navy. Not well qualified to explain Navy doctrine, Short had to make an attempt at it after repeatedly expressing confidence in Kimmel's reconnaissance. He ruminated about air patrols far from Hawaii and concluded by assuring the committee that Kimmel could accomplish more at a distance from Hawaii than he could with the same number of planes closer to the islands.[43] Barkley was unimpressed and threw Short's phrasing right back in his face. "He could accomplish more with the same number of planes if he had had them at the right place at the right time!" To that, Short could say only one word: "Yes."[44]

After his mauling by Barkley, Short needed a rest. But an hour remained before the 4:00 PM adjournment. Both Democratic and Republican members of the committee wanted to finish the investigation without another deadline extension, and with a minimum of evening and weekend sessions, so the chairman turned the witness over to Vice Chairman Jere Cooper. The Tennesseean let Short catch his breath on several easy questions then began probing the same soft spots Barkley had just battered. Continuing the next morning, Cooper criticized Short's response to the "Do-Don't" message but fastened on an aspect other than distant reconnaissance. He noted that Marshall's message writers made no mention of sabotage but that was the threat the general alerted his command against. Short responded that in Hawaii he had no indication of any threat except sabotage, and no one in Washington expected an attack on Pearl Harbor, a backward kind of proof that convinced few in the room. Cooper went on to suggest that Short had misused his radar, even though the system was in-complete, and had failed to maintain adequate liaison with Admiral Kimmel.[45]

Senator George asked few questions, but one was startlingly direct: "Was there ever any dispute about the function of the Navy?" Short answered, "Never. I am sure that they agreed fully."[46] George ended by joining Cooper and Barkley in questioning Short's choice of an antisabotage alert in response to the call for reconnaissance in the 27 November message. Short once again listed the reasons for his decision, a recital much practiced in recent years: that reconnaissance was a Navy responsibility, that General Marshall did not write the 27 November message, and that during the nine days between receipt of that message and the attack the chief of staff did not question the Hawaiian Department's alert status. Apparently not sharing Barkley's taste for skewering the witness on a halting but factual answer, George let the issue lay and yielded to the next in-terrogator.[47]

After nearly a day and a half with the top ranking Democrats on the com-mittee, Short suffered no illusions about the determination of the majority lead-ership to protect the victorious military administration of a deceased president from the charges of a disgraced soldier.

J. Bayard Clark was the first interrogator to introduce conjecture into the questioning. He wanted to know if full use of Army and Navy equipment and manpower after receipt of the 27 November message would have lessened the damage inflicted by the Japanese. Short avoided a direct answer and raised once again his primary defense, now on behalf of both himself and Kimmel. "I think to have made the maximum use of that, and felt justified in making the maximum use of it, we would have had to have something pointing to Hawaii," he replied.[48]

In questioning about other issues, Clark made clear that he liked neither Short's choice of antisabotage alert nor Kimmel's ignorance of it. Zeroing in on the thinking that led to the alert status decision, the North Carolinian got Short to reveal just how strict his interpretation of orders was. The general said his options in response to the 27 November message were limited because of the last sentence, which read, "Disseminate this vitally secret information to the minimum essential officers." He went on to elaborate, "Now, it did not say 'Officers and men.' The minute you ordered either alert No. 2 or alert No. 3 you had to tell every enlisted man that was put in position why he was there, and what he was to shoot at."[49]

More than any other of the hundreds of answers Short gave during four years of investigations, this response showed how out of touch he was with the public that could have understood his anguish and ended his disgrace. Short believed to the depth of his soul that his decision on alert status in 1941 and his explanation of it this day in 1946 were the only logical and ethical responses available to him. To him and virtually every other officer of his generation, orders must be followed to the letter or an officer should resign his commission. But to committee members, a group of ambitious men whose political calling demanded that they bend rules to gain and keep influence, and to the American people, naturally quick to bend rules and disregard authoritative pronouncements, Short's claim that he had no choice but to follow to the letter an order originating thousands of miles away and one which compromised his defenses sounded ludicrous. The general, fiercely proud of his four decades of loyal service to superiors, was incapable of understanding how anyone could consider his decision in 1941 or his answer five years later less than honorable. Tragically for his reputation, Short could not bridge that yawning gap in perception between himself and his fellow Americans.

Clark did not like Short's narrow interpretation of orders, and asked why the general did not ask for clarification of what seemed a needless limitation of a local commander's freedom of action. Short answered that he did not consider it necessary because he understood perfectly what he read in the message as the War Department's priority: "Avoiding any possible international incident that would give Japan an excuse for going to war, or for using propaganda that we had started the war."[50]

Clark soon went on record as the first committee member to suggest a solution to the different interpretations of information and different conditions of alert which grew out of the two-headed command system: unity of command. Short fell back on his main thesis, that more information from Washington to both him and Kimmel would have cleared up misunderstandings everywhere, but then appeared to contradict himself by adding, "However, I will state, on general principles, in the average situation, that I believe unity of command is a much stronger, much safer proposition."[51]

After a question about the hours of operation of radar, Clark ended in a manner that must have surprised his Democratic colleagues, anxious almost to a man to blame the Hawaiian commanders for American unpreparedness. "I want to say before I desist entirely, sir, that I have great respect for you and your honorable record as an officer in the Army. I have some sympathy for you for having gotten into a situation of the kind you encountered at Pearl Harbor. It has been a hard experience for you, sir, and I appreciate the very clear statement you have made to the committee."[52] Relieved at hearing this first expression of understanding for the ordeal he had been through the last four years, Short, with obvious gratitude, responded, "I thank you very much. I tried to be perfectly frank with the committee, and I hope that I have succeeded."[53]

Senator Scott W. Lucas of Illinois opened the afternoon session with a question about what many would consider a natural reaction to being fired and forced to live in national disgrace: "I should like to ask you whether or not you bear any ill will against the former President of the United States, Mr. Roosevelt, as a result of your retirement in December 1941?" Short quickly made clear that there was no room for personal resentment in his character. "I do not," he replied.[54]

Lucas went on to question Short's choice of an antisabotage alert and the effectiveness of Army-Navy liaison. Turning to the behavior of civilians in Hawaii, Lucas uncovered a curious difference of perspective between Hawaiian Department leadership in 1941 and outside observers like himself. The senator asked if Japanese-Americans in Hawaii had ever committed any acts of sabotage because of Army alerts. Short responded that the causation went the other way: "No; you wouldn't get sabotage as a result of an alert. You might get it because you didn't go into an alert."[55]

When this line of questioning led everyone into a maze of conjecture, Lucas turned to the two-headed command arrangement in effect in 1941 and a possible remedy:

> What I am talking about is: Assuming that in 50 years a similar situation occurs, where there is no unity of command, it is still under a joint control system. You told the committee this morning . . . that personalities were involved. That is, two men might get along all right, and two men who followed might not get along all right. If you had one man in command, where you could place all of the responsibility over the Hawaiian Islands and the fleet, would that eliminate what I am talking about here, eliminate the possibility of any confusion or conflicting interests in the future which might be responsible for a similar disaster?[56]

"I believe it would be decidedly helpful," the general answered. "When you put it at 50 years, it is hard to say whether everybody would forget."[57]

Lucas responded with his view of life expectancy—"Suit your own time on that. Most of us won't be around"—giving Barkley the chance to lighten the serious proceedings. "You don't mean that, Senator!" "Yes, I do," answered the Illinoisan with a smile, as a wave of laughter rolled across the cavernous room.[58]

The senator concluded by asking Short to evaluate himself. "Is it your contention now that with all the information available at that time you did all that any prudent commander could do to prevent or minimize such a surprise attack?" Short answered, "I believe I did all that a prudent commander could be expected to do; yes, sir."[59]

Lucas then gave Short the chance to underline his answer: "And you feel that you exercised that superior judgement necessary for one of your rank and position when you knew that war was on its way?" The general replied, "I believe I did."[60]

In his next interrogator, Short found the first committee member not interested in uncovering new evidence about Pearl Harbor. Pennsylvania Democrat John W. Murphy wanted to discredit if not destroy the witness, a purpose he made clear with a combative and sarcastic manner. He began by reading eleven alarmist newspaper headlines published in Honolulu the week before the Japanese attacked, then asked why Short had not attached much importance to them. The general answered that messages from the War Department were much more important than newspaper stories.[61]

After a dead-end exchange about the Japanese allocation of carrier-based and land-based aircraft for the attacks on Hawaii and the Philippines, Murphy turned to the correspondence between Hawaii and Washington in an effort to find gaps between Short's intentions and accomplishments. For his trouble, Murphy found nothing that was not already in the record of this and other investigations: the Aircraft Warning Service was incomplete at the time of the attack; the most likely direction of attack was from the north; antiaircraft batteries did not go into action at the same time; and infantry training for air units was a controversial policy.[62]

In his zeal to find fault with Short, Murphy soon put his foot in his mouth. Showing pictures of damaged hangars, the congressman confused the terms "fire control" and "fire department." Admiral Richardson, several rows behind the witness, laughed loudly enough for Murphy and many others in the room to hear. Short patiently explained that fire control related to the control of artillery fire rather than extinguishing blazes, but Murphy, his anger now obvious, charged ahead and promptly misquoted Short about Kimmel's reconnaissance in the weeks before the attack: "I understood you to say, sir, you expected the Navy to do complete reconnaissance."[63] The general remembered his answer perfectly. "I did not say that."[64]

Murphy offered to read the testimony he was referring to but Barkley noted the late hour, and the committee recessed. The next morning Murphy quoted Short at the Roberts commission—"The question of just how the total reconnaissance was carried out was never known by me"—and it revealed both the error of his interpretation and the tactic of his interrogation. When Short referred to the overall Navy reconnaissance effort, whatever area it covered around Hawaii, he was not saying the Navy was covering every square mile of sea around the islands. But such fine distinctions did not serve Murphy's purpose. He preferred the incriminating inference that Short believed the Navy was conducting a full 360-degree search. Though clearly unsupported by the general's testimony, this interpretation served to introduce Murphy's next tactic. By exaggerating differences of opinion between officials at various levels in 1941, Murphy sought to isolate Short from Washington, from Kimmel and the Navy, even from the two chiefs of his own Hawaiian Department staff.[65]

To complete the isolation of the general, Murphy repeatedly had to make very loose interpretations of testimony. When the congressman crossed the line between misinterpretation and outright falsification in recalling the general's testimony about the one o'clock message that arrived hours after the attack, Short could no longer cooperate. "I think you are misquoting me again," he charged.[66]

Murphy's sarcastic response—"Well, then, General, I guess I had better quote you exactly so that I won't be accused of that after this hearing"— confirmed his partisan purpose and devalued his entire examination. After a testy exchange in which Murphy agreed to quote previous testimony more carefully and Short allowed that the misquoting was probably not intentional, the Pennsylvanian pushed on.[67]

With Vice Chairman Cooper prodding him to finish, Murphy took over an hour to raise more than two dozen issues, some of them two and three times. Desperate to find inconsistencies of wording and nuance with which he could discredit Short's testimony, Murphy read many of the general's earlier statements and answers, then followed each with a question repeated in machine-gun cadence: "Did you make that statement? . . . Is that a fair statement?" Murphy's review of these issues did nothing to lead anyone to a better understanding of the Pearl Harbor tragedy.[68]

If Murphy's purpose in his belligerent examination was to uncover new facts about the attack, or even to paint Short as hopelessly incompetent in Hawaii, he failed completely. All the combative congressman revealed was that he held a different and decidedly jaundiced understanding of Short's policies in

1941, an understanding that owed much to hindsight and reflected a large measure of ignorance. But if his purpose was to deny the Republican side of the committee its fair share of time with the witness, he certainly succeeded. After taking more than four hours for himself, Murphy was leaving less than a day and a half to his Republican colleagues, much less than the two full days the partisan proportions of the committee would lead observers to expect.

ON FRIDAY AFTERNOON, Chairman Barkley turned the questioning over to the Republicans. Leading off for the minority was Owen W. Brewster of Maine, a careful and occasionally critical monitor of the wartime Pearl Harbor inquiries. While Bertrand Gearhart and Frank Keefe had charged in the House of Representatives just days before the joint committee convened that a key witness in naval intelligence had been hounded into a nervous breakdown, Brewster had raised the same cudgel in the Senate, charging that certain Pearl Harbor records had been destroyed and denouncing President Truman's executive order banning public release by the committee of information about the workings of the Magic cryptanalytic system but allowing testimony on the information gained from that system in 1941. Brewster may have gained merit within his party for loyalty, but ultimately his credibility suffered, for the investigation uncovered no evidence of deliberately destroyed documents, and the committee found the executive order protecting Magic to be no obstacle to its work.[69]

Brewster had never accepted the Roberts commission conclusion that all blame for the Pearl Harbor disaster lay with the Army and Navy commanders in Hawaii. With the wartime need to support the national military leadership no longer in effect, he was free to point out the mistakes of Washington officials. His first target was the soldier most Americans had recently come to consider above criticism, Gen. George C. Marshall, wartime chief of staff. Brewster began by giving Short the chance to bring out Marshall's errors in the days before the Japanese attack. Reading Marshall's testimony before the Army Pearl Harbor Board in 1944, Brewster let the general underline one of the bedrock positions on which his whole argument for vindication rested, that Marshall had not expected an air raid on Hawaii, in part because he shared Short's anxiety about the large Japanese-American population in the islands. The senator commented that the chief of staff's faulty analysis in 1941 indicated that "even Jupiter occasionally nods" and went on to cite more testimony from 1944 to show that Marshall did not know the contents of Short's war plans or the details of his defenses against sabotage.[70]

After a discussion among committee members about exhibits policy, Brewster let Short take nearly an hour to read letters and memoranda relating to his abrupt retirement, including documents containing the arcane legalities constructed by Army Judge Advocate General Myron C. Cramer to allow Secretary Stimson to get Short out of uniform and at the same time hold him available indefinitely for court-martial.[71]

No sooner had Short finished than Representative Murphy barged in on Brewster's time to demand of the general whether a court-martial of either himself or Admiral Kimmel in wartime would have served the interest of national security.[72] Short used Murphy's preposterous questioning of his patriotism to appeal to the national audience beyond the hearing room. "I will say that there may have been some justification in that point of view," he said, "but I do not think there was any justification in concealing the many things that were concealed; that the public had a right to know that, and that certainly I had the right to consider that the public should know it."[73]

Alarmed at the direction of the questioning, Barkley moved quickly to cut off Short's attack on off-the-record testimony. "That is a matter about which I think the committee need not spend any more time," he declared. The chairman tried to move the questioning along to Representative Gearhart but Brewster would not be sidelined. He invited Short to make clear in the public record the injustice of his treatment since the Roberts commission issued its hurried judgment: "So it is your impression, General, that the public impressions which were formed as the result of releases here in Washington and the action taken convicted you before the American public on what you term off-the-record testimony?" Short replied, "It is."[74]

Again Barkley moved to contain Brewster, this time by asking Short if he and Kimmel had the right to request courts-martial of their respective services. Short answered in the affirmative but reminded the chairman that both the War and Navy Departments reserved to themselves the power to determine when, if ever, a court-martial would be held.[75]

When the session bogged down in a discussion of legal procedures in the Army and Navy, Murphy again barged in to question Short's patriotism: "In order to have an open court hearing you would insist, during the war, on a public disclosure of the war plans we had drawn for the prosecution of the war?"[76]

"If they insisted on court-martialing me during the war, I wanted the public to know exactly what I was being tried upon," the general answered.[77]

Realizing how damaging Murphy's insinuation could be if not carefully handled, Brewster nudged between the interrogator and the witness to establish that Short's request for an open court-martial posed no threat to national security: "It should be clear in the record also that your waiver gave the War Department 6 months after the conclusion of the war to determine, so that there would be no necessity of the exposure of plans even if they did determine you should be court-martialed."[78]

For the second time Barkley tried to introduce Gearhart, but Short read one more document into the record, this one Stimson's October 1944 demand that in exchange for being allowed to read the proceedings of the Roberts commission and Pearl Harbor Board, the general agree not to disclose without Stimson's permission the contents of those inquiries. Short had refused to go along on that point, and now Murphy wanted to use Short's rejection of what amounted to a gag order to imply once again that the general was willing to compromise national security by revealing top secret information in wartime. But this time, Barkley would not allow further pursuit of the empty insinuation.[79]

Representative Gearhart began by inviting the witness to attack the limitations placed on his constitutional rights as a witness by the Roberts commission, suggesting he had been denied the right to legal counsel. The Republicans would have loved to hear Short say on the record that a Supreme Court justice had denied his right to counsel, but they were disappointed when the general's honesty overruled his self-interest. "That is not correct," he said. "I did not make a request for an attorney. I took them at their word that this was not a trial in any sense. I didn't know they were going to arrive at a finding that practically amounted to a finding of court martial. I felt that I was absolutely not guilty in any sense, and I could handle my own case, and I went before the Roberts Commission with no one assisting me in even handling documents."[80]

Already frustrated by being boxed into the last hour of the session by Barkley, Gearhart scrambled to find an issue that would highlight mistakes made in Washington. He settled on the network of six radar stations planned for Hawaii, only one of which was in operation on 7 December 1941. Gearhart asked if the contract for the fixed radar sites called for their completion before 7 December. Again the general's total lack of guile prevented his exploitation of a crack in the War Department's defense. He said there had been no contract, only a hope, and it had gone unfulfilled not only because the War Department had not sent the radar parts but also because he could not find enough skilled workmen in Hawaii. An exasperated Gearhart tried once more to find a mistake by Washington, this time asking if anyone outside Hawaii had suspended Short's antisabotage alert during the ten days preceding the attack. Short's negative answer closed the issue, and Gearhart surrendered the floor.[81]

Throughout the hearings Barkley had shown as much interest in the testimony his committee invited as in the public reaction to the proceedings. As chairman, his public concern had to be to conduct a thorough and fair investigation. At the same time, his private concern was that no one say his committee had ignored evidence or refused to take seriously any witness, for such a charge could discredit his work and lead to calls for still another Pearl Harbor inquiry. As the hearings progressed, various newspapers kept alive several of the baseless but persistent rumors still circulating since the attack. From time to time Barkley brought up these rumors and tried to use witnesses to refute them. Using Gearhart's question about Short's employment of radar as a lead, Barkley took the last few minutes of this Friday session to deal with the rumor that the young officer who had not passed along the report of approaching Japanese planes had been promoted during the war while the private who had seen the flight on his radar oscilloscope had not been promoted. If this rumor were found to be true, it would lend a measure of credibility to a larger and far more damaging suspicion—that the Roosevelt administration had known of the coming attack and conspired with key personnel to suppress every potential warning to the soldiers and sailors who died on 7 December 1941. Neither Barkley nor any other Democrat in Congress could let survive without challenge any rumor that might confirm in the public mind a conspiracy that could give them trouble at the polls for years.[82]

Despite his earlier rough handling by Barkley, Short helped the chairman kill this particular story by saying that both soldiers had been promoted during the war. Although the promotions were in the public record, the general could have used the rumor to discredit the War Department or at least embarrass the committee majority which was now obviously preparing to give him a major share of blame for the Pearl Harbor disaster. Once again, he declined to take advantage of a turn in the questioning that might have helped him.[83]

Senator Ferguson opened the Saturday morning session, Short's last day in front of the microphone. The senator would take more time than any other Republican and display more skill at examining a witness than anyone on the committee except the chairman. Even more refreshing than his technique was Ferguson's even-handed approach to a witness whom most of the committee,

Congress, and the nation had decided years before to either condemn or exonerate. By the time Ferguson got his time with Short, the committee was so
clearly politicized on the issue of blame for the Pearl Harbor disaster that no
one would have been surprised to see him simply fall in step with the Republican march against the Roosevelt administration. Instead, he carefully sifted
through the evidence one more time, feeling for sharp edges and soft spots
others had missed in the last four years.

Ferguson began with a series of questions about the messages Short had
received from Marshall and others in Washington. His purpose was not so
much to elicit what Short thought of the information Washington had sent him
—the general's strong feelings on that subject were already widely known—
but to condemn the ways the Army and Navy had communicated with their
outposts in 1941. The senator did not like the fact that Marshall's 7 December
warning had not been sent "priority." He was even more critical of the established practice of the Washington headquarters of both services in expecting
clear understanding to emerge from vague language, in particular the assumption that recipients would know which parts of a broadly composed message
would apply to one command but not to another.[84]

After getting his views on these two issues into the record, Ferguson extended his focus beyond messages received in Hawaii to the thinking that pre-
ceded their drafting in Washington. Rather than looking for facts that had not
yet leaped out at anyone poring through the Pearl Harbor documentation, the
senator looked behind policies and decisions in an effort to find the underlying
assumptions so widely held in 1940 and 1941 that no political or military leader
thought it necessary to put them on paper. This approach led Ferguson to
something previous investigators had either missed or not considered worthy
of mention. A strategic contradiction in the thinking of Washington officials
had put the Army and Navy in Hawaii on conflicting rather than cooperative
paths. President Roosevelt had justified his 1940 transfer of the Pacific Fleet
from San Diego to Pearl Harbor as a policy of deterrence. The president believed the Japanese would be less likely to mount aggression in the western
Pacific when they realized the American battle fleet was close enough to carry
out decisive retaliation. To help Tokyo get the message, the presence of the
fleet in Hawaiian waters was to be made obvious to all, with massed warships
riding at anchor in full view of tourists and the Japanese consulate.

But in the case of the Army buildup in Hawaii, visibility was to be avoided.
Repeated admonitions from Washington reminded the Hawaiian Department

leadership to refrain from any display or gesture which might reveal Army strength or appear provocative in the slightest degree to the Japanese. With the Army and Navy in Hawaii operating on opposing strategic postures—visibility for the Navy, secrecy for the Army—Washington officials made virtually impossible both the necessary cooperation between the two services and the intended interpretation of the symbols of deterrence by the Japanese.[85]

Ferguson made clear the contradictory symbolism of deterrence in Hawaii in 1941 but then went further and allowed Short to make a prideful assessment of Hawaiian Department strength on the eve of the attack. "Now, would it have been possible . . . if we had shown a full mobilization of that army, if we had shown that we were on the alert for everything that might come [,] that we would have never had an attack at Pearl Harbor?" the senator asked. "I think it quite probable that if that had been reported to the Japanese, they would have turned back the attacking force," the general answered.[86]

"That would have meant that we would have had no attack at Pearl Harbor?" the senator continued. "Yes, sir," Short answered.[87]

This was an understandable sentiment from the man who had labored effectively for nearly a year to transform his command from an undermanned, underequipped, and isolated outpost into a formidable force, but it was also an exaggeration that did little to strengthen the general's case overall.

Ferguson next gave Short the chance to repeat and elaborate on his charge that the War Department had made him the scapegoat for Pearl Harbor. The senator first wanted to know exactly who Short was pointing to when he referred to the War Department. The general named four officials, three of them in uniform in 1941 and all still receiving high praise for their accomplishments during the war: Generals Marshall, Gerow, and Miles, and Secretary of War Stimson.[88]

Taking up the second element of Short's charge, the senator asked, "Now when you use the word 'scapegoat,' will you give us the meaning that you want to convey to us in that word?" Short replied, "I meant just exactly what the common usage meant, that it was someone that they saddled the blame on to get it off of themselves."[89]

Ferguson went on to skillfully contrast the motives and behavior of the War Department during the war with those of the disgraced general. The senator succeeded in coloring Henry Stimson's War Department in shades of cunning and deceit for not only smearing Short with the damning "dereliction of duty" judgment but also thwarting his efforts to take his case to the national jury through the forum of trial by court-martial, all the while coercing the general into waiving the statute of limitations. "And you have done nothing, as I understand it, to prevent such a trial," the senator asked. "I have not," Short replied.[90]

"You are prepared, then, to defend any trial that the Government may start? Is that the way it stands?"

"That is the way it stands," the general answered.[91]

The senator then turned from a hypothetical trial to the real proceeding under way. "Do you consider that this is a fair hearing for you?" Short gave the committee more praise than it had earned thus far: "I consider that this hearing has been extremely fair, very thorough, and that I have been accorded very great courtesy by the chairman and by every member of the committee."[92]

Ferguson spent more time on the diplomacy preceding the attack than on any other aspect of the Pearl Harbor story, and he did so in such a way as to make Short's responses memorable to those who heard them in the caucus room and to the larger audience who would read them in newspapers the next day. Nine times the senator asked if Short knew of diplomatic notes being exchanged between Washington, London, The Hague, or Tokyo, and nine times the general answered "I did not." In 1941, Short had known nothing of American negotiations with the British and Dutch, intercepted messages between Tokyo and Berlin, American messages to the Japanese, British and Dutch alerts to their forces in the Pacific, and nothing of the British sighting of Japanese forces landing on the Kra Peninsula.[93]

The senator's general agreement with the thrust of Short's defense, that he was denied important information by Washington authorities, did not signal his approval of all the general's decisions in the months before the attack. Ferguson held nothing back in criticizing Lt. Kermit A. Tyler, the officer who received from the Opana radar site the report of a large number of aircraft, for not reporting the direction of approach and for making no attempt to determine the identity of the aircraft. The first error caused the Navy to search for the Japanese task force south of the islands instead of to the north, and the second allowed the attackers to preserve complete surprise. Ferguson could not believe that after making "these fatal errors," Tyler was promoted three times during the war. Short gave a feeble answer, alternating between an apology for a sincere but inexperienced young officer and an explanation of the limitations of radar in 1941. Unimpressed, Ferguson went on to ask twice in only a few minutes the question the general had come to hate more than any other in the last four years: Were the Army and Navy "asleep at the switch" when the Japanese attacked? Once again the general gave his well-practiced answer about insufficient information from Washington.[94]

Throughout his examination of Short, Ferguson took care to allow his witness the chance to comment on questionable conduct by key officials toward the Hawaiian Department in 1941 and by those involved in the various investigations of the Pearl Harbor attack. The senator found some very curious maneuvering by the War Department in a wartime inquiry known as the Clausen Investigation, a one man effort suggested by the Army judge advocate general and approved by Secretary Stimson. After reading the Army Pearl Harbor Board report, Stimson had sent Maj. Henry C. Clausen to all theaters of war to collect information beyond that taken by the Board, information supportive of War Department actions before the Pearl Harbor attack but damaging to Short. Over a ten-month period, Clausen interviewed ninety-two people, most of them Army officers. Short was well aware of Clausen's purpose, to help Stimson smear him in a possible postwar court-martial, but had said almost nothing about Clausen's work in previous investigations. Now Ferguson invited the general to condemn Clausen and his sponsors at the top of the War Department. "Do you know why the Clausen investigation was undertaken?"[95]

"I think that there is an explanation of that. You have to read between the lines," the general said.

Ferguson was not going to let this opportunity pass. "Well, will you read between the lines for us and give us that explanation?"[96]

Short explained that if a reviewing authority, Secretary Stimson in the case of the Army Pearl Harbor Board, did not agree with the findings of the inquiry, he should direct the panel to collect more evidence and reconsider its findings. Instead, Stimson had dissolved the board and then, on the recommendation of General Cramer, detailed the juniormost member of the board staff—Clausen had served as assistant recorder—to, in effect, correct the work of the board. This revelation was necessary to both the committee and the public, since few persons outside the Judge Advocate General's Corps understood the procedural differences between military inquiries, boards, and courts-martial. But Short nullified any benefit this line of inquiry might yield to him when he declined to add to his criticism of procedure a condemnation of the personalities involved. Inexplicably, he let pass the opportunity to blast Stimson, Cramer, or Clausen, although less than an hour earlier he had shown no reluctance to lambaste Stimson, Marshall, and Gerow for scapegoating him.[97]

Ferguson again tried to get Short to censure Stimson, Cramer, and Clausen by asking what the public should read between the lines. This time the general sounded like he was on the way to a specific denunciation. "And they apparently did not believe there they could get what they wanted out of the Army board, so reading between the lines." Before Short could say one more word, the irrepressible Congressman Murphy jumped in to ask that the complete record involving Clausen's investigation be entered into the record. Unwilling to waste any more time in a tussle with Murphy, Ferguson moved along to other issues.[98]

The climactic point of Ferguson's time with Short came when the senator turned to a consideration of Secretary Stimson's actions following release of the Roberts commission report. Immediately after the secretary's press release of 28 February 1942 announcing Short's retirement, the Army Judge Advocate General's office drew up a list of eleven charges on which a future court-martial of the general could be based. This document gives the clearest indication of what the War Department planned to do with Short if Senator Ferguson and other members of Congress had not pressed for a full investigation outside the confines of the military justice system and wartime restrictions on information.

All eleven charges on the list began with the word "failure," and, viewed in its entirety, the list included enough specifics to reinforce the conviction of many Americans that some kind of punitive action was warranted and, at the same time, enough generalities to make it very difficult, if not impossible, for Short to convincingly rebut every specification and implication. Four of the charges were open to interpretation, even among military specialists: "Failure to provide an adequate inshore patrol; . . . to provide an adequate anti-aircraft defense; . . . to establish a proper system of defense by cooperation and coordination with the Navy; . . . to take adequate measures to protect the Fleet and Naval Base at Pearl Harbor." Whether or not Short's policies on these issues were "adequate" or "proper" will remain topics of debate as long as the Pearl Harbor story is discussed. Before the attack, however, no one in a position to review Short's policies recommended any changes.[99]

The remaining seven charges were simply not supported by evidence presented at the series of investigations:

Failure to set up an Interceptor Command; . . . to provide a proper aircraft warning service; . . . to provide for the transmission of appropriate warnings to interested agencies; . . . to issue adequate orders to his subordinates as to their duties in case of sudden attack; . . . to provide for the protection of military personnel, their families, etc., and of civilian employees on various reservations; . . . to have his airplanes dispersed in anticipation of a hostile attack, after having been warned of the danger thereof; . . . to have his airplanes in a state of readiness for an attack.

As his correspondence and reports to General Marshall and others in the War Department clearly indicated, Short had organized an interceptor command and an aircraft warning service, had established procedures on the transmission of warnings and orders inside and outside his command, and had provided for the protection, support, and medical care of military dependents and civilians in the event of attack. All documentation reporting these activities and policies was available to both the Roberts commission and Secretary Stimson before this list of charges was drawn. Finally, Hawaiian Department aircraft were neither dispersed nor armed because Short had not received sufficient warning to justify such preparations. Curiously, the list did not include one of the few lapses the general had never tried to dispute, the failure to store ammunition at, or at least closer to, antiaircraft gun positions.[100]

Ferguson read each of the eleven charges and asked the general how he would plead if a court-martial were based on them. To each, Short replied with two words: "Not guilty."[101]

The senator ended his examination by saying he did not want the record to show that he had questioned the witness as much as he wanted. "I did the best I could," he said.

"You made a pretty good stab at it," Barkley teased.[102]

Finally, in the last hour of the last day of a grueling week, the committee reached the last Republican, Frank B. Keefe of Wisconsin. The juniormost member was not happy with his tail-end position and fired a sarcastic broadside at his colleagues. "It is always a great pleasure to find myself at the end of this whip cracking and get thrown off into the last minute of the last hour of Saturday afternoon with witnesses, so that I am under the urge, of necessity, of not consuming any time in trying to complete with the witnesses."[103]

Keefe started gently, letting Short restate many of his already well-known positions. Suddenly, however, he turned away from the course set by his Republican colleagues to question the core of Short's argument, the general's conviction that Washington had denied him sufficient men, weapons, equipment, funding, and information to mount an effective defense. Keefe suggested that the best result Short could have hoped for even if he had had all the resources he had requested in 1941 was to minimize the effect of the Japanese attack. Short agreed.[104]

From there, however, Keefe went on to make a far more damaging assertion: "Well, you could have done a pretty good job with the stuff you had out there if you had been on the alert and had been expecting an attack."[105]

Well aware of the damage he would suffer both in Congress and among the public if he ended his week before the committee by arguing with members inclined to support him, Short quietly agreed with the congressman. Fortunately for the general, Keefe ended his questioning on a more helpful note. "Now, your position in this case is that Intelligence, so far as Washington was concerned, failed?" "A hundred percent," the general answered.[106]

After several additional questions from members seeking to clarify points of testimony, Barkley asked Short if he would like to add anything not already brought out by the committee. The general then explained publicly for the first time the values that had guided his Army career for over four decades and reminded the committee of the penalty he had paid in recent years for holding those values: "As a loyal soldier, I maintained a steadfast silence for 4 years and I bore the load of public censure during this time and I would have continued to bear it so long as I thought the question of national security was involved."[107]

Short went on to thank the committee "for the attitude that they have taken," and he assured them he had tried to give a complete and frank explanation of his views. Chairman Barkley thanked Short for his cooperation, and added his hope that the general would soon recover his health. The general slowly rose and made his way out of the crowded room through scattered applause.[108]

9

Vindication Deferred

THE JOINT COMMITTEE PUBLISHED ITS RE-
PORT IN JULY 1946, AFTER TAKING SOME 15,000 pages of testimony and 183
exhibits during the examination of forty-three witnesses. The recording of testimony and preparation of conclusions and recommendations took over eight
months. Nearly 600 printed pages in length, the document includes the majority report of over 250 pages in addition to appendices of supporting documents
of about the same length, as well as 23 pages of "Additional Views of Mr. Keefe"
and a minority report of 86 pages by Senators Brewster and Ferguson.[1]

In the foreword to their report, Chairman Barkley and his colleagues fixed
overall responsibility for the Pearl Harbor attack and set forth their purposes:

> The Pyrrhic victory of having executed the attack with surprise, cunning,
> and deceit belongs to the war lords of Japan whose dreams of conquest
> were buried in the ashes of Hiroshima and Nagasaki. . . . We come today,
> over 4 years after the event, not to detract from this responsibility but to
> record for posterity the facts of the disaster. In another sense we seek to
> find lessons to avoid pitfalls in the future, to evolve constructive suggestions
> for the protection of our national security and to determine whether there
> were failures in our own military and naval establishments which in any
> measure may have contributed to the extent and intensity of the disaster.[2]

The first part of the report dealt with the diplomatic background of the attack. The major question raised in this and several previous investigations was whether the United States had in any way provoked Japan to attack Pearl Harbor. The committee found that American diplomacy during 1941 "epitomizes the traditional purpose of the United States to seek peace where compatible with national honor." The committee judged Secretary of State Cordell Hull's note of 26 November 1941, a document alleged to have provoked the Japanese, "an admirable statement of every honorable principle for which the United States has stood for many years in the Orient." Chairman Barkley and his colleagues found the Japanese guilty of whatever provocation marred Pacific diplomacy in 1941. Of Tokyo's 20 November proposal calling for an end to the oil embargo imposed in response to the Japanese occupation of Indochina and an end to American support of Nationalist China against Japanese aggression, the committee wrote, "There can now be no question that Japan intended her proposal of November 20 as an ultimatum."[3]

The second part of the report presented a narrative of the attack, including as much information on Japanese planning as was then available and the costs to both sides. While praising the Japanese for the skill of their attack, the committee judged that Army and Navy forces in Hawaii should have been capable of inflicting severe damage on the Japanese raiders and repelling the attack to a degree: "The disaster of Pearl Harbor lies in the failure of the Army and Navy in Hawaii to make their fight with the equipment at hand—it was not that they had no equipment, for they did, but that they did not utilize what they had."[4]

The third part of the report assigned responsibilities in Hawaii. The committee found enough mistakes that neither Short nor Kimmel could attribute the success of the Japanese solely to a dearth of information from Washington. Short was praised for diligently training and preparing the Hawaiian Department for war. At the same time, the committee found a major flaw in the general's strategic concept of outpost defense which, in turn, caused him to make a number of tactical mistakes as the situation in the Pacific deteriorated. He was criticized for expecting the Navy to warn him of an enemy force approaching Hawaii. This reliance contributed to the general's misreading of the 27 November warning message. The committee decided that Short made seven errors upon receipt of that message: instituting an alert against sabotage only, giving his training program a higher priority than security, not conducting reconnaissance, not training his radar officers to interpret information from the radar sites, not operating his radar on a twenty-four-hour basis, not shortening the four-hour alert status of aircraft, and not placing antiaircraft ammunition closer to mobile gun sites.[5]

However, in making its case against Short's post-warning actions, the committee overreached the evidence when it concluded that the 27 November message constituted an "adequate" warning of the imminence of war rather than the confusing "Do-Don't" set of instructions that Short struggled to interpret. The fact that the general could have based any of his three alerts on the message is just as clear as the contradictory nature of Secretary Stimson's wordsmithing. The 27 November message stands as a model of how not to compose a warning to a commander facing a poised enemy.[6]

Both Short and Kimmel were censured for their inadequate liaison in 1941. The committee found that they had developed "a cordial and cooperative relationship" but had neglected to share important information and confer on appropriate joint actions at several critical junctures. Kimmel was specifically cited for failure to share with Short information on the destruction of Japanese codes and documents on four occasions between 3 and 6 December, and to report the sinking of a Japanese submarine the morning of the attack. Short did not pass along to the Navy the radar sighting of a large number of approaching aircraft before the attack or the direction of withdrawal of Japanese planes afterward. Both commanders were criticized for failing to keep each other informed as to the content of their various alerts. This lapse accounted for the assumption by Kimmel that the Army had only one type of alert, as did Short's predecessor. In fact, both the Army and Navy in Hawaii had progressive systems of alert status, but the fact that the two services' alerts were numbered in opposite sequence —No. 1 was the highest state of alert to the Navy but the lowest to the Army— indicated an even more extensive lack of liaison. The committee also found liaison problems at lower levels of each command. The air commanders in Hawaii, General Martin and Admiral Bellinger, were criticized for not discussing in the ten days before the attack an effective distant reconnaissance to guard against the approach of enemy ships and aircraft, although earlier in the year they had authored a report which predicted in startling detail the air attack as it occurred.[7]

The committee's search for the causes of these lapses in liaison did not stop at personalities or administrative procedures. The entire arrangement of command by mutual cooperation and its implied protocol that commanders should not even ask counterparts what they were doing because such a query might arouse resentment was the target of special contempt. While such concern for the sensibilities of another may have social propriety, it is completely out of place when designed to control the relationship of two outpost commanders whose very existence is dependent upon full exchange of information and coordination of effort. It defeats the purpose of command by mutual cooperation and is worse than no liaison at all.[8]

Short and Kimmel were praised for mastering the technical aspects of their responsibilities and bringing their commands to high states of training and readiness. They were "conscientious and indefatigable commanders . . . relentless in what they regarded as the consuming need in their commands—training and preparation for war." But both were faulted for missing a number of danger signals as tension in the Pacific built through the summer and fall of 1941. The committee was especially aroused by the suspiciously worded telephone call from a Japanese reporter in Tokyo to a Mrs. Mori in Honolulu. According to the committee, the *"Mori call pointed directly at Hawaii."* The bureaucratic treatment of danger signals like the Mori call—the Fourteenth Naval District Intelligence Office put the transcript aside for further study at an unspecified time—combined with inadequate liaison caused the failure by both services to detect a hostile force and then to put into effect a state of readiness least designed to meet the onslaught. That the responsible commanders were surprised that Japan struck Hawaii is understandable; that they should have failed to prepare their defenses against such a surprise is not understandable.[9]

This third part of the report contained the single most damaging conclusion to Short as well as to Kimmel. The committee majority rejected the bedrock conviction of the two officers that Washington officials had withheld from them the information they needed to build and maintain effective defenses in Hawaii. That Admiral Kimmel and General Short were supplied enough information as reasonably to justify the expectation that Hawaiian defenses would be alerted to any military contingency is irrefutable. That there may have been other information which could have been supplied them cannot becloud or modify this conclusion.[10]

The fourth part of the report assigned responsibilities in Washington. In this, the longest of the five parts, the committee majority came closest to producing the whitewash feared by Republicans. Employing a breezy analysis that leaped gazelle-like over hill-masses of evidence, Chairman Barkley and the majority approved the president's decision to move the Pacific Fleet from San Diego to Pearl Harbor in the summer of 1940, agreed with Secretary of War Stimson and General Marshall that Hawaii was "the best equipped of our outposts" despite repeated messages from both Short and Kimmel concerning deficiencies, approved the transfer of one-quarter of the Pacific Fleet to the Atlantic in the spring of 1941, praised the Roosevelt administration for making every effort "compatible with national honor to forestall the inevitable conflict with Japan," judged reasonable the policy of not sending Magic intercepts to Army and Navy commanders in Hawaii, concluded that no Japanese "winds" code execute message was intercepted prior to the attack, found the 27 November message an accurate description of the status of diplomatic negotiations rather than a jumble of "Do-Don't" contradictions, praised General Marshall for appreciating the significance of the one o'clock message of 7 December but criticized no one for the "extremely regrettable" delay in its dispatch to Hawaii, and pronounced "the complete inadequacy of command by mutual cooperation where decisive action is of the essence."[11]

The committee majority charged Washington officials with only four mistakes. To each charge, however, the report added a qualifying condition or speculation which diluted the judgment. First, and despite a mountain of correspondence to the contrary from Short, the committee found that the only piece of equipment or weapon system the Hawaiian Department lacked in the months before the attack was enough long-range aircraft to conduct a 360-degree reconnaissance around the islands. The committee then plunged into the swamp of surmise: "It is necessarily speculative as to how additional equipment in Hawaii might have altered the situation on December 7." Second, the "bomb plot" intercept, which detailed Japanese interest in the locations of ships in Pearl Harbor, should have been sent to Short and Kimmel. The committee then added the surprising observation that it could see no connection between the intercept and an imminent attack. Third, the committee majority faulted General Gerow and his War Plans Division for "slipshod supervision" in not following up on Short's terse response to the 27 November warning. The report then relieved Gerow of lasting blame by pointing to the organization chart: "The primary responsibility, however, rests with the appropriate subordinates of General Gerow who had the duty and responsibility for supervision of details." Finally, the committee found that the War and Navy Departments were not sufficiently alerted for receipt of Japan's fourteen-part reply to the Hull Note. The committee then noted that the Japanese reply contained nothing that justified additional outpost warnings.[12]

During the more than four years since the attack on Pearl Harbor, General Short and Admiral Kimmel consistently charged that Washington officials had withheld critical information from Hawaii in 1941. After briefly addressing this allegation, the committee simply excused every official in Washington. In discussing the code-destruction information which Short never received, the committee blithely observed that the general had received "substantially the equivalent of this information," although not from the War Department. To prevent readers of the report from concluding that the War Department deserved criticism for this lapse, the committee noted that under the principle of command by mutual cooperation, Secretary Stimson and General Marshall "were properly privileged to take for granted that there was a full exchange of information between the Army and Navy commanders, particularly after General Short had specifically stated in his reply to the Department's warning of November 27 that he had established *liaison with the Navy*."[13]

Apparently not satisfied to leave in the public mind the mere suspicion of bias in the reading of evidence, the committee sealed the issue by observing that to prevent recurrences of the neglect of which the War Department was not guilty, "the intelligence as well as the departmental appraisal and estimate thereof should be supplied field commanders."[14]

In analyzing these and other instances of withheld information, the committee decided, in effect, that since no one can say for sure what the commanders in Hawaii would have done with information they did not receive, withholding it from them did no damage: "It is problematical as to what steps would have been taken by the Hawaiian commanders had they received all of the intelligence which they contend was withheld from them."[15]

Despite the title of this part of the report—"Responsibilities in Washington" —the committee managed to conclude by repeating its earlier criticism of Short and Kimmel, this time in even sharper terms. They failed to defend the fortress they commanded; their citadel was taken by surprise. Aside from any responsibilities that may appear to rest in Washington, the ultimate and direct responsibility for failure to engage the Japanese on the morning of 7 December with every weapon at their disposal rests essentially and properly with the Army and Navy commands in Hawaii whose duty it was to meet the enemy against which they had been warned.[16]

In the last part of the report, the committee majority presented its conclusions and recommendations. The committee explained the Pearl Harbor disaster in terms of twelve conclusions. Summarized, these meant Japan was guilty of aggression; no civilian official of the United States government had in any way provoked the Japanese; the disaster resulted from the failure of the Army and Navy to detect, and use all available means to repel, the enemy; and the intelligence agencies of the Army and Navy failed to appreciate key information and supply it to the Hawaiian outpost. Without naming the obvious targets—writers of the report preferred the collective term "Hawaiian commands"—the committee found Short and Kimmel guilty of "errors of judgement and not dereliction of duty."[17]

Just as important as finding out what happened on 7 December 1941 was suggesting policies to prevent a recurrence. The committee made five policy recommendations. Two dealt with administrative procedures: the institution of unity of command at all outposts, and renewed consideration of twenty-five supervisory and organizational principles violated by both Washington officials and the Hawaiian commanders in the year preceding the attack. A third recommendation called for reexamination of statutes that might assist an enemy, such as those prohibiting peacetime interception of communications but allowing the photographing and mapping of military bases. A fourth item called for further investigation of possible criminal activity in the procurement of construction materials by engineers in Hawaii before the attack.[18]

The committee's major recommendation concerned the handling of intelligence, the very same activity which had raised so many questions in previous investigations: "That there be a complete integration of Army and Navy intelligence agencies in order to avoid the pitfalls of divided responsibility which experience has made so abundantly apparent." To make such an integration effective, a number of attitudinal and organizational changes were necessary, including the selection of officers and men with the interest and aptitude for intelligence work, keeping selectees in positions for extended periods, and ending the stigma attached to intelligence work with more frequent promotions.[19]

Considering the acrimony preceding the opening of the hearings and the partisan exchanges marring the sessions, unanimity among the six Democrats and four Republicans on the causes of the nation's most spectacular military defeat could hardly be expected. Nevertheless, the signing of the report by eight of the ten members indicated a higher degree of bipartisan support than many observers foresaw. But the majority's strong censure of the Hawaiian commanders raised substantial objections from three members. Although he signed the majority report, Representative Keefe appended "Additional Views" to correct the imbalance he saw in its findings. "I feel that facts have been martialed, perhaps unintentionally, with the idea of conferring blame upon Hawaii and minimizing the blame that should properly be assessed at Washington," he noted.[20]

Keefe specifically faulted Stark and Marshall for not promptly sharing with their subordinates in Hawaii information they had on the evening of 6 December 1941 and early the next morning. This information included Japan's fourteen-part reply to the Hull Note and the one o'clock message delivered to Short hours after the attack. Keefe dismissed all wartime investigations and witnesses who contradicted sworn testimony: "The record of the high military and civilian officials of the War and Navy Departments in dealing with the Pearl Harbor disaster from beginning to end does them no credit." He also faulted the congressional investigation just concluded for refusing to consider "much vital information" and named six former officials who either gave only limited testimony or were not called by the committee, including Cordell Hull and Henry Stimson. The congressman went on to attack secret diplomacy, which he believed to be a root cause of the disaster, and to denounce President Truman's opinion that the entire nation should take the blame for the Pearl Harbor tragedy.[21]

In a second minority report, Senators Brewster and Ferguson laid out more paperwork in concluding, like Keefe, that the Democratic majority had excused too many mistakes by Washington officials and Truman's verdict of national guilt was insupportable. In a list of twenty-one "Conclusions of Fact and Responsibility," the senators charged Washington officials with failure to intercept Japanese intentions, to send sufficient information and clear warnings to outpost commanders promptly, and to equip and coordinate outpost defenses. The two senators concurred with the majority view that Short and Kimmel had failed to defend the Hawaiian coastal frontier and the Pacific Fleet, but found extenuating circumstances for that breakdown in the larger failure of Washington officials to discharge their responsibilities.[22]

Brewster and Ferguson came down especially hard on President Roosevelt. In their view, the late commander in chief "was responsible for the failure to enforce continuous, efficient, and appropriate cooperation among the Secretary of War, the Secretary of the Navy, the Chief of Staff, and the Chief of Naval Operations" in their supervision of the Hawaiian commanders. And during the last twelve hours of peace in Hawaii, the "President of the United States failed to take that quick and instant executive action which was required by the occasion and by the responsibility for watchfulness and guardianship rightly associated in law and practice with his high office from the establishment of the Republic to our own times."[23] But the senators stretched the evidence when they judged that the president and secretary of state had enough information in their possession to lead them to conclude "at least 10 days before December 7 that an attack by Japan within a few days was so highly probable as to constitute a certainty."[24]

Although clearly more helpful to Short's campaign for vindication than the majority report, Keefe's additional views and the Brewster/Ferguson minority report could not carry the same impact. By their very nature, minority views can do no more than plant seeds of doubt which, only in the most favorable circumstances, might call forth demands for another investigation. In 1946, no such circumstances were in sight, for the Congress was under increasing pressure to devote its full attention to a long list of urgent postwar problems.

In its report, the committee majority showed a strong interest in finding out what went wrong at Pearl Harbor. Just as obvious to readers, however, was the majority's reluctance to list individuals responsible for the disaster. Only General Short and Admiral Kimmel had to bear individualized blame. While concluding that some mistakes were made in Washington, the committee wanted very definitely to leave a record which showed that the really serious blunders were made in Hawaii. Thus, the lasting effect of the joint congressional investigation has been to underline the impact of the Roberts commission, the least credible of all official investigations, and its conclusion that more blame belonged in Hawaii than Washington.

For Walter Short, the congressional investigation amounted to another, and probably final, official rejection. In confirming several charges of earlier investigations, the committee made clear it would not offer him anything near the vindication he had sought for more than four years. After the exhaustive hearings, Short found only one small measure of exoneration. Senator Barkley and his colleagues specifically rejected the Roberts commission charge that the general was guilty of dereliction of duty. But the committee did so in such a way as to make virtually impossible another investigation. After taking eight months to fill twenty-one volumes with testimony and exhibits, the committee was virtually immune from the charge of wartime expediency that had fatally qualified the work of previous inquiries. If the general now requested still another hearing, he could expect little sympathy from the public and none from Congress.

To Short's dismay, the committee had shown more interest in the system of gathering, interpreting, and disseminating information in 1941 than in the conduct of individuals working within that system. Committee members felt that the systemic breakdowns it identified could be corrected more effectively by organizational reforms than by censure of the Washington officials Short blamed for his lack of information. Although deeply disappointed, the general would have to live with the majority's verdict, and he admitted as much when the committee report was published. Declaring the victory denied him in Washington, Short told reporters in Dallas, "I am satisfied that the testimony presented at the hearings fully absolved me from any blame and I believe such will be the verdict of history. As I have stated before, my conscience is clear."[25]

For the nation, the joint committee report set in motion reforms that made the armed services more effective agents of American military policy. One year after release of the report, Congress passed and the president signed the National Defense Act of 1947. This extensive reorganization of the military establishment brought into being several new agencies, military and civilian. A Cabinet-level Department of Defense combined the former War and Navy Departments and a separate Air Force. This unification of the nation's armed forces put the perennial problem of interservice rivalry on the way toward lasting solution. Another new agency addressed the problem of information gathering, interpretation, and dissemination. A Central Intelligence Agency would provide analyses and estimates to the new National Security Council, appointed and chaired by the president, as well as to the Joint Chiefs of Staff and the Defense and State Departments. If the Central Intelligence Agency functioned as planned, no commander would ever again have to interpret a "Do-Don't" message.

WHILE HIS COUNTRYMEN left Pearl Harbor behind and turned to the postwar world, Walter Short resumed the quiet rhythms of retirement. He lived each day with the same disciplined regularity of his Army career but instead of presiding over staff meetings and field maneuvers, he took walks around the neighborhood, played golf, and tended his fruit trees. The Shorts hosted a steady stream of visitors and dinner party guests, both old Army friends and new acquaintances in Dallas. When not overseeing an evening's entertainment, Isabel took them both back to a happier time with her piano playing and singing of Tin Pan Alley hits. Two months after the congressional committee released its report, the Shorts learned that one of the most joyous experiences of retirement would soon be theirs. Dean notified his parents that they were about to become grandparents. In April 1947, the Shorts' first grandchild, Emily Harrison Short, was born in West Berlin, her father's Army posting at the time.[26]

In the summer of 1948, the general learned of a new law that allowed Army officers a retirement promotion to the highest temporary grade in which they had served "satisfactorily" for at least six months during World War II. The Army and Air Force Vitalization and Retirement Equalization Act of 1948 extended to retirees of those two services the same right granted retirees of the Navy, Marine Corps, and Coast Guard two years earlier. Since Short had held the temporary rank of lieutenant general for more than ten months in Hawaii, he applied for the administrative promotion in December. His application provoked extensive research into the massive record of the Pearl Harbor investigations and memo writing by the staff of the Army Judge Advocate General's office. The JAG staff concluded, as the record made clear, that Short's tenure in Hawaii had fulfilled the statutory definition of satisfactory service. Army lawyers also showed a keen awareness of both the interservice sensitivity still alive after the unification of the armed services and the possibility that a political firestorm would engulf the Army and the Truman administration if an agency of the government made any gesture, such as promotion, that could be interpreted as a reward for a leading role in an event that took the lives of more than twenty-four hundred Americans. Of the hundreds of applications in response to this new promotion policy, only Short's carried explosive potential for the military establishment and the White House. As one staff officer wrote, "To advance General Short on the retired list will in all probability cause adverse comments from many sources and may be considered by some to have political implications. It may also place the Secretary of the Navy and the President in an embarrassing position in regard to Admiral Kimmel's advancement. I therefore consider it advisable for the Secretary of the Army, in the event he determines General Short is eligible for advancement on the retired list, to consult the Secretary of the Navy, the Secretary of Defense and the President, informing them of his proposed action."[27]

Short never received a definite answer to his application for promotion, nor did he ever read the memos relating to it. But Gen. Omar Nelson Bradley, the Army chief of staff, read all the memos, and then told an aide what to write on the bottom of the last: "Noted—C/S [chief of staff] U.S. Army—*No action to be taken*."[28]

The activities Walter and Isabel found to vary their retirement routine could not block from the general's thinking the Pearl Harbor attack, the cataclysmic event of his career, and the source of the public scorn he now had to live with. Over and over the questions came to him: What more could I have done to get ready for an attack? Why did Marshall not send the one o'clock message by the fastest method? Why would the Army not convene a real court-martial where I could present all the evidence instead of a series of political show trials? The impossibility of finding answers only made the questioning more painful.

Surprisingly, Pearl Harbor was not a forbidden topic of conversation in the Short home. When he discussed it with his wife, he heard stronger advice than others dared give: set aside loyalty to the Army and mount an aggressive defense with the assistance of civilian attorneys and journalists. The general also would discuss the disaster with anyone outside the family who expressed serious interest. He even asked the views of one of the students he hired to tend the lawn and run errands, Benjamin Purdy. Taking a worn message book out of a drawer, he would invite the young man to pull two large wicker chairs up to a marble-top table, then lay out the series of critical messages he had received in the fall of 1941. The "Do-Don't" message of 27 November still provoked him. "Now look here, Purdy," the general would say, pointing to the radiogram. "Marshall says I should do this but not that . . . do this but not that. What do you make of these instructions? . . . And look at this one that came the next day."[29]

Whoever read the messages agreed they were confusing. But the agreement Short won in these awkward sessions did nothing to relieve the deep pain he felt that none of the colleagues and long-term friends who had composed such messages and who had found excuses for not sending him the latest weapons and equipment in 1941, especially Marshall, came to his defense when the Army and the nation blamed him for unpreparedness.

In the spring of 1949, Short was given the chance to influence his reputation in history. Several months after the surrender of Japan, the Army brought together a group of civilian historians to begin the massive task of writing the history of the U.S. Army in World War II. By early 1949, a manuscript covering developments preceding the Pearl Harbor attack was completed and circulated for comment from persons having direct knowledge of events described. The Historical Division of the Army Special Staff sent Short a chapter dealing with the situation in the Pacific and the Hawaiian Department in 1941. In a detailed reply, Short recommended six changes to the manuscript, most relating to the information he had received, or not received. He made clear his desire that historians for the present and readers for all time understand that he had received none of the Magic intercepts during his time in Hawaii, and that on the day of the attack the one o'clock message from Marshall arrived too late—seven hours after the attack—to be of use. The author of the chapter, Mark S. Watson, was impressed enough by Short's objectivity in dealing with the event that ruined his career to accept five of the general's recommendations, most dealing with the information situation in 1941. But on the sixth point, Short's choice of the antisabotage alert, Watson held to his conclusions that Short's concern about sabotage had been "exaggerated," and that his brief response to the 27 November message—"Report Department alerted to prevent sabotage. Liaison with the Navy"—was "patently inadequate." The manuscript was published the following year as "The War Reaches America," chapter 15 of the *Chief of Staff: Prewar Plans and Preparations* volume.[30]

In the eighth year after the Pearl Harbor attack, the general's declining health became the dominant force in his life. With his emphysema worsening and his heart weakening, the twice weekly golf outings he loved became less frequent, and he began leaving the course after playing fewer holes. Daily walks around the neighborhood after breakfast became weekly, then stopped altogether. When the general began to need assistance with his meals and dressing, the Shorts asked the student they hired, Ben Purdy, to move from the garage apartment into the house. Isabel continued entertaining occasionally, but as the months wore on, her husband tired earlier in the evenings and had to ask for help upstairs to bed. His last outdoors activity was being driven through the Southern Methodist University campus by young Ben. To help his breathing in the heat of a Texas summer, Isabel had an air conditioner installed in her husband's upstairs window. But soon breathing became more difficult, and an oxygen tent was placed over his bed. In late August, the general began to lose strength rapidly, and Isabel called son Dean home from his teaching post at West Point. The end came at 9:32 Saturday evening, 3 September 1949, with his wife and son at Short's bedside.[31]

Dean notified the Defense Department of his father's death, called friends in the Dallas area, and requested interment in Arlington National Cemetery. Sparkman-Brand funeral home dressed the general in the uniform he had worn on his last day of active duty over seven years before. On Sunday, while two reporters and a photographer watched, porters placed the casket on a train, and Dean and his mother began the long ride to Washington.[32]

In the capital, Mrs. Short turned her husband's remains over to Arlington National Cemetery officials and completed arrangements for the funeral, scheduled for Wednesday, 7 September. Dean Short reached for a telephone and reopened an issue Army leaders did not want to be reminded of, his father's application for promotion to lieutenant general on the retired list. The application had gone unanswered for nearly a year. He called anyone he thought could help, anyone familiar with the upper reaches of the Department of the Army. On Wednesday morning, the day of his father's funeral, he was still trying. Finally, at noon, an operator put him through to the general officer branch of the office of the deputy chief of staff for personnel and administration. Lt. Col. Robert L. May answered and listened as Dean raised the promotion issue. May expressed condolences on the death of General Short, then reached for more rank. Brig. Gen. James E. Moore, secretary of the Army general staff, came on the line and explained that the chief of staff, Gen. J. Lawton Collins, had personally considered the matter and decided to take no action. Dean then asked that Moore bring the matter to the personal attention of Secretary of the Army Gordon Gray before his father's funeral, scheduled for that afternoon at three o'clock. Moore called the secretary's office and was told that Mr. Gray had left the office at noon and would not return until the next day. May called Dean Short back and told him he had missed the secretary by half an hour.[33]

Dean swallowed his disappointment, straightened his uniform, and returned to the painful duty of burying his father. At the Fort Myer chapel, next to the cemetery, he and his mother greeted guests and occupied front pews during the service conducted by an old family friend from the Army Chaplain Corps, Maj. Gen. Luther D. Miller. The warm afternoon filled with the somber sounds and bright colors of full military honors: the roll of muffled drums, escort platoons in dark blue and gleaming brass, ceremonial band in bright red, a major general's flag, the heavy hoofbeats of matched grays, flag-draped coffin on a polished black caisson, a spirited thoroughbred with boots reversed in the stirrups, the trail of black limousines, the thunder of a thirteen-gun salute, the crack of three rifle volleys, the finality of Taps echoing across rows of white stone and into the leafy distance.[34]

Few Americans noticed General Short's passing, fewer still altered routines for the event. Not one civilian official of the Army or Defense Department attended the funeral. Secretary of Defense Louis Johnson sent Maj. Gen. Leven C. Allen to represent him, and Lt. Gen. Wade H. Haislip, the vice chief of staff, represented the Army. Less than three miles from the cemetery, President Truman and Congress struggled with a vexing array of postwar problems dominated by a strange new "cold war," the threat of atomic war, and, at home, burgeoning inflation and juvenile delinquency.[35]

For Isabel, there were many more seasons of life. Remaining in the Dallas home, she wrote and copyrighted two songs, titled "Georgette" and "Old Hawaii," but neither attracted the attention of a recording studio. Two years later she scored a success when she sold lyrics titled "There Won't Be No 'If,' Baby" to Crown Music Corporation in Los Angeles. She also began writing a memoir of her life as an Army wife, with the working title "General's Lady," but a lack of interest from publishers caused her to end the effort. Abandoning a literary project, however, did not seriously threaten her standard of living. With modest amounts from various sources, she was able to maintain the Dallas home, even to pay $1,478 for fifty shares of Socony Vacuum Oil Company stock in 1951.[36]

Gone forever was the busy social life Isabel had known as a general's wife. Old Army friends settled into their own retirement routines and rarely visited. Son Dean, now involved in the frequent household moves and occasional foreign tours of his own Army career, found less time to bring the grandchildren to Dallas. About 1958, Isabel married Boyd J. Brown, a Defense Department accountant and former lieutenant governor of the Virgin Islands. The couple moved to Washington, D.C., and Isabel kept the Dallas home for rental income. In the capital she found an old friend from Hawaii days, Ruth Phillips, widow of General Short's chief of staff in 1941. When Boyd died in 1977, Isabel moved into Alban Towers, a Connecticut Avenue apartment complex. Now she found her life constricted by more than widowhood and age. In the tight society of Army widows in the capital region, some still held General Short and Colonel Phillips responsible for the disaster at Pearl Harbor decades before and refused to socialize with Isabel and Ruth. But Isabel outlived most of the grudge-holders, passing her ninetieth birthday before she died on 10 April 1984.[37]

Over the years praise came to the memory of General Short from the fast-diminishing number of Army officers who were aware of his work before 7 December 1941. Writing Isabel Short, Lt. Gen. Robert L. Eichelberger, Eighth Army commander in the Pacific, and Lt. Gen. Alvan C. Gillem, XIII Corps commander in Europe, praised Short's influence on the successful mechanized tactics they and others had used in World War II, as well as his incidental service as a role model for future general officers like themselves.[38] Kendall Fielder, who had served on Short's staff in Hawaii and retired as a brigadier general, credited Short for the excellent combat performance of the 24th and 25th Infantry Divisions in the Pacific during the war. Short had created the two units from the Hawaiian Division in October 1941.[39]

Even in death Short benefited from his earlier association with Admiral

Kimmel, just as he had during the Army Pearl Harbor Board investigation, when Kimmel told him about the Magic intercepts and other information the two commanders had not received in Hawaii. The disgraced admiral never rested in his effort to win public understanding and exoneration, and with the good fortune of nearly two decades of life after Short's demise, he had much more time to press his case. Kimmel never missed a chance to corner an editor or reporter, and from his Naval Academy class of 1904 and others of his generation he found many more friends than had Short to speak to officials and write letters on his behalf. Robert R. McCormick, publisher of the *Chicago Tribune*, offered his newspaper for more than a quarter century as a sounding board for his and the admiral's conviction that blame for the attack belonged in Washington, not Hawaii. In 1954, the admiral published a book, *Admiral Kimmel's Story*, detailing his side of the defeat. This book, and another of the same year by retired Rear Adm. Robert A. Theobald titled *The Final Secret of Pearl Harbor*, sold well, especially among those who subscribed to the view that Short and Kimmel had been singled out as scapegoats for the defeat.[40]

Short received some attention from readers of such works, including a number who had earlier blamed him for the disaster. Walter M. Harrison, president and publisher of the *Oklahoma City North Star*, was representative, with his story of 27 January 1955 headlined "Belated Apology to General Short." As gratifying to family and supporters of Short as were such changes of opinion, they did not spark the broad-based reassessment that might have forced another investigation. In the public mind, Short remained disgraced.

Nearly four decades after he first raised the issue, Short's application for a retroactive promotion under the 1948 law again came to the attention of the Army. At its 1986 convention, the Pearl Harbor Survivors Association passed a resolution of support for Short and Kimmel. Soon after, the second largest veterans group in the United States, the Veterans of Foreign Wars, passed a similar resolution. Although these actions could not carry the force of law, they provoked enough interest in the earlier treatment of the two commanders that the Army and Navy had to take note. The sons of both Short and Kimmel saw the chance to revive their fathers' applications for promotion on the retired list, and wrote letters and made appeals to reporters. Within the Army and Navy Departments, fact sheets were generated and memos written. Some who were sympathetic to the cause thought the fiftieth anniversary of the Pearl Harbor attack a suitable occasion for the promotions. But the Army and Navy would not reverse their decisions of the late 1940s. Memorial ceremonies at

Pearl Harbor on the morning of 7 December 1991, led by President George Bush, were conducted with no mention of Short or Kimmel. More than half a century after the event that ruined their careers, the Hawaiian commanders retain the reputation of being, at best, badly mistaken, and at worst, manifestly incompetent.

AFTER DECADES OF formal investigation and report writing, incredulous discussion and bitter condemnation in millions of living rooms, offices, factories, lodges, and lounges across the country, the central question of the Pearl Harbor story remains to tantalize and infuriate. How could so many intelligent, well-trained, and widely experienced officials, civilian and military, get caught so unprepared for the attack they believed they could defeat? The question has strained the understanding of three generations thus far and will likely frustrate more.

As soon as the Roberts commission, the first official investigation of the Pearl Harbor disaster, blamed General Short and Admiral Kimmel for the defeat, a number of historians and journalists put forth a different view of the event. According to the "revisionists," as they became known for their rejection of the Roberts commission report, President Roosevelt knew a Japanese naval force was approaching Hawaii in late November but let the attack occur as the pretext he needed to enter the war and help the British against Nazi Germany. Furthermore, to ensure tactical surprise in Hawaii, Roosevelt refused to warn Short and Kimmel. The revisionist interpretation has remained a compelling explanation, especially among those who find conspiracy theories attractive, and among scholars frustrated by restrictions on relevant documentation. For more than half a century, explanations of the Pearl Harbor disaster have tended to endorse one of these two interpretations despite the flaws in each. Both require that adherents overlook evidence, and both reflect political partisanship. Those who have a generally positive view of the policies of Franklin Roosevelt tend to favor the Roberts commission finding, while those critical of Roosevelt lean toward the revisionist view.[41]

The most comprehensive and useful evidence uncovered during years of research and recording of testimony by several committees and individuals came out of the Army Pearl Harbor Board and the Joint Congressional Investigation. That body of evidence makes clear that the proper location for blame lies not on the opposite poles of Roberts and the revisionists, but at several places in between. Several principal actors on the Army side of the Pearl Harbor drama evaded a measure of blame, and have retained virtually stainless reputations. Secretary of War Stimson and General Marshall failed to properly supervise the handling of crucial information in the days and hours before the attack, Stimson when he transformed a straightforward description of faltering negotiations and possible dangers into the confusing "Do-Don't" message of 27 November and Marshall when he failed to send to Short by the fastest means the one o'clock message of 7 December. Both of these officials have escaped lasting censure for their errors, Stimson because of his distinguished record of public service before 1941 and Marshall because of his preparation of the Army for World War II and his later service as secretary of state and secretary of defense.

In addition, two of Marshall's subordinates in 1941 played prominent supporting roles in the War Department's mishandling of information. Brig. Gen. Sherman Miles, chief of the Military Intelligence Division, failed to inform Short of the "bomb plot" message and related intercepts available before the attack. Brig. Gen. Leonard Gerow, chief of the War Plans Division, failed to either ask Short for an elaboration of his brief response to the 27 November war warning or advise Marshall that a higher state of alert was needed in Hawaii. But they, too, went on to compile distinguished wartime records, Gerow as a corps commander in Europe, and Miles in command of the corps area enclosing several major northeastern ports from which troops and supplies were sent to Europe. Noting the errors of these four officials in 1941 need not diminish praise for their accomplishments before and after that momentous and tension-filled year. All four made serious mistakes, and must bear a measure of blame for Army unpreparedness in Hawaii in 1941.

Where does that leave Walter Short? Pointing out the errors of others is not the same as describing him as an innocent scapegoat. Nor does one have to choose between the polar opposite interpretations of his conduct available— the condemnation of the Roberts commission report or the exoneration of the revisionist interpretation—to evaluate the general's performance of duty in 1941. Like officials in Washington, Short committed mistakes that contributed to the disaster of 7 December 1941, and they deserve to be highlighted and understood. He continued to focus narrowly on his training mission in Hawaii and internal security even after July, when the Japanese takeover of Indochina marked a dramatic, and probably irreversible, escalation of tension in the western Pacific. He declined, in deference to anachronistic service protocol, to push Navy authorities in Hawaii to either share with him the limited scope of their distant reconnaissance around the islands, or accept the use of Army long-range bombers to create a more credible search over the horizon than a handful of Navy patrol planes could accomplish. And on the eve of the Japanese attack, he displayed a surprising lack of suspicion when showed the obviously coded text of the Mori telephone call between Tokyo and Honolulu.

All of these individual lapses, both of Washington officials and of General Short, were exposed and examined at some length in the series of nine official investigations conducted during and after the war. In fact, the emphasis of the official investigations remained almost exclusively on the mistakes of individuals because, from the moment they learned of the attack on Pearl Harbor, the overwhelming majority of the public preferred to think of the debacle as the result of individual failure rather than a breakdown of some impersonal administrative system. The public's preference to look for guilty individuals was not the result of any political chicanery in the White House. Like any successful politician, President Roosevelt understood the individualistic orientation of the American people very well. He neither encouraged nor discouraged a search for guilty parties; he simply let it run its course and exercise whatever effect the series of official investigators allowed.

For Walter Short, the public's interest in finding individual rather than systemic failures had mixed results. While he clearly made mistakes of his own, the zeal of certain investigators, particularly those on the Roberts commission, resulted in a serious distortion of Short's conception of his position in Hawaii and of conditions in the Pacific in 1941. This distortion, in turn, made it more difficult for military officials and the public to understand his role in events leading to the attack. The earliest official investigators—first, Secretary of the Navy Frank Knox, who flew to Hawaii just days after the attack, and soon after, the members of the Roberts commission—were struck by Short's choice of an antisabotage alert in response to the warning message of 27 November. Almost all investigators, in fact, considered Short's concern about sabotage to be exaggerated. One respected historian of the Pearl Harbor attack has labeled the general's concern a "preoccupation," a "psychosis," even an "obsession."[42]

What such labeling overlooks is the fact that Short's awareness of the danger of sabotage in Hawaii was not at all unique to him; it was shared by virtually every Army and Navy officer of his generation. He and his contemporaries had had their views on the possibility of sabotage in overseas possessions shaped by the same events of the early twentieth century. They remembered the War Scare of 1907, when even the most knowledgeable of observers expected the

Japanese to build upon their stunning defeat of Russian forces in 1904–5 to challenge other Western powers in the Pacific and possibly lead subject peoples to overthrow colonial regimes. They remembered the 1924 mutiny of Filipino troops against their American commanders, which made U.S. Army officers wary of the loyalty of "native" populations for decades.[43]

In Hawaii, certain characteristics and activities of the Japanese population provoked questions of loyalty by other ethnic groups and kept alive in the minds of territorial and federal authorities an awareness of the threat of sabotage. The total 1941 Hawaiian Islands population of about 425,000 included 124,000 people of Japanese ancestry. Of those, 41,000 chose not to become American citizens. Within a few years of their arrival in the islands, Japanese aliens established schools to teach the language of their homeland to their children. The existence of these language schools suggested opposition to the historical American ideal of immigrant assimilation, and beginning in 1903 the FBI kept rosters of aliens teaching in them. After the Japanese Army conquered Manchuria in 1931, some Japanese-language newspapers in Hawaii took a pro-Japan editorial stance. When Japanese forces provoked hostilities at the Marco Polo bridge in 1937 and went on to attack several Chinese cities, radio broadcasts from Tokyo reminded the Japanese in Hawaii that their children belonged to the emperor. Every year a small number of young alien men went back to Japan to volunteer for the imperial armed forces or to respond to the draft. Many other aliens in Hawaii supported the Japanese military by sending "comfort kits" to the troops in China and collecting contributions for soldiers' and sailors' relief funds. Japanese-language school children responded to the encouragement of their teachers and parents by writing letters of support to soldiers in China.[44]

Walter Short could not have been the only military official in Hawaii aware of these activities and alive to the potential for disruption which they suggested. But the official investigations pictured him as some kind of aberration in his generation for being in the grip of paranoia about the sinister machinations of Japanese aliens. From that distortion of individual responsibility for the Pearl Harbor disaster, investigators went on to consider, and misinterpret, systemic causes of the debacle.

Only one systemic shortcoming in the command and reporting methods of 1941 received serious attention from investigators. This was the top-to-bottom mishandling of information in the War and Navy Departments in Washington and in the Army and Navy commands in Hawaii. After taking testimony from only a few witnesses, investigators could hardly miss the information problem, with so many accounts of messages not passed along to officials who needed them and admissions by both Army and Navy officers that they were unaware of each other's routine procedures and plans. Fortunately for the nation, recognition of the information problem led to a series of meaningful reforms, most notable among them the initiation of career military specialties in intelligence and the establishment of the Central Intelligence Agency.

The investigations, however, completely ignored another systemic failure: the lack of coordination in the national command decision-making system. Rather than coordinating their activities to support a coherent and defensible foreign policy, the State, War, and Navy Departments operated in separate spheres, guarding their historical missions and neglecting the interaction necessary to respond effectively to new developments in foreign relations. The sharp delineation of activities between the three departments was nothing new; it dated from the earliest days of the Republic. In 1898, however, it became a problem. In that year victory over Spain gave the United States government distant territories to administer and protect. The acquisition of overseas territories should have been accompanied by organizational reforms to bring about the closer interdepartmental coordination that would integrate traditional continental defense policies with the newer overseas diplomatic and military interests into a foreign policy relevant to new realities. Instead, the territories were given to the War Department to administer, and the three departments continued in their comfortable pattern of operational autonomy accented by the jealous guarding of familiar turf.

The lack of interdepartmental coordination created dangerous vulnerabilities in the Pacific. Without the endorsement of the State Department, the War and Navy Departments during the next half century were unable to secure from Congress funding sufficient to build a credible defense of the Pacific territories. In the last days of 1941, Japanese expeditionary forces made painfully clear to the U.S. government the inadequacy of its defense policy making in the Pacific by overrunning the Philippines, Guam, and Midway, and then taking nearly twenty-four thousand American prisoners of war from those islands.

The general isolation in which the War Department had to operate from the diplomacy that so extensively shaped its military missions meant that outpost commanders like Short had to go about their work in an atmosphere of uncertainty, heavily dependent on Washington officials who, while awaiting guidance from the State Department, were usually just as uncertain as officers in the field about diplomatic developments. Uninformed of current diplomatic priorities, military leaders, Short included, typically displayed constricted views of their missions and the developing diplomatic milieu around them, as the post-attack investigations revealed. What every investigation of the Pearl Harbor disaster missed, however, was the fact that this lack of strategic awareness did not result from one officer in a key position somehow missing a particular training cycle or educational experience in the course of a career. Instead, it was characteristic of almost all Army and Navy officers of Short's generation. The complete lack of experience in diplomacy, of even a rudimentary under-standing of negotiating stances and techniques, was a desirable and deliberate aspect of senior officer preparation in the U.S. Army and Navy before World War II. Diplomacy remained the prerogative of the State Department, and before World War II diplomats did not seek the advice of officials in other gov-ernment departments when formulating negotiating goals or strategies. Indeed, diplomats believed that consultation with War Department officials or mili-tary commanders who might be affected by their work somehow tainted their negotiations.

The latest expression of the separation of diplomacy from military policy making had occurred just one week before the Pearl Harbor attack when Sec-retary of State Cordell Hull turned over to the War and Navy Departments the problem of dealing with Japan. In the weeks before, the military departments had stood by as nonparticipants while the State Department had carried on ne-gotiations with Japanese special envoys about the situation in the Pacific.[45]

The handful of Army officers who had acquired some understanding of diplomacy before World War II had done so as the result of fortuitous associa-tions. The best known among these favored officers was George Marshall. He had won the respect of Henry Stimson and others, and they had offered their counsel as Marshall moved into key positions. In the course of his own career, Walter Short had not acquired a mentor of Stimson's broad experience.

With little meaningful diplomatic guidance coming from Washington, Short continued on the course set for him when he took over the Hawaiian Department, training his growing command to protect the U.S. Navy at its central Pacific anchorage and preparing to support American forces in and around the Philippines in case of a break with Japan. He saw no reason to question the conventional wisdom of 1941 that the Japanese would be foolish to directly attack an American military installation as far from the home is-lands as Hawaii, and no superior officer or diplomat made any effort to correct that view.

Conscientious to the end, neither Short nor officials in Washington realized how seriously flawed the information and control systems within which they worked had become. While the Japanese prepared to demonstrate the new power projection tactics of seaborne attack from aircraft carriers, American officials and outpost commanders struggled to respond to a rapidly deteriorating situation in the Pacific with poorly coordinated national command and regional defense procedures basically unchanged since 1898.

Notes

Chapter 1. Son of the Prairie

1. Congress, *Pearl Harbor Attack: Hearings Before the Joint Committee on the Investigation of the Pearl Harbor Attack,* 79th Cong., 2d sess., 1946 (hereafter cited as *PHA*), pt. 7, p. 3121.

2. John Toland, *Infamy: Pearl Harbor and Its Aftermath* (Garden City, N.Y.: Doubleday, 1982), 38, 46; Short quotation in *Washington Post,* 25 January 1942; editorial excerpt from *Wheeling (W.Va.) News-Register,* 26 January 1942; May speech excerpt in Husband E. Kimmel, *Admiral Kimmel's Story* (Chicago: Henry Regnery, 1955), 170.

3. Rev. William Henry Foote, *Sketches of North Carolina, Historical and Biographical* (New York: Robert Carter, 1846), 85; Col. Walter Dean Short (Ret.), interview with author, Las Cruces, N.M., 28–30 June 1985; William H. Perrin, ed., *History of Bond and Montgomery Counties, Illinois* (Chicago: Baskin, 1882), 306–7; Jacob L. Traylor, *Past and Present of Montgomery County* (Chicago: S. J. Parke, 1904), 111–12; E. H. Baumgartner to author, 5 February 1985.

4. Newspaper article, n.d., Walter C. Short Collection, Hoover Institution on War, Revolution and Peace, Stanford, Calif. (hereafter cited as WCSC).

5. University of Illinois Application No. 4277, September 14, 1897, University of Illinois Archives, Urbana, Illinois (hereafter cited as UIA).

6. Allan Nevins, *Illinois* (New York: Oxford University Press, 1917), 168–71, 359, 362.

7. *University of Illinois Catalog, 1898–99,* UIA.

8. Nevins, *Illinois,* 359.

9. *Illio 1901,* and miscellaneous correspondence, both in UIA.

10. Winton U. Solberg, *The University of Illinois, 1867–1894: An Intellectual and Cultural History* (Urbana: University of Illinois Press, 1968), 375.

11. *University of Illinois Catalog, 1897–98;* Military Department Returns, University of Illinois, 1900–1911; *Illio 1901; University of Illinois Semi-Centennial Alumni Record,* all in UIA.

12. Walter C. Short (WCS) to Council of Administration, University of Illinois, 26 October 1897, UIA; WCS transcript courtesy of Walter Dean Short.

13. WCS to President A. S. Draper, 29 April 1901 and 14 May 1901, and commencement program, 12 June 1901, all in UIA; Short interview.

14. *Champaign (Ill.) Gazette,* 12 June 1901; 1901 class day and commencement programs, UIA; The Adjutant General's Office (hereafter cited as TAG), *Official Army Register 1903* (Washington, D.C.: GPO, 1903), 419.

15. Graduate's Record, University of Illinois, 28 May 1905, UIA; Ralph B. Jackson to author, 25 August 1985, Western Military Academy Memorial Library, Alton, Ill.

16. A. S. Draper to WCS, 25 November 1901, WCSC; A. S. Draper to G. B. Cortelyou, 26 November 1901, General Correspondence of the Adjutant General's Office, 1890–1917, File 418671, Records of the Adjutant General's Office, 1780s–1917, RG 94, NARA (hereafter cited as AGO); A. S. Draper to WCS, 11 December 1901, WCSC.

17. Examination results and commission in File 418671, AGO; TAG, *Official Army Register 1902* (Washington, D.C.: GPO, 1902), 290.

Chapter 2. A Zealous Young Officer

1. From the speech titled "The Philippine Question," delivered by Senator Beveridge on 9 January 1900, printed in *Congressional Globe,* 56th Cong., vol. 33, pt. 1, pp. 704–12.

2. *Report of the Secretary of War 1901* (Washington, D.C.: GPO, 1901), 4–5.

3. Russell F. Weigley, *History of the United States Army* (Bloomington: Indiana University Press, 1984), 599; *Report of the Secretary of War 1901,* 4.

4. This and the following description of Army life in the early twentieth century are based on Weigley, *History of the United States Army,* chap. 14; William A. Ganoe, *The History of the United States Army* (New York: D. Appleton-Century, 1942), chap. 10; and R. Ernest Dupuy, *The Compact History of the United States Army* (New York: Hawthorn Books, 1956), chap. 11.

5. References to Walter Short's assignments and unit moves during 1902–7 are from Returns from Regular Army Infantry Regiments, June 1821–December 1916 (NA Microfilm Publication M665, Roll 260), RG 94, NARA.

6. *Report of the Secretary of War 1901,* 90–92.

7. Isabel Dean Short, "The General's Lady," ms., n.d., WCSC. Short's anecdotal account, written in the early 1950s, covers the period from the time she met her future husband in 1913 to his death. Because of confused pagination, the work must be cited in its entirety.

8. Short interview.

9. Weigley, *History of the United States Army,* 315–22.

10. Efficiency reports in File 418671, AGO.

11. Quotations in Commanding General, Southwestern Division, to 2d Lieutenant W. C. Short, 15 April 1907, File 418671, AGO; see also George C. Marshall, *The Papers of George Catlett Marshall,* ed. Larry I. Bland (Baltimore: Johns Hopkins University Press, 1981), 1:28.

12. Competitive marksmanship results in File 418671, AGO.

13. Col. R. W. Hoyt to the Military Secretary, War Department, 1 July 1906, AGO.

14. Jack D. Foner, *Blacks and the Military in American History: A New Perspective* (New York: Frederick A. Praeger, 1974), 95–100.

15. John M. Gates, *Schoolbooks and Krags: The United States Army in the Philippines, 1898–1902* (Westport, Conn.: Greenwood Press, 1973), 89, 133–35, 216.

16. Short interview.

17. Michael Cullinane, "Implementing the 'New Order': The Structure and Supervision of Local Government During the Taft Era," in *Compadre Colonialism: Studies on the Philippines Under American Rule*, ed. Normal G. Owen, Michigan Papers on South and Southeast Asia, No. 3 (Ann Arbor: University of Michigan Press, 1971), 13–75; Gates, *Schoolbooks and Krags*, 284.

18. References to Walter Short's assignments and unit moves during 1908–17 are from Returns from Regular Army Infantry Regiments, June 1821–December 1916 (NA Microfilm Publication M665, Rolls 180, 181), RG 94, NARA.

19. Short interview.

20. Efficiency report, 30 June 1910, File 418671, AGO.

21. Lt. Col. Lyman L. Woodman (USAF, Ret.) to author, 8 October 1986; Short interview; quotation in "A Brief History of the Sixteenth Infantry," typescript, n.d., in "Regimental Histories and Historical Notes," Entry 1568, RG 391, NARA; *Report of the Chief Signal Officer, 1910* (Washington, D.C.: GPO, 1910), 633.

22. George M. Chinn, *The Machine Gun: History, Evolution, and Development of Manual, Automatic, and Airborne Repeating Weapons* (Washington, D.C.: Department of the Navy, 1951), 196.

23. David A. Armstrong, *Bullets and Bureaucrats: The Machine Gun and the United States Army 1861–1916* (Westport, Conn.: Greenwood Press, 1982), 176–78.

24. Short interview.

25. Col. S. W. Miller, 10th Infantry, to Adjutant General of the Army, 16 October 1914, Subject: Establishment of and Regulations for the School of Musketry, Entry 25, File 1988090, RG 94, NARA; Short, "General's Lady."

26. Short, "General's Lady."

27. Quotations in Report of Physical Examination: 1st Lt. Walter C. Short, 9 October 1914, File 418671, AGO.

28. "Milady in Brown: Year Book of Belmont College," 1911, Belmont College Library, Nashville, Tennessee.

29. Newspaper article, n.d., WCSC; Short interview.

30. Short, "General's Lady."

Chapter 3. To Arms

1. This summary is based on two sources: Clarence C. Clendenen, *Blood on the Border: The United States Army and the Mexican Irregulars* (New York: Macmillan, 1969), chaps. 6–10; and Allan R. Millett, *The General: Robert L. Bullard and Officership in the United States Army, 1881–1925* (Westport, Conn.: Greenwood Press, 1975), chap. 14.

2. Clendenen, *Blood on the Border*, 220.

3. Ibid.

4. Ibid., 219, 221, 244; Returns from Regular Army Infantry Regiments, June 1821–December 1916 (NA Microfilm Publication M665, Roll 181), RG 94, NARA; "Punitive Expedition," Records of United States Army Overseas Operations and Commands, 1898–1942, RG 395, NARA.

5. Short, "General's Lady."

6. Returns from Regular Army Infantry Regiments, June 1821–December 1916 (NA Microfilm Publication M665, Roll 181), RG 94, NARA; "Punitive Expedition," Records of United States Army Overseas Operations and Commands, 1898–1942, RG 395, NARA.

7. Report of Medical Examination, 1st Lt. Walter C. Short, 10 June 1916, AGO.

8. Miscellaneous correspondence, File 418671, AGO.

9. Clendenen, *Blood on the Border,* 328–31, 334–35.

10. *Report of the Secretary of War 1916* (Washington, D.C.: GPO, 1916).

11. Clendenen, *Blood on the Border,* 315–22, 225.

12. Weigley, *History of the United States Army,* 348.

13. Millett, *General,* 307; Weigley, *History of the United States Army,* 350, 354, 561, 569.

14. John J. Pershing, *My Experiences in the World War* (New York: Frederick A. Stokes, 1931), 1:3, 20.

15. Origin unknown; contributed by Maj. Charles E. Kirkpatrick (Ret.), U.S. Army Center of Military History, Washington, D.C.

16. Short, "General's Lady."

17. Ibid.; Short interview.

18. Short, "General's Lady."

19. Ibid.

20. Newspaper article, n.d., WCSC.

21. Weigley, *History of the United States Army,* 356; Pershing, *My Experiences in the World War* 1:91–93.

22. *Report of the Chief of Ordnance 1916,* 22–25; Pershing, *My Experiences in the World War* 1:131; Armstrong, *Bullets and Bureaucrats,* 189.

23. Pershing, *My Experiences in the World War* 1:131; Ian V. Hogg and John Weeks, *Military Small Arms of the 20th Century* (Northfield, Ill.: DBI Books, 1981), 207; Chinn, *Machine Gun,* 201, 241–42.

24. Weigley, *History of the United States Army,* 351, 360; Millett, *General,* 337; Pershing, *My Experiences in the World War* 1:132.

25. All references to Walter Short's duty assignments and promotions for the period 1918–42 are from two sources: Roger J. Spiller, ed., *Dictionary of American Military Biography* (Westport, Conn.: Greenwood Press, 1984), 3:1000–1003, and biographical summary prepared by the War Department, copy in 201 File, U.S. Army Center of Military History (hereafter cited as CMH), Washington, D.C.

26. Millett, *General,* 343; Girard L. McEntee, *Military History of the World War: A Complete Account of the Campaigns on All Fronts* (New York: Scribner's, 1937), 503.

27. Telegram to WCS, June 1918, WCSC.

28. McEntee, *Military History of the World War,* 503.

29. Pershing, *My Experiences in the World War* 1:151–52; Hogg and Weeks, *Military Small Arms,* 205, 207, 250; Chinn, *Machine Gun,* 242.

30. Pershing, *My Experiences in the World War* 2:374.

31. Adjutant General of the Army, *Decorations, U.S. Army, 1862–1926* (Washington, D.C.: GPO, 1927), 767.

32. Capt. Walter C. Short, *The Employment of Machine Guns* (1922), excerpted in "Infantry Tactics: Fire," *Infantry School Mailing List, 1931–32* 4 (June 1932): 34–35.

33. Ibid.

34. *American Military Government of Occupied Germany, 1918–1920,* Report of the Officer in Charge of Civil Affairs, Third Army and American Forces in Germany (Washington, D.C.: GPO, 1943), 26; "American University on the Rhine," WCSC.

35. Report of Machine Gun Board, AEF, on Organization and Tactics, General Headquarters, American Expeditionary Forces, 29 May 1919, 6, 8, 10, in Report of Superior Board, AEF, on Organization and Tactics, GHQ, AEF, n.d. [June 1919], copy in CMH.

36. Short interview; *PHA* 23:776.

Chapter 4. Back to Barracks

1. *Report of the Secretary of War 1919* (Washington, D.C.: GPO, 1919), 4; *Report of the Secretary of War 1920,* 29.

2. Weigley, *History of the United States Army,* 353, 396–400, 403–4.

3. *Report of the Secretary of War 1925* (Washington, D.C.: GPO, 1925), 2.

4. *Report of the Secretary of War 1924* (Washington, D.C.: GPO, 1924,) 29.

5. Ibid., 23.

6. Brian M. Linn, *Guardians of Empire: The U.S. Army and the Pacific, 1902–1940* (Chapel Hill: University of North Carolina Press, 1997), 248.

7. *Report of the Secretary of War 1924,* 2–25.

8. *Report of the Secretary of War 1926* (Washington, D.C.: GPO, 1926), 35–36.

9. *Report of the Secretary of War 1923,* 14, 22; *Report of the Secretary of War 1926,* 23–24, 29.

10. *Report of the Secretary of War 1923,* 24.

11. *Report of the Secretary of War 1926,* 34; *Report of the Secretary of War 1932* (Washington, D.C.: GPO, 1932), 39–40.

12. Gen. Lucian K. Truscott Jr., *The Twilight of the U.S. Cavalry: Life in the Old Army, 1917–1942* (Lawrence: University Press of Kansas, 1989), 35.

13. Short, "General's Lady."

14. Timothy K. Nenninger, *The Leavenworth Schools and the Old Army: Education, Professionalism, and the Officer Corps of the United States Army, 1881–1918* (Westport,

Conn.: Greenwood Press, 1978), 75; General Service Schools, "Annual Report for 1920," Adjutant General's Office, RG 407, NARA; Short, "General's Lady"; Item W 26.11:2/2, RG 287, NARA Library; *St. Louis Daily Globe-Democrat*, 25 June 1934, UIA.

15. Short, "General's Lady"; General Service Schools, "Annual Report for 1920."

16. Telegram to WCS, WCSC.

17. Short, "General's Lady"; TAG, *Official Army Register 1921* (Washington, D.C.: GPO, 1921), 16.

18. John B. Wilson, comp., *Armies, Corps, Divisions and Separate Brigades* (Washington, D.C.: GPO, 1987), 218; Short, "General's Lady."

19. Short, "General's Lady."

20. Short served in the Military Intelligence Division from July 1921 to July 1924, as a student at the Army War College from September 1924 to July 1925, in the 65th Infantry from July 1925 to April 1928, at the Command and General Staff School from August 1928 to September 1930, and in the Bureau of Insular Affairs from October 1930 to June 1934.

21. Robert A. Miller, "The United States Army During the 1930s" (Ph.D. diss., Princeton University, 1973), 25 and 25 n.

22. George S. Pappas, *Prudens Futuri: The U.S. Army War College 1901–1967* (Carlisle Barracks, Pa.: Alumni Association of U.S. Army War College, 1967), 119.

23. Ibid., 93–94.

24. Army War College, "Outline of the Course 1924–1925," War Department General and Special Staffs, Adjutant General's Office, RG 165, NARA; Pappas, *Prudens Futuri*, 121, 123.

25. Burke Davis, *The Billy Mitchell Affair* (New York: Random House, 1967), 55; Army War College, "Outline of the Course 1924–1925."

26. Lucian K. Truscott Jr., biographical summary in 201 File, CMH.

27. Chief of Military History, *The Army Lineage Book* (Washington, D.C.: GPO, 1953), 78. Short commanded 6th Infantry from July 1934 to June 1936.

28. Newspaper article, n.d., WCSC; Short interview; Short, "General's Lady."

29. Newspaper article, n.d., WCSC. Short served as assistant commandant of the Infantry School from July 1936 to February 1937.

30. *Army List and Directory*, 20 October 1936, 139–41; TAG, *Official Army Register 1937* (Washington, D.C.: GPO, 1937), 2, 643; Col. Wendell G. Johnson (Ret.) to author, 6 May 1985; Short interview.

31. Short interview.

32. Col. Wendell G. Johnson (Ret.) to author, 6 May 1985.

33. Col. (Ret.) and Mrs. Walter Dean Short, interviews with author, 28–30 June 1985.

34. Richard C. Brown, *Social Attitudes of American Generals, 1898–1940* (New York: Arno Press, 1979), 3–17. Thirty-eight percent of the generals were born in the Midwest, 49 percent in a small town, 27 percent were sons of professionals, and 91 percent were Protestants.

35. Ibid., 172, 212, 244–45, 296, 390.

36. Short interview.

37. William Jay Smith, *Army Brat* (New York: Persea Books, 1980), 159–60, 172.

38. Short interview.

39. Ibid.; Richard Stockton VI, *Inevitable War* (New York: Perth, 1932).

40. John W. Killigrew, *The Impact of the Great Depression on the Army* (New York: Garland, 1979), chap. 1, pp. 1–2; chap. 2, pp. 1, 26; chap. 8, p. 1.

41. *Army Navy Journal*, 9 July 1932, 1; *Army Navy Journal*, 1 April 1933, 1; Killigrew, *Impact of the Great Depression*, app. 1.

42. Killigrew, *Impact of the Great Depression*, chap. 10, pp. 15–16; app. 1; *Army Navy Journal*, 3 February 1934, 1; *Army Navy Journal*, 30 June 1934, 1; *Army Navy Journal*, 16 February 1935, 1.

43. Killigrew, *Impact of the Great Depression*, chap. 6, pp. 16, 21; *Report of the Secretary of War 1933* (Washington, D.C.: GPO, 1933), 6, 8–11; *Report of the Secretary of War 1934* (Washington, D.C.: GPO, 1934), 7, 198; *Report of the Secretary of War 1935* (Washington, D.C.: GPO, 1935), 127.

44. *Report of the Secretary of War 1936* (Washington, D.C.: GPO, 1936), 40; *Report of the Secretary of War 1937* (Washington, D.C.: GPO, 1937), 33; *Report of the Secretary of War 1940* (Washington, D.C.: GPO, 1940), 66; Killigrew, *Impact of the Great Depression*, chap. 13, pp. 12–20; D. Clayton James, *The Years of MacArthur, 1880–1941* (Boston: Houghton Mifflin, 1970), 1:424–25; *Report of the Secretary of War 1933*, 8; *Report of the Secretary of War 1934*, 7.

45. James MacGregor Burns, *Roosevelt: The Lion and the Fox* (New York: Harcourt, Brace & World, 1956), 254; James, *Years of MacArthur* 1:440–41.

46. Bruce W. Bidwell, *History of the Military Intelligence Division, Department of the Army General Staff: 1775–1941* (Frederick, Md.: University Publications of America, 1986), 330–31; *PHA* 34:84–85, 36:311–12.

47. Capt. R. G. Howie to the Assistant Commandant, Infantry School, 16 April 1937, subject: Design and Development of a Machine Gun Carrier, Decimal 470.8, Office of Chief of Infantry Correspondence 1921–1942, Records of Chiefs of Arms, RG 177, NARA.

48. Ibid.

49. Report, Department of Experiment, the Infantry School, 28 February 1938, subject: Test of Howie Machine Gun Carrier; Lt. Col. J. G. Ord, Director, the Infantry Board, to the Chief of Infantry, 1 March 1938, subject: Howie Carrier, both in Decimal 470.8, Office of Chief of Infantry Correspondence 1921–1942, Records of Chiefs of Arms, RG 177, NARA.

50. Weigley, *History of the United States Army*, 4:17–18, 561, 568–69.

51. Newspaper article, n.d., WCSC.

52. Scrapbook, WCSC; Arnold J. Heidenheimer et al., *Vanguard to Victory: History of the 18th Infantry* (Aschaffenburg, Germany: Main-Echo Verlag, 1954), 63; Short commanded in succession 2d Brigade, 1st Division from February 1937 to June 1938; 1st

Brigade of the same division from June 1938 to October 1939; and 1st Division from October 1939 to September 1940.

53. Newspaper articles, n.d., WCSC.

54. Col. Wendell G. Johnson (Ret.) to author, 6 May 1985.

55. Newspaper articles, n.d,, WCSC; Short commanded IV Corps from March to May 1940.

56. Mark S. Watson, *Chief of Staff: Prewar Plans and Preparations*, vol. 4, pt. 1 of *United States Army in World War II* (Washington, D.C.: GPO, 1950), 165–71, 175.

57. Short, "General's Lady"; WCS to National City Bank of New York, 27 December 1940, WCSC; Short commanded I Corps from October 1940 to January 1941.

58. *PHA* 22:32.

Chapter 5. The Seriousness of This Situation

1. Marion Hoyt Lewis, interviews with author, Pana, Illinois, 30 December 1984 and 19 June 1985.

2. Watson, *Chief of Staff*, 460–61.

3. Gordon W. Prange, *At Dawn We Slept: The Untold Story of Pearl Harbor* (New York: McGraw-Hill Book, 1981), 39, 44.

4. Gen. George Marshall to Maj. Gen. Walter Krueger, 14 April 1941, in Marshall, *Papers* 2:473–74.

5. *PHA* 22:32; Charles D. Herron, biographical summary in 201 File, CMH; change of command ceremony, film, Fort Shafter, Territory of Hawaii, 7 February 1941, WCSC.

6. War Department General Orders No. 9, 6 February 1913, and GO 16, 5 April 1921; Stetson Conn, Rose Engelman, and Byron Fairchild, *Guarding the United States and Its Outposts*, vol. 12, pt. 2 of *United States Army in World War II* (Washington, D.C.: GPO, 1964), 150–53.

7. Prange, *At Dawn We Slept*, 51; *PHA* 23:1227.

8. All quotations in *PHA* 15:1601–2.

9. Quotations in ibid.; see also *PHA* 15:1428, 18:3136, 22:165, 28:1355–56; *Jane's Fighting Ships 1941* (New York: Macmillan, 1942), 313.

10. *PHA* 24:1835.

11. *PHA* 24:1822–23.

12. *PHA* 39:75.

13. *PHA* 23:776, 790, 827; 24:1793.

14. *PHA* 24:1787, 18:3126.

15. Watson, *Chief of Staff*, 49.

16. *PHA* 15:1606.

17. Conn, Engelman, and Fairchild, *Guarding the United States*, 12, 31, 354, 374–75; *PHA* 15:1631.

18. Conn, Engelman, and Fairchild, *Guarding the United States,* 167.

19. *PHA* 24:1786–88; Conn, Engelman, and Fairchild, *Guarding the United States,* 169.

20. Conn, Engelman, and Fairchild, *Guarding the United States,* 170; *PHA* 12:318–19, 18:3096.

21. *PHA* 15:1626.

22. Ibid.; Short quotation on 1609, Marshall quotation on 1612.

23. Truman Temple, "Crippling Blow by Swordfish," *World War II* 4 (May 1989): 34–41.

24. Quotation in *PHA* 15:1606; see also *PHA* 14:973–74, 1000–1004.

25. Conn, Engelman, and Fairchild, *Guarding the United States,* 167–68; *PHA* 1:38, 22:35.

26. *PHA* 15:1432.

27. *PHA* 15:1635.

28. *PHA* 33:696.

29. Conn, Engelman, and Fairchild, *Guarding the United States,* 166–67; *PHA* 1:54, 7:3047, 22:38, 32:172.

30. Wesley Frank Craven and James Lea Cate, eds., *The Army Air Forces in World War II* (Chicago: University of Chicago Press, 1948), 1:172; ibid. (1955), 6:267.

31. Conn, Engelman, and Fairchild, *Guarding the United States,* 168–69; *PHA* 12:320.

32. Short quotation in *PHA* 15:1622–23; see also *PHA* 7:3086.

33. Brig. Gen. Walter Krueger, Assistant Chief of Staff, War Plans Division to Colonel Sherman Miles, memo, WPD, 29 July 1937, WPD 3878-3, in Conn, Engelman, and Fairchild, *Guarding the United States,* 154.

34. Diary of Henry L. Stimson, 23 April 1941, Manuscripts and Archives, Yale University Library, New Haven, Connecticut.

35. David Kahn, "The United States Views Germany and Japan in 1941," chap. 16 of Ernest R. May, ed., *Knowing One's Enemies: Intelligence Assessment Before the Two World Wars* (Princeton, N.J.: Princeton University Press, 1986), 482–83.

36. *PHA* 7:2932.

37. Both quotations in ibid.

38. Ibid.

39. *PHA* 22:32; see also *PHA* 27:138–39, 218–19, 230–31.

40. *Biennial Report of the Chief of Staff of the United States Army July 1, 1939, to June 30, 1941, to the Secretary of War* (Washington, D.C.: GPO, 1941), 10–11; Prange, *At Dawn We Slept,* 178.

41. Conn, Engelman, and Fairchild, *Guarding the United States,* 172–73.

42. Watson, *Chief of Staff,* 361–66.

43. *PHA* 7:2933.

44. Ibid.

45. *PHA* 18:3187, 29:2077.

46. Watson, *Chief of Staff,* 438–48.

47. *PHA* 15:1635, 12:320, 22:36.

48. *PHA* 7:2934.

49. *PHA* 7:2942.

50. *PHA* 7:2935.

51. *PHA* 14:1406.

52. *PHA* 6:2581–82, 7:2950, 2983.

53. *PHA* 3:1019–23, 1096, 5:2154–57, 7:2942–43.

54. *PHA* 7:2935; see also 3:1024, 2:919, and 23:1106.

55. Short quotation in *PHA* 7:2935; alerts defined in 7:2941 and 15:1440–44.

56. *PHA* 22:36, 28:1369–70.

57. *PHA* 7:2941–44.

58. *PHA* 7:2936, 6:2581–82, 28:1597.

59. Gerow quotation in *PHA* 23:1106; see also 23:1111 and 7:2948.

60. *PHA* 6:2582, 7:3228.

61. *PHA* 7:2936.

62. *PHA* 7:2937.

63. *PHA* 14:1061–62.

64. *PHA* 11:5356.

65. *PHA* 10:4680.

66. *PHA* 7:2950, 2984.

67. *PHA* 14:1408, 27:789, 6:2596–97, 2764.

68. *PHA* 24:1780.

69. *PHA* 22:191.

70. Conn, Engelman, and Fairchild, *Guarding the United States,* 183.

71. *PHA* 27:737–39; the transcript of the Mori call is in 35:274–76.

72. WCS to Walter Dean Short, 18 November 1941, WCSC.

73. Short quotation in Prange, *At Dawn We Slept,* 481; *PHA* 22:87, 156.

74. *PHA* 22:57.

75. Mrs. Walter C. Phillips, interview with author, Washington, D.C., 8 October 1985; *PHA* 22:57; Lt. Gen. Louis W. Truman (Ret.), telephone interview with author, 5 August 1986.

76. *PHA* 1:54–55, 24:1784, 39:119.

77. *PHA* 7:2939.

78. Truman interview; *PHA* 27:109, 114, 35:212–13; Ladislas Farago, *The Broken Seal: The Story of "Operation Magic" and the Pearl Harbor Disaster* (New York: Random House, 1967), 382.

Chapter 6. The Glare of Investigation

1. Truman interview; Conn, Engelman, and Fairchild, *Guarding the United States,* 192–93.

2. *PHA* 22:63, 61.

3. *PHA* 22:47.

4. Ibid.

5. *PHA* 22:62.

6. Quotations in "Report of the Battle of Oahu," 2, typescript in WCSC; see also 1, 3–5.

7. *PHA* 3:1530, 7:3260.

8. *PHA* 22:94–95.

9. *PHA* 24:1749.

10. *PHA* 24:1753.

11. *PHA* 22:75, 193; Delos C. Emmons, biographical summary in 201 File, CMH.

12. Truman interview.

13. Prange, *At Dawn We Slept,* 592–94; Officer Biographies, Operational Archives Branch, Naval Historical Center, Washington, D.C.

14. *PHA* 22:1–3; *PHA* 7:2921–22, 3155.

15. *PHA* 22:1–3; *PHA* 7:3278–80, 3262.

16. Truman interview.

17. Quotation in *PHA* 35:31; see also 22:7–28.

18. *PHA* 22:32–33.

19. *PHA* 22:34–75.

20. *PHA* 22:47.

21. *PHA* 22:82–83.

22. *PHA* 22:72–79.

23. *PHA* 23:1109.

24. *PHA* 22:104.

25. Ibid.

26. *PHA* 22:105.

27. *PHA* 23:976–77.

28. *PHA* 23:981–87.

29. Quotation in *PHA* 22:37; see also 22:42–43.

30. Quotation in *PHA* 22:44; see also 22:58–59, 50–53, 70–71.

31. Quotation in *PHA* 22:72–73; see also 22:75 and 23:1106, 1111, 977.

32. Quotation in *PHA* 22:103, 22:41; see also 22:320–21, 88, 156, 162, 168.

33. *PHA* 27:753, 19:3797.

34. *PHA* 39:20.

35. *PHA* 39:21.

36. *PHA* 7:3133.

37. *Oklahoma City Daily Oklahoman,* 25 January 1942.

38. Marshall quotation in *PHA* 7:3133; Short request for retirement in 7:3135; see also 7:3134, 3136.

39. *PHA* 7:3135.

40. Marshall quotation in *PHA* 7:3139; Stimson quotation on 11:5429.

41. *PHA* 7:3139–47.

42. WCS to Walter Dean Short, 8 February 1942, WCSC.

43. *PHA* 7:3142.

44. Short interview; WCS to TAG, 9 March 1942, and TAG to WCS, 17 March 1942, WCSC; TAG, *Official Army Register January 1, 1941*, 1304–6.

45. Louis Morton, *United States Army in World War II: The Fall of the Philippines* (Washington, D.C.: Department of the Army, 1953), 24, 42.

46. *New York Times,* 26 March 1942.

47. William Manchester, *American Caesar: Douglas MacArthur, 1880–1964* (Boston: Little, Brown, 1978), 152.

48. Sidney Fine, *The Automobile Under the Blue Eagle: Labor, Management, and the Automobile Manufacturing Code* (Ann Arbor: University of Michigan Press, 1963), 77–78.

49. WCS to James C. Colvin, 24 January 1943, UIA.

50. Short interview; Toland, *Infamy,* 47-48; *Army and Navy Journal* 79 (30 May 1942): 2.

51. Short interview.

52. Ibid.

53. Maj. Gen. Robert L. Eichelberger to WCS, [February 1942], and Maj. Gen. Frederick L. Martin to WCS, [April 1942], both in WCSC; Short interview.

54. Miscellaneous correspondence, WCSC; Short interview.

55. Short interview.

Chapter 7. Toward Vindication

1. *PHA* 19:3823–25, 7:3172.

2. *PHA* 7:3152–53.

3. Stimson Diary, 10 December 1943.

4. Public Law 208, 78th Congress; War Department Bulletin No. 2, 1 February 1944; Public Law 339, 78th Congress, *PHA* 35:3; *New York Times,* 29 May 1945.

5. Kimmel, *Admiral Kimmel's Story,* 158.

6. Quotation in Prange, *At Dawn We Slept,* 617; see also *PHA* 19:3848–53.

7. *PHA* 29:2239–40, 19:3930–31, 27:11, 32:5–6.

8. *PHA* 19:3840–43, 3846–47, 3854, 3857, 3861, 3864, 3870–73, 3876–77.

9. *PHA* 7:3149–50.

10. WCS to Col. Otis K. Sadtler, July 9, 1944, WCSC.

11. Prange, *At Dawn We Slept,* 637; *PHA* 27:11–34, 35:104–5.

12. WCS to Harry H. Bennett, 28 June 1944, WCSC.

13. *PHA* 27:187.

14. *PHA* 27:153–87.

15. *PHA* 27:218.

16. Ibid.

17. *PHA* 27:222.

18. Ibid.

19. *PHA* 27:223-24.

20. *PHA* 27:226.

21. *PHA* 27:227.

22. Ibid.

23. Grunert question in *PHA* 27:227; Short answer on 228.

24. *PHA* 27:229, 231.

25. *PHA* 27:232.

26. *PHA* 27:232–34.

27. *PHA* 27:254–57, 284.

28. Walter C. Phillips, biographical summary in 201 File, CMH.

29. *PHA* 27:581, 580, 586.

30. *PHA* 32:1–14, 169.

31. *PHA* 32:73.

32. *PHA* 32:171–72, 203.

33. Quotations in *PHA* 32:175; see also 176.

34. Quotation in *PHA* 32:207; see also 176–204.

35. *PHA* 32:205.

36. Col. and Mrs. Walter Dean Short (Ret.), interviews with author, 28–30 June 1985.

37. Kimmel, *Admiral Kimmel's Story,* 129–31.

38. *PHA* 32:53–54, 21, 103–4, 119–21, 130–31.

39. *PHA* 28:946–47.

40. Farago, *Broken Seal,* 230–32. The text of the bomb plot message is in *PHA* 12:261.

41. *PHA* 29:2284, 2148, 2371–72, 2391, 33:771, 39:225; *PHA, Report,* 486.

42. *PHA* 32:521, 684, 33:735, 35:104; Brownlow, *Accused,* 156.

43. Brownlow, *Accused,* 156; Toland, *Infamy,* 91; Short interview.

44. *PHA* 29:2252–53.

45. Quotation in *PHA* 29:2258–59; see also 2255–57.

46. *PHA* 29:2259.

47. Ibid.

48. Ibid.

49. Ibid.

50. *PHA* 19:3879–80.

51. *PHA* 29:2256–57.

52. Quotation in *PHA* 29:2267; see also 2262–66.

53. *PHA* 19:3881.

54. *PHA* 19:3931.

55. *Congressional Record,* vol. 90, pt. 6, pp. 7573–76; ibid., pt. 10, appendix, pp. A3870–71.

56. *PHA* 39:175.

57. Ibid.

58. Emphasized words in *PHA* 29:2073; see also 29:2075, 2193–95, 2079, 23:1106, and

39:84–86. See also Richard N. Current, *Secretary Stimson: A Study in Statecraft* (New Brunswick, N.J.: Rutgers University Press, 1954), 166.

59. Quotation in *PHA* 39:175; see also 176.

60. *PHA* 39:176.

61. Quotation in *PHA* 39:321; see also 303, 308–9, 63–66, 96–97, 178.

62. *PHA* 27:575, 723; *PHA* 28:1005, 1533; *PHA* 29:1627.

63. Quotation in *PHA* 39:60; see also 27:578, 730, 586, 597, 733, 28:1012–14, 1023, 1541, 1368.

64. Phillips interview.

65. *PHA* 35:4.

66. *Dallas Morning News*, 2 December 1944.

67. *PHA* 35:5, 29:2266–67; Short interview. Clausen took testimony from 23 November 1944 to 12 September 1945. General Marshall verbally initiated another limited investigation, this one by Col. Carter W. Clarke, to look into rumors about the destruction of secret documents. Clarke took testimony during 14–16 September 1944 and 13 July–4 August 1945. He did not attempt to contact Short.

68. Short interview; Miscellaneous Correspondence, Morgue File, UIA.

69. Col. and Mrs. Walter Dean Short (Ret.), interviews with author, 28–30 June 1985.

70. Short interview; War Department General Order 389, 7 August 1945.

Chapter 8. A Full and Complete Investigation

1. Truman quotation in *Public Papers of the Presidents of the United States: Harry S. Truman, 1945* (Washington, D.C.: GPO, 1961), 29 August 1945, 244; see also *PHA* 35:13–19; see also Current, *Secretary Stimson*, 180.

2. *Washington Post*, 30 August 1945.

3. *Public Papers of the Presidents of the United States: Harry S. Truman, 1945*, 30 August 1945, 249.

4. *PHA* 1:3–4; see also *New York Times*, 31 August 1945.

5. *Biographical Directory of the American Congress, 1774–1949* (Washington, D.C.: GPO, 1950), 815, 888, 982, 1017, 1151, 1201, 1203, 1395, 1481, 1604; *Congressional Directory*, 2d ed. (Washington, D.C.: GPO, 1945), 10–11, 20, 24, 38, 43, 50, 89, 103, 116, 131, 162–63, 180–81, 188–89, 191, 193, 217–18, 221, 225, 228.

6. Executive memoranda, 28 August 1945 and 23 October 1945, in *Congressional Record*, vol. 91, pt. 8, 6 November 1945, pp. 10445–46; remarks of members of Congress in ibid., 2 November 1945, pp. 10342–43, 10352–53; 6 November 1945, pp. 10446–48; 14 November 1945, 10685.

7. *PHA* 1:26–231.

8. *Washington Post*, 20 November 1945; *PHA* 1:265–66, 305–6, 343–44.

9. *Washington Post*, 21 November 1945.

10. *PHA* 39:137; 2:455–56, 559, 614; see also 2:406–45, 458–73, 477–549, 560–603, 615–773.

11. *PHA* 2:777, 5:2477; *Washington Post,* 7 December 1945; *Washington Post,* 27 November 1945; *Washington Post,* 28 November 1945.

12. Quotation in *PHA* 32:553; see also 29:2313, 2317–19.

13. *PHA* 3:1081.

14. *PHA* 3:1173, 1177.

15. *Washington Post,* 9 December 1945.

16. *PHA* 3:1276, 1434.

17. *Washington Post,* 14 December 1945.

18. *Washington Post,* 15 December 1945; *Washington Post,* 16 December 1945.

19. *PHA* 6:2518; see also 6:2540–52.

20. Quotation in *PHA* 6:2574; see also 6:2799–2811, 14:1000–1001, 16:2225, 2227.

21. *PHA* 6:2859–2902, 2907–10, 2642–50, 2660–63, 2763–65, 2902–4.

22. *PHA* 7:3154, 2956–57, 6:2493.

23. *Washington Post,* 25 December 1945.

24. Short's statement in *PHA* 7:2921–22; see also *Washington Post,* 23 January 1946.

25. *PHA* 27:187, 7:2921–64.

26. *PHA* 7:2964.

27. *New York Times,* 23 January 1946.

28. *Washington Post,* 23 January 1946; *New York Times,* 24 January 1946.

29. *PHA* 7:2971.

30. Ibid.

31. Ibid.

32. *PHA* 7:2984.

33. *PHA* 7:2986–87.

34. *PHA* 7:2993–3013.

35. *PHA* 7:3014.

36. *PHA* 7:3014–15.

37. *PHA* 7:3016.

38. Ibid.

39. *PHA* 7:3017.

40. Ibid.

41. Ibid.

42. *PHA* 7:3018.

43. Ibid.

44. Ibid.

45. *PHA* 7:3029, 3032–44.

46. *PHA* 7:3047.

47. *PHA* 7:3048–49.

48. *PHA* 7:3050.

49. Quotations in *PHA* 7:3055–56; see also 7:3054.

50. *PHA* 7:3056.

51. *PHA* 7:3057.

52. *PHA* 7:3058.

53. Ibid.

54. Ibid.

55. Quotation in *PHA* 7:3067; see also 7:3062–65.

56. *PHA* 7:3073.

57. Ibid.

58. Ibid.

59. *PHA* 7:3078.

60. Ibid.

61. *PHA* 7:3079–81.

62. *PHA* 7:3082–89.

63. *PHA* 7:3090.

64. Ibid.

65. *PHA* 7:3094.

66. *PHA* 7:3105; see also 7:3094–3109.

67. *PHA* 7:3106.

68. Quotations in *PHA* 7:3120–21; see also 7:3106–24.

69. *Congressional Record,* vol. 91, pt. 8, 6 November 1945, p. 10446; ibid., 2 November 1945, p. 10342.

70. Quotation in *PHA* 7:3128; see also 7:3127, 3129–30.

71. *PHA* 7:3133–47.

72. *PHA* 7:3147–48.

73. *PHA* 7:3148.

74. Barkley quotation in *PHA* 7:3148; other quotations in 7:3149.

75. *PHA* 7:3149.

76. *PHA* 7:3152.

77. Ibid.

78. *PHA* 7:3153.

79. *PHA* 7:3154–55.

80. *PHA* 7:3155.

81. *PHA* 7:3156–59.

82. *PHA* 7:3159.

83. Ibid.

84. *PHA* 7:3162–68.

85. *PHA* 7:3168.

86. Ibid.

87. Ibid.

88. *PHA* 7:3169.

89. Ibid.

90. *PHA* 7:3172.

91. *PHA* 7:3172–73.
92. *PHA* 7:3173.
93. *PHA* 7:3173–76.
94. *PHA* 7:3179-80; see also 7:3177–78, 3181.
95. Quotation in *PHA* 7:3186; see also 35:1–5.
96. *PHA* 7:3186.
97. *PHA* 7:3187.
98. Quotation in *PHA* 7:3187; see also 7:3188.
99. *PHA* 7:3191–94.
100. Ibid.
101. Ibid.
102. *PHA* 7:3209.
103. Ibid.
104. *PHA* 7:3209–23.
105. *PHA* 7:3223.
106. *PHA* 7:3224.
107. Quotation in *PHA* 7:3231; see also 7:3230.
108. Quotation in *PHA* 7:3231; see also *Washington Post,* 27 January 1946.

Chapter 9. Vindication Deferred

1. *PHA, Report,* xiv.
2. *PHA, Report,* xi.
3. *PHA, Report,* 48, 40, 33.
4. *PHA, Report,* 71–72.
5. *PHA, Report,* 119–30, 154.
6. *PHA, Report,* 125; see also 123–24.
7. *PHA, Report,*150; see also 151–53.
8. *PHA, Report,* 153.
9. *PHA, Report,* 154, 137, 154–55.
10. *PHA, Report,* 156.
11. *PHA, Report,* 163, 172, 226, 240; see also 164–67, 181, 192, 200–201, 227–28.
12. *PHA, Report,* 167, 204; see also 164, 190, 220–22.
13. *PHA, Report,* 205–6.
14. *PHA, Report,* 206.
15. *PHA, Report,* 234.
16. *PHA, Report,* 238.
17. *PHA, Report,* 252; see also 251.
18. *PHA, Report,* 252–66.
19. *PHA, Report,* 253.
20. *PHA, Report,* 266-A.

21. *PHA, Report,* 266-S; see also 266-H, 266-T, and 266-U.

22. *PHA, Report,* 503–5, 506–73.

23. *PHA, Report,* 505–6; see also 540–43, 565–70.

24. *PHA, Report,* 504.

25. *Washington Post,* 21 July 1946.

26. Short interview.

27. Lt. Gen. Edward H. Brooks to the Secretary of the Army, Summary: Advancement of Major General Walter C. Short on the Retired List to the Grade of Lieutenant General, n.d. [noted 19 April 1949], WCSC.

28. Lt. Gen. Wade H. Haislip, Memorandum for the Chief of Staff: Advancement of Major General Walter C. Short to the Grade of Lieutenant General on the Retired List, 18 May 1949, WCSC.

29. Short interview; Benjamin Purdy, interview with author, Austin, Tex., 12 May 1991.

30. WCS to Maj. Gen. Harry J. Maloney, 7 April 1949; Mark S. Watson to Maj. Gen. Orlando Ward, memo, 3 June 1949, WCSC; Watson, *Chief of Staff,* 509.

31. Purdy interview; Short interview.

32. Short interview; newspaper article, n.d., WCSC; *New York Times,* 5 September 1949.

33. Lt. Col. Robert L. May, Memo for Record, 7 September 1949, WCSC.

34. Short interview; *New York Times,* 8 September 1949.

35. *New York Times,* 8 September 1949.

36. Short interview; confirmation receipt, Merrill Lynch, Pierce, Fenner and Beane, 18 April 1951, WCSC.

37. Short interview; Phillips interview; *Washington Post,* 20 July 1977 and 12 April 1984.

38. Lt. Gen. Robert L. Eichelberger to Isabel Short, 15 September 1949; Lt. Gen. Alvan C. Gillem to Isabel Short, 12 September 1949, both in WCSC.

39. A. A. Hoeling, *The Week Before Pearl Harbor* (New York: Norton, 1963), 208.

40. Admiral Kimmel died on 14 May 1968; Kimmel, *Admiral Kimmel's Story;* Rear Adm. Robert A. Theobald, *The Final Secret of Pearl Harbor: The Washington Contribution to the Japanese Attack* (New York: Devin-Adair, 1954).

41. Prominent early revisionists and their works are Harry Elmer Barnes, ed., *Perpetual War for Perpetual Peace* (Caldwell, Id.: Caxton Printers, 1953; Westport, Conn.: Greenwood Press, 1969); Charles A. Beard, *President Roosevelt and the Coming of the War, 1941: A Study in Appearances and Realities* (New Haven, Conn.: Yale University Press, 1948; Hamden, Conn.: Archon Books, 1968); John T. Flynn, *The Truth About Pearl Harbor* (privately printed pamphlet, New York, 1944); George Morgenstern, *Pearl Harbor: The Story of the Secret War* (New York: Devin-Adair, 1947); Charles C. Tansill, *Back Door to War: The Roosevelt Foreign Policy, 1933–1941* (Chicago: Henry Regnery, 1952); Theobald, *Final Secret of Pearl Harbor.* More recent examples of revisionist literature include Toland, *Infamy;* James Rusbridger and Eric Nave, *Betrayal at Pearl Harbor: How Churchill*

Lured Roosevelt into World War II (New York: Summit Books, 1991); and Edward L. Beach, *Scapegoats: A Defense of Kimmel and Short at Pearl Harbor* (Annapolis, Md.: Naval Institute Press, 1995).

42. The three terms appear in Prange, *At Dawn We Slept*, 153, 403, 597, respectively.

43. Linn, *Guardians of Empire*, 84–85, 148–49.

44. *PHA* 35:287, 536, 270, 343–44, 263; Farago, *Broken Seal*, 141 n.

45. Secretary of State, Memorandum of Conversation, 29 November 1941, *Foreign Relations of the United States 1941*, vol. 4, *The Far East* (Washington, D.C.: GPO, 1956), 685–87.

Suggested Reading

Primary Sources

Archives and Collections

Sources on the life of Walter C. Short are readily accessible but widely scattered. The public libraries of Hillsboro and Litchfield, Illinois, have collections of genealogical materials and nineteenth-century local histories containing biographical sketches of the Short family and other early settlers in Montgomery County and adjacent areas of southwest Illinois. The University of Illinois maintains in its archives at Urbana a collection of items on Short's class of 1901 as well as a clippings file compiled on the general by the alumni affairs office. The Belmont College Library in Nashville, Tennessee, has a small number of items on Isabel Dean Short's student years.

Materials on the many units in which Walter Short served can be found in the National Archives and Records Administration facilities in Washington, D.C., and College Park, Maryland. Nine record groups were of central importance to this study: RG 94, Records of the Adjutant General's Office, 1780s–1917; RG 407, Records of the Adjutant General's Office, 1917–; RG 120, Records of the American Expeditionary Forces (World War I), 1917–23; RG 165, Records of the War Department General and Special Staffs; RG 177, Records of Chiefs of Arms; RG 350, Records of the Bureau of Insular Affairs; RG 391, Records of United States Regular Army Mobile Units, 1821–1942; RG 394, Records of United States Army Continental Commands, 1920–42; and RG 395, Records of United States Army Overseas Operations and Commands, 1898–1942. Two other government agencies in Washington, D.C.—the United States Army Center of Military History and the Naval Historical Center—have extensive collections on Army and Navy doctrine, commands, units, operations, and personalities. Among government publications, the series *War Department Annual Reports* provides extensive information on Army activities during Walter Short's career, especially the yearly compilation, *Report of the Secretary of War*. The *Biennial Report of the Chief of Staff of the United States Army, July 1, 1939, to June 30, 1941, to the Secretary of War* recounts the hurried expansion and modernization of the Army in a time of building threat. Two other annual publications, the *Official Army Register* and the *Army List and Directory*, provide useful information on the careers of Short and his contemporaries.

The most concentrated source on the general's military career is the Walter

Campbell Short Collection at the Hoover Institution on War, Revolution and Peace at Stanford University, Palo Alto, California. The Short Collection contains much personal memorabilia and a modest amount of official correspondence and documentation but very few personal letters. Short did not keep a diary.

The most complete account of Short's activities as commanding general of the Hawaiian Department is contained in the record of the joint congressional committee convened soon after World War II to investigate the Japanese attack on Hawaii. Titled *Pearl Harbor Attack: Hearings Before the Joint Committee on the Investigation of the Pearl Harbor Attack* (79th Cong., 1st sess., 1946), the hearings record is augmented by the testimony and reports of all official investigations of the attack conducted during the war. Publication of an index to the hearings in 1990 brought the compilation to forty volumes.

Interviews

A number of persons who had personal dealings with General Short generously shared their impressions of an unforgettable personality. Their memories provided the rich human detail that often escapes capture in libraries and archives. Col. Walter Dean Short (Ret.), General Short's only son, generously hosted me in his home in Las Cruces, New Mexico, and, along with his wife, Emily Irby Short, patiently answered countless questions on the lives of both the general and his wife, Isabel Dean Short.

Marion Hoyt Lewis, a niece of the general, recounted experiences with Walter and other members of the Short family in the 1920s and 1930s. Her son William offered impressions of the general in his later years. E. H. Baumgartner, Claire Cress, Cora Landers, and A. L. Whitten, all of Fillmore, Illinois, provided information on early generations of the Short family and described life in rural Illinois in the early twentieth century.

Two of General Short's former aides described in illuminating detail an officer they greatly admired as well as the United States Army in a pivotal period of American history. Col. Wendell G. Johnson (Ret.) served with General Short on three occasions: at Puerto Rico in 1925–28, at Fort Benning, Georgia, in 1936–37, and as aide when the general commanded 1st Division and Provisional Corps in 1939–40. Lt. Gen. Louis W. Truman (Ret.) served two tours of duty with the general, first at Jefferson Barracks, Missouri, in 1934–36, and later as aide when the general commanded in Hawaii.

Mrs. Walter C. Phillips, widow of General Short's chief of staff in Hawaii, offered impressions of several personalities in the top echelon of the Hawaiian Department in 1941, and recounted harrowing and humorous experiences during and after the Japanese attack.

Mr. Benjamin Purdy of Austin, Texas, gave a vivid portrait of General Short in his retirement years.

Secondary Sources

Unpublished Materials

Miller, Robert A. "The United States Army During the 1930s." Ph.D. diss., Princeton University, 1973.

Moenk, Jean R. "A History of Large-Scale Army Maneuvers in the United States, 1935–1964." Historical Branch, Office of the Deputy Chief of Staff for Military Operations and Reserve Forces, U.S. Continental Army Command, Fort Monroe, Va. December 1969.

Short, Isabel Dean. "The General's Lady." Manuscript. Walter Campbell Short Collection, Hoover Institution on War, Revolution and Peace, Stanford, Calif. N.d.

Tate, James P. "The Army and Its Air Corps: A Study of the Evolution of Army Policy Towards Aviation, 1919–1941." Ph.D. diss., Indiana University, 1976.

Books and Articles

Armstrong, David A. *Bullets and Bureaucrats: The Machine Gun and the United States Army, 1861–1916.* Westport, Conn.: Greenwood Press, 1982.

Beach, Edward L. *Scapegoats: A Defense of Kimmel and Short at Pearl Harbor.* Annapolis: Naval Institute Press, 1995.

Bidwell, Bruce W. *History of the Military Intelligence Division, Department of the Army General Staff: 1775–1941.* Frederick, Md.: University Publications of America, 1986.

Brown, Richard C. *Social Attitudes of American Generals, 1898–1940.* New York: Arno Press, 1979.

Brownlow, Donald G. *The Accused: The Ordeal of Rear Admiral Husband Edward Kimmel, U.S.N.* New York: Vantage Press, 1968.

Burns, James MacGregor. *Roosevelt: The Lion and the Fox.* New York: Harcourt, Brace & World, 1956.

Chinn, George M. *The Machine Gun: History, Evolution, and Development of Manual, Automatic, and Airborne Repeating Weapons.* Washington, D.C.: Department of the Navy, 1951.

Clark, Ronald. *The Man Who Broke Purple: The Life of Colonel William F. Friedman, Who Deciphered the Japanese Code in World War II.* Boston: Little, Brown, 1977.

Clendenen, Clarence C. *Blood on the Border: The United States Army and the Mexican Irregulars.* New York: Macmillan, 1969.

Collier, Thomas W. "The Army and the Great Depression." *Parameters* 18 (September 1988): 102–8.

Conn, Stetson, Rose C. Engelman, and Byron Fairchild. *Guarding the United States and Its Outposts.* Vol. 12 of *United States Army in World War II.* Washington, D.C.: GPO, 1964.

Craven, Wesley Frank, and James Lea Cate, eds. *The Army Air Forces in World War II.* 7 vols. Chicago: University of Chicago Press, 1948–58.

Current, Richard N. *Secretary Stimson: A Study in Statecraft.* New Brunswick, N.J.: Rutgers University Press, 1954.

Davis, Burke. *The Billy Mitchell Affair.* New York: Random House, 1967.

Dupuy, R. Ernest. *The Compact History of the United States Army.* New York: Hawthorne Books, 1956.

Eaton, Maj. George B. (USA). "General Walter Krueger and Joint War Planning, 1922–1938." *Naval War College Review* 48 (Spring 1995): 91–113.

Farago, Ladislas. *The Broken Seal: The Story of "Operation Magic" and the Pearl Harbor Disaster.* New York: Random House, 1967.

Fine, Sidney. *The Automobile Under the Blue Eagle: Labor, Management, and the Automobile Manufacturing Code.* Ann Arbor: University of Michigan Press, 1963.

Foner, Jack D. *Blacks and the Military in American History: A New Perspective.* New York: Frederick A. Praeger, 1974.

Foote, Rev. William Henry. *Sketches of North Carolina: Historical and Biographical.* New York: Robert Carter, 1846.

Ganoe, William A. *The History of the United States Army.* New York: D. Appleton-Century, 1942.

Gates, John M. *Schoolbooks and Krags: The United States Army in the Philippines, 1898–1902.* Westport, Conn.: Greenwood Press, 1973.

Hamm, Diane L. "William F. Friedman: Dean of American Cryptology." *INSCOM [Intelligence and Security Command] Journal* 7 (December 1984): 7–9.

Heidenheimer, Arnold J., et al. *Vanguard to Victory: History of the 18th Infantry.* Aschaffenburg, Germany: Main-Echo Verlag, 1954.

Hoehling, A. A. *The Week Before Pearl Harbor.* New York: Norton, 1963.

Hogg, Ian V., and John Weeks. *Military Small Arms of the 20th Century.* Northfield, Ill.: DBI Books, 1981.

Holley, I. B. "Of Saber Charges, Escort Fighters, and Spacecraft: The Search for Doctrine." *Air University Review* 34 (September–October 1983): 2–11.

James, D. Clayton. *The Years of MacArthur.* Vol. 1, *1880–1941.* Boston: Houghton Mifflin, 1970.

Johnson, Capt. Wendell G. "The Howie Machine-Gun Carrier." *Infantry Journal* 44 (November–December 1937): 529–31.

Kahn, David. "The United States Views Japan and Germany in 1941." In *Knowing One's Enemies: Intelligence Assessment Before the Two World Wars,* edited by Ernest R. May. Princeton, N.J.: Princeton University Press, 1984.

Killegrew, John W. *The Impact of the Great Depression on the Army.* New York: Garland, 1979.

Kimmel, Husband E. *Admiral Kimmel's Story.* Chicago: Henry Regnery, 1955.

Linn, Brian M. *Guardians of Empire: The U.S. Army and the Pacific, 1902–1940.* Chapel Hill: University of North Carolina Press, 1997.

Marshall, George C. *The Papers of George Catlett Marshall.* Edited by Larry I. Bland. 4 vols. Baltimore: Johns Hopkins University Press, 1981–96.

McEntee, Girard L. *Military History of the World War: A Complete Account of the Campaigns on All Fronts.* New York: Scribner's, 1937.

Melosi, Martin V. *The Shadow of Pearl Harbor: Political Controversy over the Surprise Attack, 1941–1946.* College Station: Texas A&M University Press, 1977.

Millett, Allan R. *The General: Robert L. Bullard and Officership in the United States Army, 1881–1925.* Westport, Conn.: Greenwood Press, 1975.

Nenninger, Timothy K. *The Leavenworth Schools and the Old Army: Education, Professionalism, and the Officer Corps of the United States Army, 1881–1918.* Westport, Conn.: Greenwood Press, 1978.

Nevins, Allan. *Illinois.* New York: Oxford University Press, 1917.

Owen, Norman G., ed. *Compadre Colonialism: Studies on the Philippines Under American Rule.* Michigan Papers on South and Southeast Asia, no. 3. Ann Arbor: University of Michigan Press, 1971.

Pappas, George S. *Prudens Futuri: The U.S. Army War College, 1901–1967.* Carlisle Barracks, Pa.: Alumni Association of U.S. Army War College, 1967.

Perrin, William H., ed. *History of Bond and Montgomery Counties, Illinois.* Chicago: Baskin, 1882.

Pershing, John J. *My Experiences in the World War.* 2 vols. New York: Frederick A. Stokes, 1931.

Pogue, Forrest C. *George C. Marshall: Education of a General, 1880–1939.* New York: Viking Press, 1963.

Prange, Gordon W., with Donald M. Goldstein and Katherine V. Dillon. *At Dawn We Slept: The Untold Story of Pearl Harbor.* New York: McGraw-Hill, 1981.

Rusbridger, James, and Eric Nave. *Betrayal at Pearl Harbor: How Churchill Lured Roosevelt into World War II.* New York: Summit Books, 1991.

Sasso, Maj. Claude R. (USA). "Scapegoats or Culprits: Kimmel and Short at Pearl Harbor." *Military Review* 63 (December 1983): 28–47.

Short, Capt. Walter C. "Machine Guns as an Aid to the Scheme of Maneuver." *Infantry Journal* 34 (February 1929): 115–20.

———. "Machine Guns of an Infantry Division." *Infantry Journal* 17 (September 1920): 261–63.

———. "Machine Guns on the Defense." *Infantry Journal* 30 (June 1927): 579–88.

Smith, William Jay. *Army Brat.* New York: Persea Books, 1980.

Solberg, Winton U. *The University of Illinois, 1867–1894: An Intellectual and Cultural History.* Urbana: University of Illinois Press, 1968.

Spector, Ronald H. *Eagle Against the Sun: The American War with Japan.* New York: Free Press, 1985.

———. "The Military Effectiveness of the US Armed Forces, 1919–39." In *Military Effectiveness.* Vol. 2 of *The Interwar Period,* edited by Allan R. Millett and Williamson Murray. Boston: Allen & Unwin, 1988.

Spiller, Roger J., ed. *Dictionary of American Military Biography.* Vol. 3. Westport, Conn.: Greenwood Press, 1984.

Temple, Truman. "Crippling Blow by Swordfish." *World War II* 4 (May 1989): 34–41.

Theobald, Rear Adm. Robert A. *The Final Secret of Pearl Harbor.* New York: Devin-Adair, 1954.

Thorpe, Elliott R. *East Wind Rain: The Intimate Account of an Intelligence Officer in the Pacific, 1939–1949.* Boston: Gambit, 1969.

Toland, John. *Infamy: Pearl Harbor and Its Aftermath.* Garden City, N.Y.: Doubleday, 1982.

Traylor, Jacob L. *Past and Present of Montgomery County.* Chicago: S. J. Parke Publishing, 1904.

Truscott, Gen. Lucian K., Jr. *The Twilight of the U.S. Cavalry: Life in the Old Army, 1917–1942.* Lawrence: University Press of Kansas, 1989.

Underwood, Jeffery S. *The Wings of Democracy: The Influence of Air Power on the Roosevelt Administration, 1933–1941.* College Station: Texas A&M University Press, 1991.

U.S. Army. Adjutant General of the Army. *Decorations, U.S. Army, 1862–1926.* Washington, D.C.: GPO, 1927.

———. Chief of Military History. *The Army Lineage Book.* Washington, D.C.: GPO, 1953.

Vogel, Victor. *Soldiers of the Old Army.* College Station: Texas A&M University Press, 1990.

Watson, Mark S. *Chief of Staff: Prewar Plans and Preparations.* Vol. 4 of *United States Army in World War II.* Washington, D.C.: GPO, 1950.

Weigley, Russell F. *History of the United States Army.* Enlarged ed. Bloomington: Indiana University Press, 1984.

Wilson, John B., comp. *Armies, Corps, Divisions and Separate Brigades.* Washington, D.C.: GPO, 1987.

Wohlstetter, Roberta. *Pearl Harbor: Warning and Decision.* Stanford, Calif.: Stanford University Press, 1962.

Index

About the Author

Charles Anderson, who passed away in 2003, was a long-standing historian at the Center for Military History. A Marine rifle platoon leader in Vietnam, he was the author of a number of books on various military-related subjects, including contributions to the official history of the Vietnam War. *Day of Lightning, Years of Scorn* is the capstone of a highly regarded military author's career.